ooks are to be returne.
ne last date below.

D1356117

LEEDS CITY BUSINESS 1893-1993:
ESSAYS MARKING THE CENTENARY OF THE INCORPORATION

Leeds City Business 1893-1993: Essays Marking the Centenary of the Incorporation

JOHN CHARTRES and KATRINA HONEYMAN
Editors

Leeds University Press

Published by
Leeds University Press, 1993.

© The authors, 1993.

ISBN 0 85316 157 7

Typeset, Printed and Bound by The Charlesworth Group, Huddersfield, UK, 0484 517077

CONTENTS

LIST OF FIGURES

LIST OF PLATES

LIST OF TABLES

PREFACE

This publication of this collection of essays has a two-fold purpose. It forms a significant contribution to the celebrations of the Centenary of the Incorporation of the City of Leeds from its business and academic communities. It is the outcome of extensive collaboration between the Leeds Chamber of Commerce and Industry and its members, the City, and the University of Leeds. The essays examine some of the major companies of Leeds, whose histories have spanned that century, and explore their fortunes as key influences upon the city economy.

This book also begins to rectify the dearth of business history in Leeds. Earlier studies have covered the overall economic context, as in Professor Maurice Beresford's volumes to celebrate the visit of the British Association and to celebrate the centenary of the Leeds Chamber of Commerce, and in Derek Fraser's collection, *A History of Modern Leeds*, which provided a valuable introduction to the key features of the City's history. In the 1950s, Gordon Rimmer and others produced a series of short, exploratory essays on the principal sectors of Leeds commerce and industry, published in the *Leeds Journal* by the Chamber, under the series title "Leeds and its Industrial Growth". Gordon Rimmer was also responsible for an outstanding study of the local linen industry with *Marshall's of Leeds, Flax Spinners* 1788–1886 (1960). There have also been important studies of Tetley, Fowler, and Greenwood and Batley. The great bulk of the business history of the City is as yet unwritten, and represents a great wealth of experience to be recovered.

All of the companies covered in this present volume are Leeds-based or Leeds founded, and their history has been set into the wider context of the City's economic development from the 1890s to the 1990s. They have been chosen as representative of the principal characteristics of the City's economic base over the period. The firms covered are therefore among the most enduring in Leeds, and together their histories reflect and illuminate much of the industrial and commercial experience of the City as a whole. They show the diversity of the Leeds economy, through these studies of clothing, printing, the production of chemicals and toiletries, financial services, food and drink, the utilities, the media, and medicine-related industries. Each of the representatives of these sectors of the Leeds economy is studied in that context, to identify

some of the ways in which it contributed to their establishment and development, and its reciprocal contributions to the life of the City. Our first and last
chapters place the studies into that wider context, the introduction setting the
industrial context of Leeds over the last century, and the last examining the
City's current position and future prospects in the light of the challenges of
the 1990s. Some at least of these challenges echo those of the previous century.

Most of the business historians who have produced this book are located
within the new Centre for Business History at the University of Leeds. This
Centre, formally established this year, will we hope represent a further enduring
element of the City's centenary celebrations, and one that will be the focus for
many future studies. The aim in this volume has been to produce a series of
short histories that will meet the interests of a wide range of readers. We very
much hope that they appeal to the general reader, particularly those who live
and work in Leeds, and help to administer the City, and the current and past
employees of the firms or businesses represented here. They are also of wider
interest to those concerned with the academic discipline of business history.

The research of these essays has been co-ordinated and conducted through
the Centre for Business History and the School of Business & Economic
Studies, University of Leeds. It has also drawn upon the wider scholarly
resources of the University, principally the Brotherton Library. Particular debts
of gratitude are owed to the Leeds Chamber of Commerce and Industry and
to Leeds City Council. Much of the primary research work was conducted by
Jane Durham and Graham Sykes, who made use of the valuable collection of
business records at the Leeds District Archive Office, at Sheepscar, and who
received a great deal of help and guidance from the participating companies
and organizations.

Yorkshire Post Newspapers Ltd, the Leeds Permanent Building Society,
Joshua Tetley & Son, and John Waddington PLC all provided access to records
in their possession. In addition, Jeremy Burton generously loaned documents
relating to his grandfather's company, and provided other information. Peter
Collins, formerly Technical Director of Elida Gibbs, enthusiastically identified
source material relating to Joseph Watson and Sons Ltd, other than that which
is available at the Unilever Historical Archives at Port Sunlight. Many others
have given generously and enthusiastically of their time and advice, and are
thanked in the individual chapters to which they made their contribution. The
research work received the generous financial support of British Gas PLC,
Elida Gibbs Ltd, The Leeds Permanent Building Society, Joshua Tetley and
Son Ltd, the Thackray Family Trust, and John Waddington PLC. In addition,
Price Waterhouse, whose partnership was formed in Leeds in 1865, and who
have been auditors to many of the companies in this study, also kindly provided
financial support.

As editors, we are especially grateful to the support and advice we have received from the other members of the Editorial Committee: Peter Coles-Johnson, Director, Leeds Chamber of Commerce and Industry; Peter Collins, Associate Director of Elida Gibbs Ltd; and Victor H. Watson, Chairman of John Waddington PLC until July 1993. Their enthusiasm and support throughout the project has been critical to its successful completion.

This volume is therefore the outcome of a partnership between the University of Leeds, the Leeds business community, and the City from which we hope the study of business history to grow and prosper. Its completion is itself a strong signal of the community interest in the subject. We are particularly happy to signal the positive developing links between the University and the City Council. The generous assistance provided by Stan Kenyon, the Director of Planning, and the Economic Development Unit at the Leeds Development Agency is gratefully acknowledged.

We hope that this volume will be the first of many to be produced through the new Centre for Business History. Above all, we hope that it will be read and enjoyed by many as a fitting contribution to the centenary of our City.

JAC,
KH,
August 1993.

Acknowledgements

Many thanks are due to those who granted permission for the reproduction of illustrations: to Yorkshire Post Newspapers Ltd for the plates in Chapters 1 and 2; to the Leeds Permanent Building Society for the plates in Chapter 3; to Leeds City Council Department of Leisure Services, Local History Library for Plate 4.1; to Joshua Tetley and Son for the plates in Chapter 5; to John Waddington PLC for the plates in Chapter 6; to Jeremy Burton for permission to use material in the Leeds District Archives for the plates in Chapter 7; to Jeanette Strickland for locating illustrations in the Unilever Historical Archives for use in Chapter 8. Penny Wainwright provided the illustrations for Chapter 9 with the exception of plate 9.1 which is reproduced by kind permission of the Thackray Medical Museum.

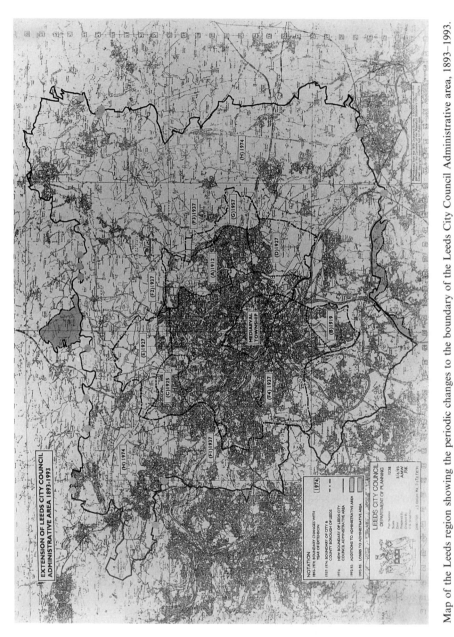

Map of the Leeds region showing the periodic changes to the boundary of the Leeds City Council Administrative area, 1893–1993.

CHAPTER 1

Introduction: The city of Leeds and its business 1893–1993[1]

Stephen Caunce and Katrina Honeyman

'LEEDS is at last a city' remarked the *Yorkshire Factory Times* in 1893 and it may seem surprising that this status had been so long delayed, for Leeds was then the largest town in Yorkshire and it had long been an economic centre of national importance. Though incorporation by royal charter now brought Leeds into line with comparable urban centres, it is not an ancient town like York, Ripon, or Pontefract. It only received a borough charter in 1626, it has never had a cathedral of the established church, and it has never been a county town. Instead, its steady rise in importance has always rested on its role as a regional centre of business activity. People came to this spot on the edge of the Pennines simply because it offered them a chance to earn a good living through trade and industry, all of it originally centred on wool and woollen cloth. It rose above its early local rivals, notably Wakefield and Halifax, because merchants found it the most effective base for their operations. Leeds is in many senses a self-made city and its prosperity still rests on its ability to deliver the economic goods.

Because of this, Leeds' continuing success has been based on diversity and on change, not on trying to protect the relics of past prosperity or past privileges. Even in local government terms, though Leeds had a continuous existence as a city with county borough status between 1893 and the radical reorganization of local government in 1974, the area administered by the city council grew substantially through periodic boundary changes. (See Map) Roundhay, Shadwell, Cross Gates, and Seacroft were taken over in 1912, Middleton in 1919, and Adel and Cookridge in 1926. In 1927, Halton and Temple Newsam, in the east, and Alwoodley and Eccup, in the north, further substantially enlarged the city. Finally, small parts of Rodley, Upper Armley, Alwoodley, and Seacroft were added in 1937. The changes of 1974 were not just a renewal of this process of growth, but had a genuinely different character. As well as Leeds itself, the former municipal boroughs of Morley and Pudsey, and the urban districts of Rothwell, Horsforth, Aireborough, Otley, and

1

Plate 1.1   The site of City Square as it looked in 1893, looking from the junction of Park Row and Boar Lane. The creation of City Square three years later was a conscious attempt to impress those emerging from the railway station, and it can be said to symbolize the growing self-confidence of the new city. However, this was no overnight transformation for it was not until 1933 that the LMS decided to revamp the station itself and to erect the Queen's Hotel across the front, completing the new look.

  The building in the centre is the old Mixed Cloth Hall, built in 1758 where the Post Office now stands.

Garforth, together with large parts of the former rural districts of Wetherby, Tadcaster, and Wharfedale were all now joined together to form the Leeds Metropolitan District, which as its name suggests is a small region rather than a unitary city, and which currently has a population approaching three-quarters of a million. It covers an area of 213 square miles, including substantial rural areas. This doubled the administrative area run from Leeds, but also created a council with wider interests than those of the city alone. Minor alterations of the Leeds/Bradford boundary in 1992, and of the borders with Wakefield, Selby and Harrogate a year later, are the only changes made since then, and they were of little significance.[2]

I

In assessing the economic history of Leeds it is essential to include this sense of constant change and this wider vision. Thus, Leeds has always had a strong manufacturing base, but it attained definite regional pre-eminence because of its long tradition of commercial activity. Situated on the edge of a manufacturing region in the Pennines that is unable to grow much food, next to a productive agricultural belt to the east which has little industry, Leeds was a natural centre for the exchange of the commodities produced by each side.[3] It has thus always functioned as the hub of the wider regional economy, in addition to having a thriving local economy of its own. It is this that explains the much wider range of industries and services that have made Leeds their base rather than Wakefield, Halifax, Huddersfield, and Bradford, its traditional rivals. Its multi-faceted and outward looking economy was symbolized by a variety of mercantile institutions: the old Cloth Halls, which reflected the central position of Leeds in the West Riding woollen trade during the eighteenth and early nineteenth century; the Corn Exchange, which served the region's farmers;[4] and the Leeds Stock Exchange, established by 1844.[5] The merchants of Leeds provided entrepreneurial skills and linked manufacturers throughout West Yorkshire to national and international markets that they could never have reached directly. Local banks mobilized capital for manufacturing activity, but the city's financial services developed far beyond this in range and sophistication during the nineteenth century.

The importance of business was reflected in continuing efforts to build up a comprehensive infrastructure, and especially good communications. Leeds is in a good position to benefit from traffic through the Aire gap, the easiest transpennine route, but it lies away from the main north-south corridor that runs through the Vale of York, and towards the west, where most of the cloth production was located, the hills rise to over a thousand feet in less than twenty miles. Packhorse roads can still be seen in many places, and if they are used as footpaths today they were the motorways of the seventeenth-century cloth trade, used by enormous trains of laden horses. Turnpike roads encouraged much wider use of wheeled vehicles, which greatly increased the flow of traffic in the eighteenth and nineteenth centuries, but bulky, low value goods were best moved by water. The river Aire was not naturally navigable to Leeds, but the construction of the Aire and Calder Navigation gave the city its long-desired link eastwards to Hull and the North Sea as the eighteenth century began. To the west, access to the port of Liverpool was the aim of the Leeds and Liverpool canal, though its route was so tortuous and progress so slow that more direct contact had been made via Sowerby Bridge and then Huddersfield before it was finished in 1816. Coalfields developed all around

Plate 1.2   Infirmary Street in the early nineteenth century, with the Mixed Cloth Hall visible on the left. It housed 1,770 stalls for the sale of woollen cloth dyed either in the yarn or in the wool, rather than woven in its natural state for dying later. This was the speciality of manufacturers from the Aire Valley and in the eighteenth century the hall, where they made contact with the Leeds merchants, was the essential hub around which their whole trade revolved. The undyed cloth of the Calder Valley townships was sold in the White Cloth Hall, whose front still stands on Crown Street, behind the Corn Exchange. As the trade grew, however, and as factories spread, this type of arrangement became obsolete and the halls were in decline by the mid nineteenth century.

Note the stagecoach, laden with passengers, and the lack of any other traffic. Coaches operated mostly from inns on Briggate, and Leeds was the centre of the whole West Yorkshire network of services, which closely resembled the present day rail network in this respect.

Leeds in the eighteenth and nineteenth centuries, reinforcing the demand for this kind of low-cost transport, and horse-drawn waggonways were built to feed coal down to the canals and into the heart of the city. This, and the steam engines fired by the coal, provided a focus for engineering innovation, and Matthew Murray is credited with running the world's first successful haulage system based on steam locomotives on the Middleton Railway in 1812.[6] By 1893, there was an extensive regional railway network, and a regular and relatively rapid train service to London had greatly eased commercial relations between Leeds and the capital. On the other hand, it also opened up London as a competitor in the provision of financial services, and if this had little impact at the time, it has transformed the ownership and outlook of most of the city's financial institutions today.

For consumers, the railway reinforced the city's ability to offer retail facilities to the better-off that outclassed anywhere else in the West Riding, and it was referred to as the 'London of Yorkshire'. Consumption patterns and preferences were transformed in the years around 1893, a trend precipitated by the development of the multiple (general) store, of which the Leeds Industrial Cooperative Society was the most striking local example, opening its first shop in Albion Street in 1884. By the late 1890s there were seventy shops, mostly in the working-class industrial suburbs.[7] The *Arcades*, which continue to bring pleasure to the Saturday crowds, were developed with the middle-class shopper in mind. The first of these, completed in 1877, was the brainchild of Charles Thornton, proprietor of the Varieties Music Hall. The remainder, built 15 or 20 years later, were municipal creations. The last to be constructed, the Grand, Victoria, and County, were all finished in 1898.[8] Other locations for specifically middle class shopping included the suburban shopping parades and the department stores, of which the most remarkable was Schofields. Originally a draper and milliner in the Victoria Arcade, Snowden Schofield prospered sufficiently to purchase adjoining shops until in 1947 he

Plate 1.3 The Leeds Basin in the days when it was a thriving internal port, looking towards the parish church.

5

had acquired the whole arcade.[9] The store remained in family hands until its purchase by a London property developer in 1984 and following a period of restructuring, the £16 million Schofield Centre opened in 1989, converting the store into a mall in line with the preferences of the 1980s. It retains a clearly upmarket image, but the class distinctions that marked so much of the early development of retailing in Leeds as elsewhere are now very muted. Leeds remains the leading centre for shopping in West Yorkshire today, and it increasingly overshadows its neighbours and draws in shoppers who would rarely have visited it before the Second World War. Moreover, Leeds has not so far acquired a major out-of-town shopping centre[10] and the effort put into developing the traditional shopping areas has kept them lively and accessible to all.

The citizens of Leeds were served by a thriving local press in 1893, and the reputation of its newspapers outside the city reflected its status as a major regional centre. The *Leeds Mercury* was now a shadow of the crusading Liberal paper it had been, but the *Yorkshire Post* attracted increasing respect as one

Plate 1.4   Leeds City Market. The impressive market hall dates from 1904, and this bustling market is still one of the liveliest to be found in any English urban centre. The recent controversy over redevelopment plans shows that it remains at the heart of shopping in Leeds for many families, especially those seeking bargains. Michael Marks ran a penny bazaar here in the 1880s which was perhaps the most successful stall in the market's history since the business later grew into Marks and Spencer.

Plate 1.5   The top end of Briggate in the 1890s. This was the heart of the shopping district. The entrance to Queen's Arcade, built in 1888–89, is signposted on the left by its clock, while Thornton's Arcade, 1877–78, emerges higher up through the arch beyond Lockhart's Cocoa Rooms.

Note the horse tram, the first successful urban public transport system, but one that was soon replaced first by steam and then by electric traction as the demand for transport grew beyond all precedent in the late nineteenth century.

of the leading Conservative titles outside London. It spoke for the business community of the region, not just for the city of Leeds. *Yorkshire Post* leaders were read at home and abroad as indicators of what West Yorkshire thought at a time when regional diversity was much more pronounced than it is now. It played a leading part in the opposition to appeasement in the 1930s and it is generally credited with lighting the fuse that set off the Abdication crisis. Its history is described in Chapter 2, and it is now one of the very few remaining daily morning regional newspapers, having swallowed its old rival, the *Mercury*, in 1939. The 1880s and 1890s were particularly prolific decades for the press of Leeds, when thirty-nine new publications appeared catering to both general and specialist readership. Hobby and interest magazines, suburban newspapers, and evening newspapers all stem from this time. The most enduring, the *Yorkshire Evening Post*, was founded by the owners of the *Yorkshire Post* in 1890, and it has been vital as the profitmaker that has supported its more prestigious sister title ever since.[11]

Plate 1.6   The County Arcade, the finest of the arcades opening off Briggate, now refurbished as part of the modernization of the city centre shopping facilities. It was finished in 1898 on the line of the former Wood Street which was demolished to make way for it.

It would be wrong, however, to imply that the external perception of Leeds in 1893 as a vibrant commercial and industrial centre meant that the city had no problems. The proclamation of incorporation in the *Yorkshire Factory Times* was closely followed by criticism of the city's uncivilized state,[12] and many of the ordinary people who had helped create the city's wealth felt the celebrations ignored deep-seated problems that often reduced their lives to misery. Physically, the Leeds of 1893 was very different from the one we see around us, despite the continuity that is evident in the central street patterns and in some of the city's leading buildings. The population was little more than one-third of what it is today but was much more closely packed together, partly because of the difficulties that arose from living beyond walking distance from work and shops. The result was a built-up area confined within very narrow limits by modern standards, and the squalid central residential areas combined with a heavily polluted atmosphere to create a degraded and short life for many. It was less than half a century since cholera epidemics had raged in the city and ironically it was in 1893 that the peak rate of infant mortality— 21 per cent—was recorded.[13] The city's population had doubled in the last forty years of the nineteenth century and it was growing by 4000 per year in the 1890s, creating an urgent demand for housing which could not be adequately met. It was the immigrant communities which experienced the worst degradation. First the Irish, and then east European Jews congregated in the Leylands, Quarry Hill, and Wellington Road districts where slum housing was tightly packed together and large numbers of factories and workshops offered jobs.

The growth of the Leeds Permanent Building Society, which forms the subject of Chapter 3, is a fine example of the utilization of the financial expertise that existed within the city to try to tackle this problem. However, the construction of back-to-back houses, the solution favoured by private builders since they could be erected rapidly and achieved high densities such as 80–90 houses per acre, did little for the working-class residents of the city since they were cramped, ill-ventilated, and insanitary. Although an improved type was developed by the 1890s, in many of the working-class districts of Leeds the older type predominated until the 1930s. Their shortcomings earned Leeds, and other West Riding towns, a good deal of notoriety and the Housing Act of 1909 seemed to prohibit further building. However, plans approved before May of that year were exempt and since large numbers had been so approved, the construction of the 'better' type of back-to-backs continued

Plate 1.7 Wood Street before demolition. The Boy and Barrel Inn can be seen on the left and a yard named after it lay behind Wood Street. This intricate pattern of development preserved the lines of the tenements of the original inhabitants of the town, who bought long plots of land with a frontage on Briggate. As the town grew, the gardens behind were built up as yards, courts, and side streets, and most became the sites of coaching inns and public houses.

9

until 1937, by which time the clearance of the earlier versions was well under way. Slum clearance began in 1900, and was initially concentrated in the Leylands. Many of the small clothing factories and workshops were also demolished, hastening the movement out of the area which had begun as the immigrants established themselves. The Jews in particular moved north, first to Chapeltown and then to more enduring settlements in Moortown and Alwoodley.[14]

Most housebuilding of the 1890s was concentrated in an arc from Harehills through Holbeck to Armley Road and new suburbs and social neighbourhoods emerged as the middle class moved out of the formerly fashionable areas around Woodhouse Hill, which became the location of subletting to a mostly rootless population. The new suburbs were typified by estates of small semi-detached houses of which 26,000 were built between 1926 and 1940 through public and private efforts, linked to a more comprehensive slum clearance programme which was instigated in the 1930's.[15] It was this sprawling of both people and houses which necessitated the almost constant enlargements of the city's boundaries in this period, and apart from a temporary halt to both construction and demolition caused by the Second World War, consistent efforts have been made ever since to ameliorate the living conditions of the Leeds population through new building and renovation. Despite this, the legacy of more than a hundred years of back-to-back house building continues to cast a shadow over the local housing stock as many streets of the later types still exist and they remain bleak places. Many houses have been improved, however, and they do fulfil a useful role in providing students, single people, and first time buyers with cheap accommodation that has vanished in many other cities.

Alongside the problems stemming from poor housing, acknowledgement that life in a city had to be differently organized from that in villages was finally forcing the universal provision of the basic requirements of modern urban life by 1893. Water supply, the removal of sewage and refuse, the provision of heat, light, and transport were all being transformed, and all were municipalized during the nineteenth century: water in 1850, gas in 1870, and electricity during the 1890s. This was partly due to dissatisfaction with the performance of the private companies, but it was also recognized that the profit motive would never induce the building of expensive facilities for the poverty-stricken sections of the city. The way this affected gas manufacture and supply is shown in Chapter 4, and the results were very mixed despite the high hopes at the start. The difficulties of running an enterprise like this within a political framework were exacerbated by the growing competition of electricity, itself run by the council, for markets that had once seemed to be natural monopolies. Electricity came to dominate domestic lighting since it was safer

Plate 1.8 Quarry Hill flats. Planned from 1935 in imitation of Continental ideas, this was the largest scheme for municipal flats in England at the time. It was to be built on the site of some of the worst slums in Leeds, and it was intended as a self-contained community with a wide variety of facilities. The first section was occupied in 1938, but the war prevented the scheme proceeding as planned. Rents were high in comparison with the slum housing replaced, and no lasting sense of community ever developed. By the 1960s it had itself become a problem and demolition was seen as the only solution.

and brighter, and it was also the basis during the 1890s of the development of the local tramway system into a real city-wide network, replacing the horse and steam traction that had powered the pioneer efforts of the 1870s.[16] The cheap internal transport provided by the Leeds network was undoubtedly the key factor in allowing the city to spread out as it did, and it also linked up with those of adjoining townships. It was said that it was possible to travel most of the way from Leeds to Liverpool by tram, though it is unlikely anyone tried it given the slow speeds and boneshaking ride of early trams. Locally the transport network was further enhanced by the petrol bus, introduced in 1905, and the trolley buses, which operated between 1911 and the 1930s. Governmental recommendation to scrap the tram on safety grounds at the same time as the trolley buses was ignored and efforts were made to improve the system instead. Lines like the one to Temple Newsam, with its tracks separated from the road traffic and its high carrying capacity foreshadowed the rapid transit systems of today, but at the time they did not seem justified by traffic congestion as they now do. Trams therefore played a diminishing role alongside the more flexible buses until 1954, when they were finally abandoned.[17] The traffic problems of the 1990s may cause a renaissance of the tram in Leeds, however, as in other northern cities.

If life is to be more than bed and work, people have to have the facilities to allow them to entertain and enjoy themselves. Leeds has long had a high cultural reputation, though in the 1890s it was better known for its four music halls, including the City Varieties of *The Good Old Days* fame, than for its more meagre 'straight' theatrical output. Moving pictures caught on very fast and the first cinema, opened in 1906, was quickly followed by many more.[18] This is fitting for it was in Leeds that the first moving picture was shot, in 1888 on Leeds Bridge, by Louis Aime Augustan le Prince.[19] Leeds is justifiably proud of its University which acquired independent status in 1904.[20] Although the West Riding had a strong temperance movement, beer has always played an important role in lightening everyday life as well as lubricating most celebrations, and there were thirty breweries of varying size in 1893. As in every city, this number dwindled over the years, so there were fifteen in 1914, seven in 1940, and just three in 1956.[21] Given the increasing size of breweries this can be seen as concentration rather than decline, but certainly customer choice was greatly reduced. In 1993, Joshua Tetley and Son, the subject of Chapter 5, was the sole survivor. The firm is now part of Allied-Lyons Retailing, which has many interests outside brewing and an international outlook, but Tetley's retains a high profile within the group and a good deal of regional autonomy, so there is still a local tradition active in this industry. For those with a taste for the outdoors, Leeds has always been better than most cities as a place to live. Its Pennine location has helped to ensure that it has always been well provided with open spaces, including the 'moors' and the steep valleys that bring the countryside right into the city even today. Old mansions and their grounds have also been preserved, though Roundhay Park was the centre of controversy when it was acquired by the Corporation in 1868 since it lay beyond the City boundary and out of reach of most of the citizens.[22] Visiting

Plate 1.9 Trams at Bridge End in the 1930s, looking over Leeds Bridge to the bottom of Briggate. The bridge was the original cloth market, described as the busiest in the country by Defoe in the early eighteenth century, but two hundred years later it was swallowed up in urban sprawl. The electric trams were first introduced in 1890 and by the inter-war years they had become the backbone of the city's internal transport system. However, in this photograph the replacement of horses by internal combustion engines has already gone a long way and was soon to become a formidable rival to trams as well. A trolleybus is visible behind the line of trams.

13

was sparse until the trams reached the park, but since then its landscaped areas have proved invaluable to those seeking quick escape from an industrial environment, while it is now also the site for major international rock music events.[23]

Roundhay also provides outdoor sports facilities used by thousands of people every year, and Leeds has a long and active tradition in sport. Cricket of a high standard has been played here since the mid-nineteenth century, yet it was only after the completion of the Headingley ground in 1892 and a fierce battle with Sheffield that Leeds finally became the headquarters of Yorkshire County Cricket Club in 1902.[24] The origins of soccer locally are much more muted, and it is only recently that the city has had any claim to dominance in Yorkshire. Until 1905, when the Leeds City Association Football Club took over the Elland Road ground from the Holbeck Rugby Union Football Club, rugby had monopolized the football scene. It still maintains a strong presence, with well known rugby union clubs like Headingley (now merged with Roundhay into Leeds) attracting national attention, and despite a recent lack of trophies, Leeds Rugby League club has always stood out as one of the small group of affluent clubs that usually seem to live in a different world from their humbler brethren like Bramley, also within the Leeds boundary. Neither Leeds City nor Leeds United distinguished themselves in the Football League before the late 1960s, but since then Leeds United, despite some barren periods, have established a national reputation.[25]

II

By 1893 Leeds had developed into one of the largest concentrations of industrial activity in the UK, with national and international reputations in many sectors. Coal, engineering, and tanning were the core industries, supplemented on the margin by expanding trades such as clothing and contracting trades such as pottery.[26] Textiles in particular were in heavy decline, which may seem strange for the city that had traditionally been at the heart of the West Yorkshire wool trade. It was Bradford rather than Leeds that dominated the manufacture of wool textiles, particularly in the worsted section of the trade, but in the long run this has done Leeds no harm, and it is Bradford which has had to cope with the effects of the almost continuous decline of Britain's wool textile industry during the twentieth century.

The organic industrial structure of Leeds was a powerful source of develop-ment and key factors in the long term regional pre-eminence of Leeds were its ability to shift investment into new fields; the interaction between many diverse industries and firms; the support they provided for each other; and the flexibility of the economy as a whole.[27] This was recognized in 1893, when the 'good fortune' of Leeds in having an economy based on a diversity of manufacturing and commercial activity was emphasized by the Chamber of Commerce.[28] In the first decade of the twentieth century it was said that, 'the district is favoured by reason of the variety of its industries and the effects of bad trade are never felt to the same extent as in districts which are dependent on one or two industries merely'.[29] Labour, capital, and buildings were transferred from one activity to another with remarkable speed and apparent ease. Thus linen had employed 10 per cent of the local labour force at its peak in the mid-nineteenth century, but it succumbed to foreign competition after 1870, and by 1890 less than 2 per cent of Leeds workers were engaged in linen production.[30] The gap this left was quickly filled by clothing and other expanding trades and an examination of redundant flax mills reveals that most were soon in use again for other purposes.[31] That manufacturing was concentrated in a small number of well-endowed locations facilitated the change in use of industrial buildings. During the nineteenth century, industry was located sectorally along the Aire and Meanwood valleys, converging in those parts closest to the town centre, including the Leylands and the Beck. Thus in the 1890s most manufacturing took place in Woodhouse Carr, Burmantofts, Cardigan Fields, Gipton beck and near the centre of town around Park Square, Cookridge Street, Wade Lane and Call Lane, where manufacturers 'invaded or re-invaded commercial property'. Insurance, banking and legal services became concentrated in the area between Park Row and Briggate; while warehousing and merchanting was located predominantly in Wellington Street and Park Square.[32]

Engineering dominated the core trades in 1893. As steam became increasingly important in the nineteenth century, the legacy of engineers like Matthew Murray led to continuing success in building railway locomotives and rolling stock, traction and ploughing engines, and road rollers, all of which were to remain profitable well into the twentieth century. The steady demand for specialist machinery for mills and factories also put Leeds in the forefront of many other branches of this diverse industry and provided well-paid jobs for thousands of men in a multitude of firms across the city.[33] Their expertise benefited the city's other industries in return, as with the expanding printing industry whose most rapid growth took place between the 1880s and 1911, when its 8000 employees formed the fourth largest occupational category in the city.[34] Leeds engineers were responsible for innovations in printing press technology and lithographic machines which allowed the city's firms to develop an early specialization in colour printing, resulting in international recognition. The local industry's vitality and flexibility led to a high concentration of printing firms, with a myriad small firms coexisting alongside several giants. The general 'jobbing' printers served local demand, while the larger, more specialist firms reached a wider market. Heterogeneous organizational forms therefore characterized the structure of the industry. The firm of John Waddington, which forms the subject of Chapter 6, began in the jobbing sector, but from early links with the world of theatre, it built a reputation for quality and innovation that allowed it to grow in a most unusual manner. Although its public image is most strongly linked to playing cards and board games these have never formed the real basis of its prosperity. This came mostly from packaging, which supplied many local firms. Alf Cooke, which in 1893 was reputed to be the largest colour printer in Europe, subsequently acquired the status of Royal Printer and specialized in playing card printing alongside Waddingtons. E. J. Arnold had exploited the educational printing niche as the number of schools multiplied in the wake of the 1870 Education Act, becoming the 'largest school stationers and furnishers in Europe', and also producing long runs of railway timetables and fulfilling HMSO contracts. Other notable printing firms included Petty, which specialized in colour advertising work.[35]

An even more striking example of the mutual benefits of such co-operation is the success of tailoring from the late nineteenth century, which made it the largest tailoring centre in Europe at its peak in the inter-war years. Almost 40 per cent of the local workforce were then employed in the industry, making it the largest local employer of labour and its history touches many facets of Leeds life, something that is reflected today in the collective local memory. On the eve of the Second World War just one firm, Montague Burton Ltd., whose story is told in Chapter 7, employed 10,000 people at Hudson Road Mills. Striking though the development of Burton's was, several other local tailors, including Collier, Price, Jackson, and Hepworth were equally enduring and almost as successful. The industry depended on the willingness of local engineering firms to meet its technical needs and John Barran, who is credited with introducing the ready-made clothing trade to Leeds, worked closely with Greenwood and Batley in realizing his 'band knife', which allowed the bulk precision cutting of cloth. By 1893, not only were all the major clothing firms using Greenbat band knives, but the city contained no fewer than five sewing-machine making firms. Leeds soon earned an international reputation as a developer and a producer of clothing technology as a result.[36]

Leather tanning and boot and shoe making were more minor core trades which peaked in the 1890s, when Leeds was the country's premier tanning town, with a healthy trade in leather for footballs as well as being a major boot making centre.[37] The military demands of World War One brought a substantial, if short-lived boost, but then the majority of the town's boot and shoe firms failed to keep pace with technical innovations and changes in taste towards lighter leathers and shoes.[38] The trade as a whole settled at a low plateau by the late 1930s and though Stead and Simpson remains a name in high street shoe shopping today, Leeds shoe production sank virtually without trace. Some leather works specializing in coats and jackets have survived to the present, however, mostly in their traditional location of Sheepscar and Buslingthorpe.[39] The woollen and worsted industries similarly enjoyed a temporary revival in the early decades of the twentieth century, largely because of the buoyant market created by the local clothing trades but by 1925 this reprieve was over and the industry had virtually disappeared by the end of the Second World War.[40] Other sunset trades included pottery,[41] and dyestuffs.[42] While none of these was crucial to the Leeds economy, and in the long run the local economy was probably stronger without many of them, their demise was regretted. Echoes of vanished industries remain in any case, for instance the firm of Joseph Watson, the subject of Chapter 8, which moved successfully from tanning into soap production, had originally been based on the demand for soap from woollen manufacturers and the supply of lanolin that cleaning fleeces produced. The firm acquired the nickname 'Soapy Joe's', which has survived as it branched out into toiletries, and as part of Elida Gibbs it is still a major employer of women in the city.

Although engineering was exceptional in the extent and depth of its linkages, the majority of Leeds firms found the bulk of their custom with other Leeds businesses in the same way. All local industries of any size were supported by a group of ancillary trades, which were established and developed through the demand created by the location leaders. The clothing industry flourished partly because, in the 1890s, production was located in two concentrated areas: in and around Park Square, which maximized commercial contact, or in the Leylands district, where manufacture was largely based in workshops subcontracting for the larger factories.[43] The large, centrally-located firms thus developed close links with the secondary concentration to the benefit of both, especially by the creation of economies of scale which were only otherwise available to the very large enterprises. This was particularly rewarding for this type of highly innovative, newly established industry. Although the importance of close contact among firms had lessened by 1914, these groupings of trades into locational concentrations in some respects resembled the industrial districts that are currently viewed as a component of flexible production methods, which are again being promoted as an effective method of encouraging new types of manufacturing enterprise.

III

For the engineering industry the very lack of specialization that had been one of its strengths has begun to cause difficulties and its overall growth has been slower than the national average for several decades. Moreover, expansion was least impressive in the new sectors of the industry where potential for growth was greatest. An exception to this is the firm of Thackray, the subject of chapter 9, which, as a maker of surgical instruments and supplies, can be seen to have specialized in precision engineering and survived profitably through a process of continuous innovation. There was also some success with bicycle production, and Leeds even gained a place in the annals of aircraft manufacture, but production was not large enough to form the basis of new growth sectors. Particularly serious in the long term was the absence of automobile production, for although one Leeds firm had enjoyed a brief excursion into car production[44] and another manufactured motor car parts, the loss of metal making to those areas with a comparative advantage in steel production severely reduced the capacity of the Leeds industry to compete. New specialities in heating and ventilation plant, and in conveying and elevating machinery developed, but growth was most pronounced in cast and pressed metal products such as dustbins, lawnmowers and metal furniture, which incorporated very little in the way of 'state of the art' engineering technology.[45] Today, a small number of dynamic high-tech firms exist in Leeds, but the overall impression of the industry is one of heavy producer goods production for which future demand is limited.

Until the 1960s Leeds remained without question the centre of Britain's tailoring trade and the city's manufacturers enjoyed enormous success through encouraging and facilitating the universal male practice of suit-wearing after the war. They were slow to respond to the move away from suits after the mid-1950s, however, and many of the names from the early days disappeared in the recession of the 1970s. Heaton's, whose striking building at the corner of North Street and New York Road (at one time known as Heaton's corner) still bears testimony to its former greatness, collapsed. So did the firm of David Little, after more than 100 years in the business. Other firms were taken over, such as John Barran, now owned by Beau Brummel. Some became part of larger groups: Joseph Hepworth was incorporated into Next; and Montague Burton Ltd. no longer manufactures, existing as Montague Burton Retailing within the Burton Group. The shake-out of clothing firms was a reflection of the industry's failure to respond to market changes and to technical and product innovations introduced by foreign competitors in the post-war years. Of those firms that have survived to the 1990s, the majority have succeeded through niche marketing and a judicious use of new and flexible technologies. The three most important, Berwin, Sumrie, and Centaur, are firms of moderate size, producing quality garments for top-of-the-range retail outlets. Their future prospects are reasonable but the Leeds clothing industry as a whole is a shadow of its former self.

Printing is still a major industry and Waddingtons have developed a stream of new products over the years including jigsaws, waxed containers, and printed plastic margarine tubs. Despite some spectacular failures alongside these successes, and notwithstanding two hostile takeover bids from the redoubtable Robert Maxwell, the firm has survived in relatively good shape to the present. Many other Leeds printers also suffered from Maxwell's attentions and few escaped so lightly: E. J. Arnold's resulting demise has left a hole in the local printing trade. Alf Cooke has ceased to exist in its earlier form, but the name is perpetuated by the new firm Alf Cooke Transfer Print (1982) Ltd. Apart from a small number of medium sized firms, most of the rest of the local trade is still carried on by small letter press and jobbing printers among whom there is substantial turnover. The traditional strength of Leeds printing, however, is still apparent in the supply of new entrants to take the place of those giving up.

IV

The variegated nature of business activity in Leeds continues to be viewed as its major strength, 'based equally on a wide range of manufactures and the full complement of ... commercial and other services which characterize a regional centre',[46] but the dynamic and flexible quality of its industrial structure has become less pronounced over recent decades and the industrial symbiosis of 1893 is less apparent today. The cohesion of the business community as reflected in the activities of the Chamber of Commerce remains, yet the flexibility of production and the fluidity of industrial structure are much less pronounced. The replacement of declining sectors by those with long term growth potential, which was so evident in 1893, almost ceased until recently. In purely industrial terms, Leeds can therefore no longer be regarded as a growth point in the national economy.[47] Evidence from the annual reports of the Leeds Chamber of Commerce and elsewhere indicates that the underrepresentation of the 'new' industries of the twentieth century and the failure to share in the growth sectors of vehicles, chemicals, and electrical goods from the 1920s, has posed enduring problems. Manufacturing activity as a whole declined in the 1950s when industrial employment rose by 12 per cent nationally, precisely because Leeds has not produced the goods for which demand is expanding fastest. Since the 1960s, moreover, Leeds has failed to keep pace with changes in the structure of demand, technical expertise, industrial organization and communications, leading in the 1970s to a preponderance of old-established industries and too many low-tech, labour-intensive manufacturing processes undertaken in small scale units of production.[48]

This does not mean that the Leeds economy is in danger of collapse, however, and if manufacturing output has declined absolutely, service sector activities are expanding substantially and employment in the distributive trades and professional services has expanded more than commensurably. Accountancy has been a particular growth area in the past decade, with the major national firms all turning to Leeds as the location for their north-eastern branches, making it the fastest growing centre in the north and second only to Manchester in absolute terms. Such trends have to be seen in the context of the city's position as a regional centre, and a growing role as a provider of services for the surrounding towns and cities, allowing them to concentrate more on manufacturing, is only to be expected in an era of ever-greater specialization and ever-faster communications. Such developments simply mirror on a regional scale the national trends in sectoral shifts.

The impact of the economic downturn of the 1980s and 1990s has therefore been muted, as was the depression of the early 1920s, when it was said that, 'because of the various nature of its industries... [Leeds] may not have suffered as severely as some other towns. The outlook for the future ...is more hopeful than in some centres'.[49] The difference this time is that recovery starts from a much weaker manufacturing base, and while there is nothing inherently unsound about the shift of employment into the service sector, allowing industries like engineering to vanish is much more contentious. The prospects for the local economy after 1993 forms the subject of Chapter 10, and it is certain that Leeds will have many more adaptations to make if it is to continue to provide its inhabitants with a high standard of living over the next century.

In the same way, while it is clear that solutions have been found to most of the social and environmental problems reformers of 1893 would have considered the most pressing, other problems have arisen to take their place. All parts of the city now have access to basic services, and despite the mistakes of recent decades, the housing stock is incomparably better than it was a century ago, but this has not meant the end of poverty and of personal misery for the poorest. There are still homeless people and some housing is still clearly below any acceptable modern standard, yet building is at its lowest ebb since the Second World War. Standards have risen, moreover, and what was once accepted, such as ragged, barefoot children, would now cause immediate concern. These are not problems and issues unique to Leeds, but they still have to be faced locally. If the aim is to have a city where all have jobs and an adequate income to cover their needs, then there is much still to do, and getting the economy right will be at the heart of any solution.

In closing, it is interesting that the preoccupations of the business community in 1993 bear a surprising resemblance to those of 1893. The local economy was depressed, but, 'the year closes with a more hopeful feeling than for some time past', recorded the Chamber of Commerce Annual Report of that year. Throughout the continent and the USA, and even Britain's own colonies and dominions, tariffs continued to restrict the export trade of local business. The Chamber took a broad view of its role, and its solutions to the immediate problems of the business community included the active promotion of decimalization and of a Channel Tunnel. Members had a long wait for both, but perhaps now that both have been achieved, Leeds will prove to be on the verge of new-found prosperity.

Bibliography

M. W. Beresford and G. R. J. Jones (eds) *Leeds and its Region*, 1967.
Ivan Broadhead, *Leeds*, 1990.
Derek Fraser (ed) *A History of Modern Leeds*, 1980.
A. C. Price, *Leeds and its Neighbourhood*, 1909.
A. N. Shimmin, *The Ninety-seven industries of Leeds*, 1926.

Notes

[1] Peter Coles-Johnson of the Leeds Chamber of Commerce, and Stan Kenyon, Director of the Department of Planning, Leeds City Council, provided documentary and other information helpful in the writing of this chapter. Their assistance is gratefully acknowledged.

[2] Stan Kenyon very kindly provided the information on boundary changes and the associated map contained in this chapter.

[3] E. M. Sigsworth, 'The industrial revolution', in M. W. Beresford and G. R. J. Jones (eds), *Leeds and its Region*, 1967, p. 149.

[4] For an excellent survey of the development of Leeds's Cloth Halls and markets, see Kevin Grady, 'Commercial, marketing and retailing amenities, 1700–1914', in Derek Fraser (ed), *A History of Modern Leeds*, 1980, pp. 177–99.

[5] The Leeds Stock Exchange has only recently ceased to exist. For further information on the development see J. R. Killick and W. A. Thomas, 'The provincial Stock Exchanges, 1830–1870', *Economic History Review*, 2nd ser, XXIII, 1970, pp. 96–111.

[6] H. Parris, 'Leeds and its railways', *Leeds Journal*, 1955, pp. 157–68.

[7] The co-op in Leeds was a large and highly integrated concern. In 1896, the *Yorkshire Factory Times* proclaimed it to be 'the largest on earth'. More information on the Co-op can be found in W. G. Rimmer, 'Retailing', in *Leeds Journal*, 1955, pp. 379–82.

[8] The impetus for the Arcades came partly from the shortage of vacant land fronting the main streets. see Grady, *op cit.*, p. 194.

[9] Ivan Broadhead, *Leeds*, 1990, pp. 100–103.

[10] Out-of-town shopping is threatened at a site identified near the ring road at West Park.

[11] E. M. Sigsworth, 'Development of the Press', *Leeds Journal*, 1958, pp. 441–4.

[12] 'Leeds is at last a city but is no more civilised for that', *Yorkshire Factory Times* 10 February 1893.

[13] C. J. Morgan, 'Demographic change, 1771–1911', in Fraser, *Modern Leeds* p. 67.

[14] Much of the information in this paragraph comes form W. G. Rimmer, 'Historical Survey', *Leeds Journal*, 1954, pp. 391–4.

[15] *ibid.*

[16] In 1891, Thomson-Houston, an American company, electrified three miles of tram track between Sheepscar and Roundhay. In 1894, Leeds Corporation took over the Leeds Tramway Company and electrified the entire tramway system, supplying power from a station at Crown Point Bridge. Information from W. G. Rimmer, 'Electricity', *Leeds Journal*, 1958, pp. 299–303.

[17] F. J. Glover, 'Transport', *Leeds Journal*, 1956, pp. 299–304.

[18] W. G. Rimmer, 'Stage and Screen', *Leeds Journal*, 1957, pp. 7–11.

[19] Broadhead, *Leeds*, p. 78.

[20] The Yorkshire College opened in 1874 and became part of Victoria University in 1887. Its independence in 1904 was prompted by the departure of the other Victoria University participants, Manchester and Liverpool. P. H. J. H. Gosden and A. J. Taylor (eds), *Studies in the history of a university, 1874–1974*, 1974.

[21] The three breweries were Tetley, Melbourne, and Hemingway. E. M. Sigsworth, 'Brewing', *Leeds Journal*, 1956, pp. 79–81.

[22] John Barran, clothing manufacturer and notable local citizen, was instrumental in the purchase of the park, and financed a commemorative fountain which remains today.

[23] 80,000 fans congregated for the Rolling Stone concert in 1982, fewer than the 100,000 who gathered for the Military Tattoo in 1926 for the tercentenary (of Leeds's incorporation as a municipal borough) celebrations.

[24] E. M. Sigsworth, 'Sport', *Leeds Journal*, 1957, pp. 71–79.

[25] E. M. Sigsworth, 'The rise of Football', *Leeds Journal*, 1957, pp. 149–58.

[26] The Leeds mining district produced 25 per cent of the West Riding's coal output in the second half of the nineteenth century when it supplied the energy requirements of many Leeds industries. W. G. Rimmer, 'Coal', *Leeds Journal*, 1954, pp. 3–6.

[27] This is illustrated in great detail in M. F. Ward, 'Industrial development and location in Leeds north of the river Aire, 1775–1914', unpublished PhD thesis, University of Leeds, 1972; and E. J. Connell, 'Industrial development in south Leeds, 1790–1914', unpublished PhD thesis, University of Leeds, 1975.

[28] Leeds Chamber of Commerce, Annual Report, 1893. Thanks to Peter Coles-Johnson for access to this document.

[29] Leeds Chamber of Commerce, Annual Report, 1902.

[30] W. G. Rimmer, 'Flax', *Leeds Journal*, 1954, pp. 175–8. For a comprehensive account of the history of the Leeds linen industry, see W. G. Rimmer, *Marshall's of Leeds, Flax Spinners 1788–1886*, 1960.

[31] Ward, Thesis, passim.

[32] *ibid*, pp. 135–6.

[33] In 1914, Leeds contained 50 different branches of engineering, an industry that had links with the majority of Leeds' trades. Ward, thesis, pp. 123–9.

[34] W. G. Rimmer, 'Printing', *Leeds Journal*, 1958, pp. 269–75.

[35] *ibid*, pp. 353–7; and Ward, thesis, p. 131.

[36] Ward, thesis, p. 129. see also Joan Thomas, *A History of the Leeds clothing industry*, 1955, pp. 37–40.

[37] By 1890, demand for footballs was so great that manufacturers ordered their hides in 'quantities of 500 at a time', J. Buckman, 'The later phases of industrialisation', in Beresford and Jones (ed), *Leeds and its region*, p. 163. Leeds was still 'the most famous and productive town in the world' for football leather in the 1920's. Leeds Chamber of Commerce, Annual Report, 1922.

[38] Ward, thesis, p. 119.

[39] For more detail see W. G. Rimmer, 'Leather', *Leeds Journal*, 1957, pp. 377–82.

[40] Leeds Chamber of Commerce, Annual Reports, 1922–27.

[41] W. G. Rimmer, 'Pottery', *Leeds Journal*, 1958, pp. 185–9.

[42] E. M. Sigsworth, 'Dyeing', *Leeds Journal*, 1955, pp. 3–5.

[43] Thomas, *Leeds clothing*, passim.

[44] Buckman, 'Later stages', p. 165, makes reference to some experimentation in the 1890's.

[45] W. G. Rimmer, 'Engineering', *Leeds Journal*, 1955, pp. 305–8.

[46] Leeds Review Plan, 1968, p. 64. (Submitted to the Secretary of State 1968; approved by the Secretary of State, 1972). Stan Kenyon kindly provided this report.

[47] G. F. Rainnie, 'Economic Structure', in Beresford and Jones (eds) *Leeds and its region*, p. 236.

[48] 'very few firms in Leeds are large by national standards...most are small family run businesses'. *ibid*, p. 224.

[49] Leeds Chamber of Commerce, Annual Report, 1922.

CHAPTER 2

Yorkshire Post Newspapers Ltd: perseverance rewarded[1]

Stephen Caunce

A S BRITAIN entered the 1990s, daily morning newspapers were still published in only ten English towns and cities outside London.[2] The *Yorkshire Post*, based in Leeds, was one of them and surveys of journalism usually accord it a higher status than the vast majority of the regional press and thereby support its claim to be 'Yorkshire's national newspaper'. John Merrill of the University of Missouri School of Journalism wrote in 1968 that 'along with Edinburgh's *Scotsman* and Manchester's *Guardian*, it stands at the top of Britain's provincial dailies in general quality and national prestige,'[3] and it has had several editors of national stature, most notably Sir Linton Andrews (1939–60).

In 1988 Alistair Hetherington wrote that, 'the primary news priority is in the political, social and industrial category, with a preference for Yorkshire or North-eastern events. That must be the proper priority for a serious newspaper. Sex, scandal and gossip are absent from the *Yorkshire Post*'s pages. The

Plate 2.1 Sir William Linton Andrews, 1886–1972, editor of the *Leeds Mercury* 1923–39, editor of the *Yorkshire Post* 1939–60. Surprisingly, he was the first Yorkshireman to edit the *Post*. During his time with the newspaper he came to be recognized as a leading figure in the newspaper industry, chairing the Press Council 1955–59 and working hard to raise the professional status and training of journalists. His knighthood was a reflection of the general esteem in which he was held.

coverage of national news is necessarily more limited than in the 'quality' nationals, and only the most pressing of international news is carried. The business and financial pages provide a competent service, again with a leaning towards Yorkshire news but altogether on a smaller scale than the major nationals'.[4] With the largest sale among English regional morning newspapers, averaging around 92,000 copies per day in recent years,[5] it is the last English regional title that is generally given the sort of quasi-national status that the *Glasgow Herald* and the *Scotsman* still preserve north of the border. Most other regional mornings serve scattered rural constituencies and are very different, while its old rival the *Guardian* is now a London newspaper in nearly every way, and the *Birmingham Post* has accepted a largely local role. Before the Second World War, however, together with the *Yorkshire Post*, they had spoken for large, economically significant regions whose interests often diverged from those seen in London newspapers, and their editorials were taken very seriously at home and abroad.

I

The *Yorkshire Post*'s strong sense of its own identity is reinforced by proud claims of a continuous production history since 1754,[6] but such continuity should not be taken to indicate inertia. Virtually nothing about the present operation resembles the early days, and during its long history the ownership and management structures have been radically transformed several times as the scale of the enterprise has grown more and more complex. Thus it began life as a weekly, the *Leeds Intelligencer*, and it only acquired the present title and began daily publication in 1866, a year after the Yorkshire Conservative Newspaper Company Limited (YCN) had been formed to bring a professionalism impossible under the ramshackle partnerships and sole proprietorial regimes previously in control. During the past century YCN has started new titles alongside the *Post*, most notably the *Yorkshire Evening Post*, and it has also bought up both complementary and rival titles in an attempt to dominate the market for news in Leeds and in Yorkshire. All have had a role to play in the group, but most have been short-lived and few of those currently published have a long history. Since 1969 Yorkshire Post Newspapers Limited (YPN), as it is now known, has been a part of the United Provincial Newspapers Group, though it is run as a separate company for most purposes. The acquisition of the *Daily Express*, the *Sunday Express*, and the *Star* in 1985 caused the group to rename itself United Newspapers, but did not affect the operational independence of the Leeds company. Today its modern headquarters building is a Leeds landmark housing a large number of news-related

Plate 2.2   The new headquarters at Bean Ing, Wellington Street, officially opened by the Prince of Wales on 9 December 1970. This is an uncompromisingly modern design, purpose built for newspaper production, and winner of a RIBA award in 1971. The tower on the right, with its digital clock and temperature readout, has become familiar to all users of the Leeds inner ring road system.

companies and when Yorkshire was given its own ITV franchise in 1967, YPN even branched out into television for a time by joining the successful YTV consortium by invitation after its own bid failed.[7]

The *Yorkshire Post* has always been the flagship title of the group, but the business must be seen as an enterprise concerned with a generic product, news and information, which can be disseminated profitably in a wide and increasing variety of ways, and not simply as an extension of its leading title. Moreover, the fact that, 'nothing is more perishable than news',[8] as an anonymous YPN writer recently commented, means that the whole newspaper industry operated and continues to operate in ways that set it apart from the average business. Before we can see why YCN developed as it did, we have therefore to consider some of these generalized forces that constitute the operational matrix of such a firm. Thus, in the nineteenth century, local newspapers gained enormously from improvements in communications, which aided them both in gathering and selling news, but which also exposed them to competition from larger operations based outside their original catchment area.

This pressure has grown during the present century as newspaper readerships have grown beyond any early expectations and enormous economies of scale have thereby been opened up, though even now there still seems to be no market for daily continental newspapers in either Europe or the USA. The market for newspapers has always been segmented in this and other ways, and it is the positioning both of individual titles and of groups of titles that often determines the success and failure of companies. This is a dynamic rather than a static operation, and standing still is simply not an option for very long, so marketing assumes an overriding importance characteristic of few other industries. The evolution of the company's marketing strategy and the way this has affected the company structure over the past hundred years forms the basis of this article. Since a short study cannot be exhaustive, three occasions where radical change occurred have been chosen for detailed examination with the intention of pointing up the wider issues they all illuminate, despite their widely-varying immediate origins.

The company's location in Leeds is a key factor in itself, for British newspaper publishing has always been more geographically concentrated in the capital than that of any comparable country: Paris, for instance, has never dominated the French press in the same way.[9] Moreover, Leeds was never a newspaper town like Manchester and Glasgow, the most important centres outside London. After Manchester, in 1947 Leeds apparently had the largest number of journalists in England outside London,[10] but it played no real part in the national press network. The only known occasion when a national newspaper set up in Leeds was a short-lived attempt by the *Daily Chronicle* between 1925 and 1930, and its failure seems to show that the general strategy of clustering in a few main centres was a wise one for titles without clear local roots.[11] The most basic consideration in this century for all newspapers outside London has been whether the protection offered by remoteness, which makes London news slow to arrive and of less interest to local people, is balanced or even overwhelmed by the difficulties of gathering national and international news, which mostly has to be done in London and which has been of growing importance for a mass audience as well as the upper classes.

This is not simply a matter of local versus national papers. The *Yorkshire Post*'s title proclaims a county status rather than identifying with Leeds alone, and this is worth examining. The territory YPN has traditionally claimed as its own extends over everything 'twixt Trent and Tweed', as the *Post*'s masthead asserted for much of the past century. In practice, most of its sales are made within a sort of greater Yorkshire that extends over the old county boundaries to the north to some extent, extensively to the south, and hardly at all to the west. Its heartland is naturally in the textile area around Leeds, and Sheffield's sense of a separate identity has made it hard to dominate the urbanized parts of the southern portion of the West Riding, but it has a strong hold on those involved in agriculture throughout all three ridings. Bradford, Halifax, Huddersfield, Hull, Middlesbrough, Scarborough, and York all maintain daily newspapers even today, and there is a multitude of weekly titles serving smaller centres. Based in the largest conurbation in the county, however, the *Post* inevitably has advantages in regional news operations, similar to those a London base gives in the national field. Thus the *Yorkshire Post* is always poised somewhere between the nationals and the truly local newspapers. It constantly tries to persuade readers in urban areas of Yorkshire to desert their local titles, while trying to fend off outside titles trying to persuade its own readers to do the same thing. It had less chance than a Manchester paper of joining in the twentieth-century race for really big circulations, but it was in a dominant geographical position in a heavily-populated and clearly-defined region of its own.

Competition between newspapers is often presented in terms of relative journalistic quality, and this is important. It can, however, obscure the simple fact that an unprofitable but beautifully written newspaper cannot survive forever, however worthy it may seem. The various changes of ownership of the *Times* in the last few decades, together with the recent history of the *Observer*, shows a widespread willingness to persevere with prestige, quality titles even when commercial criteria would indicate immediate closure, but also that in the end a hopeless financial position will force drastic action. YPN's policies can similarly best be explained by a mixture of commercial and other factors. Thus, in its first issue, on Monday 2 July 1866, the *Yorkshire Post* stated that 'the political principles of this journal are Conservative; while supporting every practical improvement, it will resist organic changes.... It will be at once conservative and progressive, a foe to democracy and revolution, but the firm friend of all constitutional reform'. The original company name makes it clear how deep this commitment ran, and in 1939 A. J. Cummings of the *News Chronicle* described the paper as the leading Conservative organ in the provinces.[12] For most of its history as an independent company, shares could only be transferred after the Board of Directors was satisfied that new owners held appropriate political convictions, and the evidence to the 1947 Royal Commission on the Press makes it clear that this was taken seriously.[13] The political affiliation was dropped from the company name in 1967 only because it was an unavoidable part of buying into the YTV franchise, and support for Conservatism is still written into the articles of association,[14] if it is now usually muted in the editorial content of the company's newspapers.

Proprietorial egotism has been another notable feature of the newspaper industry, but it has never been particularly evident at YCN. There were roughly 1500 shareholders at the end of the Second World War[15] and no single share-holding ever dominated the company before the 1960s. However the Becketts, by origin a Leeds banking family, had been prime movers in the company's formation and for most of its independent existence they played a large part in directing its affairs. They were prominent local Conservatives and several of them were MPs at various times, including the first chairman, William Beckett Denison. Every chairman thereafter was also a family member until the retirement of William's son, the Hon. Rupert Beckett in 1950. In the 1920s he was described as 'a heavy-jowled, heavily-built, slow-moving Yorkshireman, who looked more like a squire from Henry Fielding's pages than a city magnate, a chairman of newspapers and a director of Westminster Bank, the L.N.E.R., the Royal Exchange Insurance Co., and the Aire and Calder Canal.... In his prime [he] did not merely preside at Board meetings. He ruled them. He inspired the utmost respect and wielded powerful influence.... [Yet] it would be astonishing to most people that ... [he] would not dream of forbidding the editor to have a leader on a certain subject'.[16] The Becketts seem to have had no desire to be the Yorkshire equivalent of the Scott family who owned and edited the *Manchester Guardian*, let alone the Harmsworths, even though the company history cannot be disentangled from their own.

Finally, we must not allow the present monopoly that YPN holds over news in Leeds to blind us to the fact that in 1893 the *Yorkshire Post* was not pre-ordained to succeed. The *Leeds Mercury* had always had a far higher circulation than the *Post*, and it had also been the more prestigious title when it was owned and edited by the famous Liberal propagandist, Edward Baines, earlier in the century. Thus, James Grant, surveying the provincial press in 1870, said of Leeds that 'Until about twenty years ago ... the *Leeds Mercury* was published weekly, and probably had the largest circulation, the greatest number of advertisements, and was the most profitable provincial newspaper

Plate 2.3 The Hon Rupert Evelyn Beckett, 1870–1955. A highly successful and respected banker and businessman, and chairman of the Yorkshire Conservative Newspaper Company 1920–50. His career began in his family's two Yorkshire banks, whose amalgamation with the Westminster he masterminded in 1921. After ten years on their board he was elected chairman, making him a businessman of genuinely national stature. He died a millionaire and left four daughters.

of any in Great Britain.... It was transformed into a daily paper, published at a penny.... about fifteen or sixteen years ago.... [and] a weekly edition, with supplement... is said to have an enormous circulation'.[17]

II

The launch of the *Yorkshire Evening Post* by YCN in 1890 is the first episode to be examined here. It stemmed from a dramatic alteration in the environment in which newspapers were operating, one that offered both huge opportunities and warnings of novel difficulties ahead. The opportunities derived from the rapid rise in the sales of newspapers to groups which previously had not bought them at all in the late nineteenth century. The trend was first visible in the success of the *Daily Telegraph* as the first penny newspaper[18] and the immense popularity of magazines like *Tit Bits*. This culminated in the new journalism of the *Daily Mail*, whose first issue in 1896 sold 400,000 copies, something completely unprecedented for a daily. The huge extra flow of revenue from both sales and advertising transformed the industry, and even at a local level it allowed the employment of significant numbers of journalists on the larger titles, whereas previously general printing work and the sale of books and stationery were essential sidelines: as late as 1831 the *Intelligencer*'s circulation was only about 1,500 per week.

Charles Pebody, who became editor in 1882, could therefore talk of making the *Yorkshire Post* into 'the *Times* of the North of England', something that would have been inconceivable in earlier decades. He moved away from a heavy concentration on politics and the frequent verbatim reprinting of long speeches towards cultural features, and foreign dispatches from the *Times* and the *Telegraph* were reprinted, the latter contributing a great deal to the *Post*'s reporting of the Boer War. The formation of the Press Association as a co-operative venture by provincial newspapers in 1870 had gradually improved their national news coverage, and then Reuters similarly improved foreign coverage in ways no one paper could have afforded on its own. The circulation grew steadily as a result, and a weekly supplement called the *Yorkshire Weekly Post* added a further dimension, but something more radical was needed to keep abreast of the times. If there was now a substantial market for news in Yorkshire, with transport improving so markedly the danger was that it would be invaded by London titles, offering themselves as superior products. Local news was therefore seized on in the regions as a commodity nationals could not provide, and since evening publication reinforced the local advantage, many evening titles were founded at this time. Thus the *Leeds Daily News*, founded in 1872, changed its name to the *Yorkshire Evening News* in 1905, and while it never equalled the circulation of the *Evening Post*, Leeds proved able to sustain both titles until after the Second World War. Newspapers like the *Leeds Intelligencer* did not begin as local news sheets, as might be expected. While local advertisements were always important, their local news content was frequently very slight in the eighteenth century. They relied rather on lifting standard items from official dispatches or from London newspapers to fill their pages as cheaply as possible.[19]

The *Evening Post* moved YCN for the first time from dependence on one title towards a strategy of aiming separate products at particular groups, thus allowing the morning title to maintain the quality orientation so important to its owners without surrendering the chance to serve a mass readership. Its circulation soared from an initial annual total of nearly nine million to twenty million by 1896, overtaking the *Yorkshire Post* in its fifth year, as fig 2.1 shows, and peaking initially at nearly fifty eight million in 1901. In 1905 it nearly reached fifty nine million, and with an average of well over fifty million down to 1914, it became 'one of the most successful evening newspapers in the world'.[20] In contrast, the morning title peaked at just over twenty three million in 1900, and it was averaging around twenty million when the war came. The *Evening Post* also proved a valuable boost to advertising revenue with its larger

Figure 2.1   Circulation 1881–1922

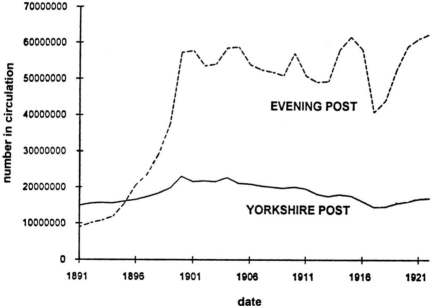

Source: YCN Accounts Ledger, Yorkshire Post.

Figure 2.2   Sources of income, Yorkshire Post

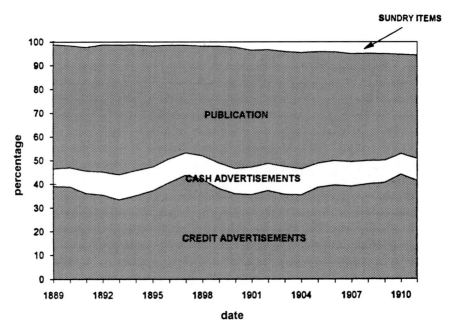

Source: YCN Accounts Ledger, Yorkshire Post.

and different readership, for just as with readership the advertising market is highly segmented.[21] Advertisers get value for money by selecting those papers and magazines which most nearly reach their potential customers and no-one else. Local newspapers are very cost-effective where saturation coverage of one area is the aim, and they may also serve particular trades that are based in their locality. Linton Andrews noted that between the wars the Saturday *Yorkshire Post* was so full of property advertising that 'it was often the largest issue of any daily paper in Britain'.[22] Personal, classified advertising has proved a great strength of the local press, and many people buy the paper mainly for the adverts. Historically, advertising revenue is usually at least as high as that from sales, and is frequently higher. Items like the sale of waste paper provided a small income as well, but they were of little significance as figs 2.2 and 2.3 show.

The *Evening Post*'s performance in terms of profit does not match that suggested by its sales, however, as fig 2.4 shows. Starting a new title was not an easy or cheap option, even though it needed no London office of its own, and its more modest journalistic aims allowed staffing levels well below the *Yorkshire Post*'s. The total staff employed by YCN still increased significantly. It shared Change Court, the *Yorkshire Post*'s headquarters in Albion Street in

Figure 2.3   Sources of income, Evening Post

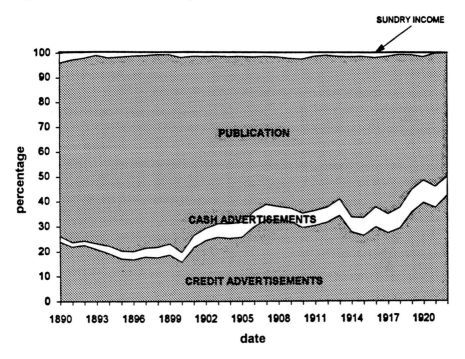

Source: YCN Accounts Ledger, Yorkshire Post.

the centre of Leeds. New printing machinery, consisting of six four-rolled web machines, was installed to cope with the massive increase in output that would be required. With such start-up costs, the new title did not break even until 1895, and though it surpassed the profits of the *Yorkshire Post* in 1904, it was not until 1912 that it became the consistent moneymaker for the company that it has been ever since. Wartime conditions led to a huge temporary boost to sales of the morning title, but in normal times it was now the junior partner in profit terms. YCN as a whole, therefore, had now secured a much stronger base of sales in its region, something it could never have done by concentrating on a *Yorkshire Post* run as they wished it to be run.

III

The threat to regional morning titles from bigger units based in London but producing and printing northern editions in Manchester grew rapidly after 1918. With Manchester's privileged access to very densely populated areas in

Plate 2.4   In June 1866, the newly formed Yorkshire Conservative Newspaper Company began preparing Change Court, Albion Street, its new headquarters, for the production of the first copy of the *Yorkshire Post*. As the company expanded, extra adjoining buildings were incorporated, some of which had begun life as houses. None were intended for industrial use and by the middle decades of this century it resembled a rabbit warren. While it is remembered with affection by many, it was not an environment that encouraged efficiency and modern working practices.

the north west, several locally-based titles were also able to build up impressive circulations, which put Leeds in a dangerous position since it was less than fifty miles away. The *Daily Despatch* sold 414,000 copies per day in 1930, for instance, and the *Empire News* and the *Sunday Chronicle* achieved 1,286,000 and 930,000 in sales every Sunday in the same year, both higher than the *Sunday Express*. Greater literacy and longer journeys to work by public transport continued to enlarge markets for news, and titles which aggressively built such big circulations, and especially those selling throughout the country, could then guarantee a huge audience for advertisers. This justified premium rates, which kept down sale prices to readers, so further increasing circulations and enhancing the demand for advertising space.[23] Moreover, as Rupert Beckett said in 1947, 'your editorial expenses are just as large if you have a circulation of 100,000 as they are if you have a circulation of 1,000,000'.[24] In essence, the decades between the wars consisted of a long struggle to keep the *Yorkshire Post* viable in its traditional form in the face of such formidable rivals, a

Figure 2.4   Gross profits, Yorkshire Post Newspapers

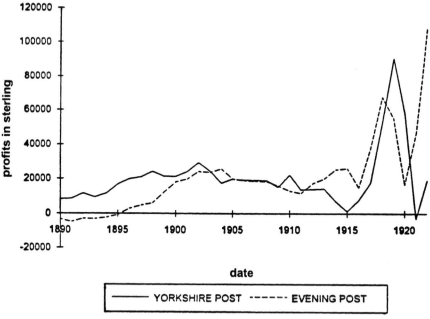

Source: YCN Accounts Ledger, Yorkshire Post.

struggle which was ultimately unsuccessful. This struggle constitutes the second of our pivotal episodes.

Many national titles also found it hard to cope in this environment, and out of the eight nationals published in 1900, only three still existed as separate titles in 1938. Of seven new titles started in the same period, three failed.[25] While it was possible to sustain the *Times* on a daily circulation of 187,000 in 1930, 132,000 proved inadequate to keep the *Morning Post* profitable, and in 1937 it merged with the *Daily Telegraph*, the only quality paper that really prospered. Halving its price from 2*d.* to 1*d.* in 1929 increased its circulation from 90,000 to 175,000 in a year, and then to 637,000 in 1937. Pricecutting alone was not enough, however, for the *Morning Post* had tried it and failed to pick up enough extra circulation to make up for the lost revenue, or to boost its very poor advertising sales.[26] In this context, the *Yorkshire Post*'s circulation of 30,000 in the 1930s was clearly inadequate to sustain its aspirations, and the total provincial morning daily sale of around 2,400,000 throughout the 1930s was the same as that of the *Daily Express* alone in 1937.[27] Its only reason for hope was that it was not competing directly with the titles with mass readerships, and a survey in 1935 showed that no real national market yet existed in the quality sector that it wished to be part of. The 'national' qualities actually functioned almost as regional newspapers of southern England, with 28 per cent of their sales made in the south east, and a further 31 per cent in East Anglia and the West Country in almost equal proportions.[28] They took 13.7 per cent of the whole market in the south east, but only 3.6 per cent in Lancashire and 1.6 per cent in the northeastern counties.

The merging of these regional markets was to be expected in the near future and the *Yorkshire Post* needed a strategy to cope. It could, in theory at least, seek national sales, just as they were trying to sell in Yorkshire. There was a proven demand for the *Manchester Guardian* and the *Yorkshire Post* in the south, based on their distinctive points of view rather than their geographical base, for both were more anti-Hitler than the London press, and the *Post* was the only Conservative newspaper to take this line. In practice, however, news-paper distribution relied chiefly on specially chartered trains to achieve the speed and reliability that were essential to such an ephemeral product, and building national circulations in the twentieth century depended heavily on proximity to the natural hub of the national transport system, which was London. National papers took to printing in Manchester and Glasgow to get speedy access to the best networks serving the north of England and Scotland respectively. They co-operated with locally based operations in this, but they would certainly not assist a move to send papers south as that threatened their London editions' market share there. Northern newspapers wishing to reach a wide market in the south had either to act alone, and chartering trains was only economic if it was done by many titles acting together, or else to send their papers via London, which would mean printing long before their London rivals as well as incurring additional costs.

Both the *Manchester Guardian* and the *Yorkshire Post* were forced to the conclusion during this period that the only long term options were to produce a London edition, or else to remodel themselves according to the example of their evening titles. Even winning sales locally from the popular national papers was difficult, however, for great circulation battles were being fought out through free gifts to new readers. Advertising rates responded very sensitively to passing circulation benchmarks, such as a million, which was the goal at first, and then two million. The returns in terms of sales income were bound to be small given the expense involved, and might even be counter-productive on the surface, but in terms of overall revenue the market leaders found it worthwhile to commit enormous resources. In contrast the best the *Post* group could afford were very modest efforts.[29]

The *Manchester Guardian* always rejected the notion of 'Manchesterising' itself, as it called it and this is why, after the war, it saw no alternative to a move to London.[30] Since the *Yorkshire Post* has stayed in Leeds, it is generally believed that they never considered any other option but the local one. In 1923, however, Countess Bathurst put the *Morning Post* up for sale due to its perilous financial situation.[31] Soundings were made for purchasers who would maintain it as an avowedly Conservative newspaper, and to the *Yorkshire Post* it seemed a natural partner. Negotiations began in the summer and a price was agreed in October, but Lady Bathurst wavered over accepting it and as YCN needed time to raise the money and to get full approval of its board, a hiatus ensued. The true state of the London paper's finances now became clearer, and the offer was reduced in December. As 1924 progressed YCN became ever cooler, and in March a consortium of rich Conservatives headed by the Duke of Northumberland made a higher bid for overtly political reasons, which was accepted, and the project was abandoned in Leeds. There were probably few regrets as the years went by, for the *Morning Post* proved to be little more than a licence to lose money for its new owners, who had no experience of newspaper management. It is interesting to speculate, however, whether association with a more enterprising company, and one with a strong regional base, might have made a difference. Most certainly it would have altered the future course of YCN.

Despite this misfire, 1923 was still a significant year for it was then that the *Leeds Mercury* was acquired. The last decades of the nineteenth century had not been good ones for the *Mercury*, and in 1901 it had been sold to the Rothermere group,[32] which had taken it decisively down market. Relying chiefly on a light style and good sports coverage to hold a largely working-class readership, it easily outsold the *Post* and was making reasonable profits. After the purchase Linton Andrews was recruited from the *Daily Mail* to become editor, but he found a very ambivalent attitude among the directors when he suggested improvements. 'Go ahead if you think it necessary, but you know we shall be quite happy if you keep the *Mercury* running on an even keel without losing money',[33] he was told. The editorial staff all fitted into two rooms of no great dimensions, and it had little equipment. The editor had no typewriter of his own, for instance, and there were only two telephones. Many of the reporters saw it merely as a stepping stone on the way to Fleet Street, and an ethos had developed of selling stories on to other papers to supplement earnings rather than using them in the *Mercury* itself.

It is hard to escape the conclusion that if the *Mercury* made profits when run like this, a more thrusting approach might have turned it into a north-eastern version of Manchester's *Daily Despatch*. Linton Andrews increased sales by careful use of what resources he had, and even saw off the threat of the *Daily Chronicle* as a local competitor, aided by ingenious but low-cost ideas like printing lists of birthdays in each issue which allowed readers to claim a free gift if their own date appeared. Once again we are up against perceptions of the *Yorkshire Post* that have nothing to do with commercial logic, however, and if the *Mercury* had a real role in this period it was a blocking title that completed YCN's control of morning newspaper sales in Leeds, leaving no gaps that might attract an outside competitor. This was important because of the *Post*'s determined political stance, for Leeds and the other urban centres of West Yorkshire, where the bulk of its potential readership lived, were particularly unlikely territories for a mass Conservative movement or a high-selling Conservative newspaper at this time. Though the *Post* was not losing sales, it had to retain a twopenny cover price to maintain itself, whereas popular titles, including the *Mercury*, sold for a penny. With the remnants of its Liberal past left unchanged the *Mercury* had a wider appeal than the *Post*, but it could do little to gain readers. The real growth in circulations was now either among new readers who had little interest in politics and responded to new methods of presentation and a more sensational approach, or those who wanted a more overtly radical message.[34]

Between 1936 and 1946 the *Mercury* and the *Post* between them were reputed to have lost £148,000, something not denied by Rupert Beckett during

Plate 2.5 Paper sellers rushing to get the news onto the streets of Leeds. Whereas most of the editorial and production staff enjoyed relatively secure and well paid jobs, distribution was characterized by casual employment, low earnings, and payment by results. Yet such men were vital to sales within the city centre, where YCN was at its strongest.

questioning by the Royal Commission on the Press in 1947, and this situation could only be tolerated because the *Evening Post* continued to make high profits.[35] In 1932 it was selling nearly 170,000 copies per day, but even so the Board of Directors had to ask several times in the 1930s if there was a future for the *Post* in its existing form.[36] The obvious way out was to merge the two morning titles, which, if it worked, would graft the *Mercury*'s larger circulation and greater popular appeal onto the Conservative outlook and higher-quality orientation of the *Post*, concentrating the whole morning sales available to the company in one title. The danger, one that many of the directors saw only too clearly, was that a hybrid paper would appeal to neither readership and would shed readers rather than gain them. Such apprehensions, linked to an emotional commitment to the *Post* as it was, were always decisive, especially as Linton Andrews was then fighting for the *Mercury* and its own proud history.

The survival of the *Post* as it stood depended therefore on the willingness of its wealthy supporters, to whom the *Post*'s Conservative message was highly desirable, to shield it from the full effects of competition. It is largely the support of the Beckett family, with their banking connections, that explains YCN's ability to buy up a more commercially successful title, but in 1939 a verbal agreement between Beckett and Lord Kemsley for the latter to buy YCN and add its titles to his extensive publishing empire showed that even this commitment had its limits. It took the intervention of Anthony Eden, who had strong family connections with the chairman, to prevent this going ahead, and it was again politics that decided the issue. Arthur Mann, the *Post*'s editor between the wars, was the architect of the *Post*'s opposition to appeasement and it was strongly suspected that an underlying motive behind this purchase was a desire to silence him.[37] Eden convinced the company that it would be unpatriotic to allow this to happen.

Almost by default, then, the *Yorkshire Post* approached the end of the inter-war years much as it had begun them, and this was dangerous. Ownership of the *Mercury* had only bought time and by 1938, only five other English towns and cities had two local morning newspapers.[38] It was the impending war that really seems to have broken the deadlock in Leeds, for producing two newspapers in the anticipated hard times seemed impossible. As it became clear that paper rationing would be severe, the chance to incorporate the *Mercury*'s ration with that of the *Post* was a compelling practical reason for amalgamation.[39] Lists of staff to be retained and dismissed were prepared in the late autumn of 1939, but the actual event was kept completely secret until November 26th, when the last edition of the *Mercury* had already been published, in order to prevent Fleet Street flooding the area with canvassers to encourage readers to switch to their titles rather than try the new paper. The price was to be dropped to one penny, despite misgivings about the implications for the image of the joint title, and the *Mercury*'s name was retained for some years as a subtitle, but there was never any question of which would be the senior partner in the merger.[40] With Arthur Mann keen to retire, Linton Andrews was the obvious man to take the combined editorship, but otherwise the redundancies that were an essential part of the process were always going to come mainly from the staff of the *Mercury*. Rupert Beckett put up £5000 of his own money to compensate those who lost their jobs, but under wartime conditions labour was soon in short supply and so the exercise proved far less traumatic than had been anticipated.

The war also brought a breathing space for the whole newspaper industry since government regulations and a strict quota allocation system for paper, based on pre-war performance, put an end to real competition for sales.[41] People were hungry for news and everything that could be printed could be sold. Advertising was severely restricted, and most goods were rationed in any case, so the previous advantages of the national titles were largely nullified. War conditions also partially insulated Linton Andrews from the pressure exerted by some directors who were worried by some of the hostile comments about the new look. He could honestly say that many of the changes to layout which were needed to get the approval of the new readership were also necessary to cope with paper rationing. Sales told their own story after a while, moreover: circulation was now twice the old level for both titles combined, and six times that of the *Yorkshire Post*.[42] Assessing profitability is more problematical because with the wartime reduction in advertising, and increases in costs, mere sales increases were not an unmixed blessing, but it is certain that the position was better than it would have been otherwise. With hindsight, perhaps the most important aspect of all was the break made with the concept that the *Post* must position itself in the market on the same level as the quality nationals.

IV

Many regional morning papers entered the 1950s not only in a far healthier financial condition than anyone could have predicted twenty years previously, but they also seemed to be in a better position to compete, for the war had allowed the whole industry to drop the expensive relics of the circulation wars which no company had dared risk being the first to abolish. Yet it rapidly became clear that nothing fundamental had changed, for in the decade after 1953, when market forces were again decisive, seventeen daily and Sunday newspapers ceased production, most of them based outside London. Birmingham still had two morning titles, two evenings, and one on Sunday in 1947, but it was simply too close to London, and the 1950s saw a retreat into relative parochialism. The position of English regional quality titles became untenable in the 1950s and 60s, as the *Manchester Guardian*'s move to London illustrates.[43] Because it is further from London, and the sense of separateness is still strong in Scotland there were still five morning and six evening titles published in Scotland in 1988, and significantly the mornings had three times the circulation of the evenings, but this was impossible in any English region.[44] Manchester's own titles quickly found themselves outgunned by the greater resources of the northern editions of London newspapers, and then as London found it did not need editorial facilities in the north, Manchester withered completely. Apart from printing operations, in 1990 only the *Manchester Evening News* was left. In these circumstances the decision not to make the *Mercury* the main morning title suddenly paid dividends, for it would have had no chance of survival, whereas the distinctive nature of the *Post* gave it something to hold its readers with.

Rupert Beckett's retirement in 1950 is therefore symbolic of the ending of an era at YCN. His family's monopoly of the chairmanship ended and appointments to the Board from now on came increasingly from within the company, starting with Linton Andrews, so that for the first time the editorial and production sides were being allowed to play a formal and significant role in directing company strategy. Previously the Board had been entirely the preserve of notables selected for their status and their suitability as guardians of the newspaper's political traditions. This coming to terms with a very difficult situation when much of the old elbow room had vanished constitutes our final episode. Could a course be plotted that would keep a big enough circulation to pay for the staffing needed to run a serious newspaper in Leeds?

The best place to start was completing its monopoly of the local market in Leeds, where the *Yorkshire Evening News* still remained outside its control. It printed in Leeds and Doncaster like the *Evening Post*, and their circulation areas were nearly identical, but the *Post* was always well ahead in circulation. Whereas the *Post* was selling 237,403 copies in July 1963, the *News* could only manage 115,000. This was no longer enough to return a profit to its owners since 1929, Provincial Newspapers. Leeds was by this time the last English city outside London to be served by two evening newspapers, for Birmingham, Manchester, and Leicester had all lost their second title earlier in the year.[45] The *News* was not part of the core of Provincial's business, which was mostly concentrated in Lancashire and the London area, so it was no great surprise when a sale to YCN was announced on December 3rd for 130,000 £1 ordinary shares in YCN, giving the *News* a value of roughly £450,000 at current share values. The economies that resulted from the sale were impressive: YCN recouped £300,000 of its notional outlay very quickly by selling off the Leeds offices and printing plant of the *News*,[46] and of its 400 staff of all types, very few got jobs within the *Evening Post*.

41

There was a paradoxical side to this deal, however, for the new shares now made up nearly 21 per cent of YCN's equity.[47] Provincial specifically denied any interest in a takeover, but they continued to build up their holding and under the terms of the 1965 Monopolies and Mergers Act they soon met the legal definition of proprietorship. Moreover, as the two companies' interests now fitted well together, they began to co-operate closely, even setting up a new joint enterprise, Doncaster Newspapers Ltd, in the one area where they overlapped. YCN and Provincial's existing weekly titles were merged to form the *Doncaster Gazette* and *Chronicle*, and this and a new *Doncaster Evening Post* were both now published from a new, purpose-built base.[48] This developed YCN's existing policy of publishing both the *Post* and the *Evening Post* in several local versions to gain local appeal outside Leeds. It was the editor of the south Yorkshire edition of the *Evening Post* who took charge of the new title, and the emphasis YCN put on this region reflected its high population and its feeling of remoteness from Leeds. Sheffield, after all, still had its own morning title, the *Sheffield Telegraph*, and here YCN was the outsider seeking to overwhelm the local product with greater resources. The importance attached to the county-wide function is reflected in the twenty staff employed in 1988 in strategic centres round the county, notably Bradford, Hull, and York, as well as Sheffield, and they also had offices in places like Huddersfield and Middlesbrough.[49] Evening sales in particular were still very competitive in the county, for successful local titles existed in all the larger towns.

The purchase of East Yorkshire Printers in 1964, brought in three weekly newspapers in the East Riding,[50] another type of newspaper that YCN could not hope to overwhelm with its existing titles, and five years later the Goole Times Printing and Publishing Company was acquired with its four weeklies.[51] There were no closures or savings here, just empire building to protect the company's overall position. Having been one of the companies that seemed to prize independence from chains above almost anything, YCN was now both forming a local chain of their own and linking it informally to Provincial's. This issue of concentration of newspaper ownership in a few companies continues to be a very contentious one today, and the Royal Commissions on the Press of 1947 and 1961 had both investigated its impact on the delivery of news.[52] In fact, the competitive strength of newspaper chains actually proved to be rather limited, as YCN's own experience in Leeds confirmed. Rather than strangling local titles, it was arguable that forming chains had helped them survive through pooling resources.

This raises the whole issue of the role competition actually plays in the newspaper industry. It often seems to outsiders to be its most characteristic feature, but even at the point of sale market segmentation means that individual titles compete with no more than a handful of rivals, not the entire list of titles published. Thus the *Sun* and the *Independent* are not in any meaningful sense of the word direct competitors today, and newsagents sell them as complementary products so as to offer something to all their customers, rather than as alternatives to each other. Complementarity extends much more widely, for even the fiercest competitors actually need other newspapers to work with them. Distant routine news gathering has always relied on a common effort by the whole industry, for instance, and the training of journalists has always been, and continues to be, based upon a massive exchange of personnel between newspapers, and especially up from small local newspapers, via the regionals, to the nationals. Organizations like the Press Council deal with the industry as a whole, which often acts in unison to defend common interests. Even in marketing, a successful strategy by one newspaper is almost certain to be copied by others in a very short time, perhaps within days, and papers aiming at similar markets usually resemble each other closely. Planning a successful survival strategy as markets change therefore does depend on competing fiercely, but within a basically co-operative and imitative framework. YCN needed collaborators more than most after the war as the market for regional dailies shrank steadily in relation to the resources required to remain in business. The relaunch of the *Sun* during 1969 as a downmarket tabloid brought relief from a surprising direction, however. It caused one of the massive shifts in the pattern of segmentation which happen from time to time, and this one worked to the advantage of the *Yorkshire Post*. By 1971 the *Daily Sketch*, the *Daily Express*, and the *Daily Mail* were all in financial difficulties due to the explosive growth of tabloids, and this led to the virtual extinction of serious national middlebrow papers.[53] The *Mail* merged with the *Sketch* under the *Sketch*'s editor, and then it and the *Express* both moved steadily downmarket in content and appearance. The *Post*'s unsensational, serious, but not overly intellectual journalism could have been designed to meet the needs of many readers in the north dissatisfied by this trend. Fig 2.5 shows the circulation trends for both YCN's titles in this period

There were completely new challenges as well, however, which had no such silver lining. Television increasingly won over whole classes of advertising in the early 1960s. Sales were now producing only 35 per cent of revenue,[54] and the pressure on advertising was therefore all the more keenly felt. Classified advertising remained plentiful, but was only marginally profitable, and YCN's evidence to the 1961 Royal Commission on the Press shows that a radical rethinking of the basics was in train as a result, looking to a move towards more of a magazine format, with colour printing, and drawing on American experience of how to coexist with television. This was the background to YCN's move into television ownership in 1967, but this actually proved a short-lived deviation from the business of running newspapers and not a new start.

Figure 2.5   Circulation 1933–85

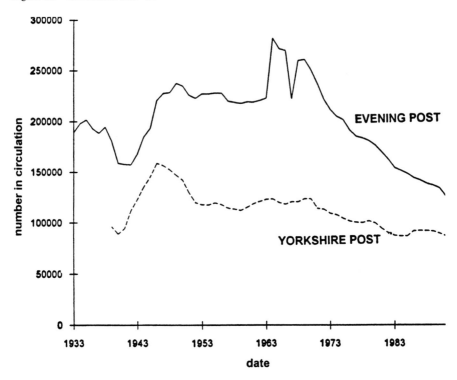

Source: YCN Accounts Ledger, Yorkshire Post.

    The company's control over many vital aspects of operating policy was also then constrained by the corporate structures of the industry. Cover prices could only be changed by agreement with the Yorkshire Newspaper Society, for instance, and experience in the 1950s had shown that any rises led to losses of readers that were never made good.[55] As British circulation levels were the highest in the world, there seemed no prospect of gaining extra readers now that local competition had been eliminated. Costs were extremely inflexible with paper suppliers operating in unison,[56] for instance, and the wage structure of the industry was largely determined by national bargaining with strong trade unions, especially on the production side. Before the war YCN had relied on the extensive use of casual labour to cope with the frequent fluctuations in sizes of editions, but now it was a matter of expensive overtime. Mechanization was not ruled out by the unions, but they insisted that those displaced by new machinery should not be summarily dismissed, and the extra costs of winding down the labour force through natural wastage undoubtedly made certain technology uneconomic.[57]

44

Plate 2.6   Linotype compositing machines in use at Albion Street. Invented in 1886 and perfected by 1890, these had revolutionised typesetting by allowing one man to set a line of type (the origin of the name) four times as fast as a team of three men could do it previously. This mid twentieth-century scene had changed little from that time, but the technology was nearing the end of its life then and was replaced in 1966.

Pressure for change therefore built up during the 1960s. Automation was clearly a vital issue, but so was the creation of a much enlarged professional management structure, in place of the traditional dual dominance of the editor of the *Post* on journalistic questions, and of the Board over everything else. New, Leeds-made Viscount presses had been installed in July 1963, financed by a share issue, to speed up printing and allow it to be done in colour.[58] They also marked a move to a new type of technology as they were centrally controlled from a console. In 1965 the publicity department was completely reorganised and much expanded in a drive to win back display advertising, and the aggressive pursuit of customers is something which since then has become ever more important for survival.[59] In 1966 an Organization and Methods department was set up, and the relative passivity of previous management strategies was overturned.[60] In 1966 linotype setting began to be replaced by teletype setting, and the retraining involved was partly financed by setting up a subsidiary operation under franchise from Sight and Sound Ltd to offer the same training in keyboard skills to other organizations.[61] Thereafter there was a steady switch to computer technology, which spread gradually into virtually every part of the operation over the next two decades.[62]

Plate 2.7   The next stage in preparing a page for printing in the traditional manner normal until the early 1970s. The metal type produced from the linotype machines is made up by hand and the appearance of the printed page depended entirely on this manual skill.

Despite these improvements, a huge investment programme was clearly needed by the end of the 1960s, especially since newspaper printing technology had been revolutionized by web offset litho presses during the 1960s. Symbolically perhaps, the old headquarters were now judged beyond further adaptation. If the group was to remain competitive it had to make a fresh start in every sense, and when the City Council refused permission for a redevelopment at Albion Street, a new site was acquired at Bean Ing on Wellington Street for a new, purpose-built headquarters. Large, open-plan editorial areas were created in line with the latest concepts in modern design, and this allowed rational planning of working methods for the first time. The whole scheme eventually cost £4.1m, with £715,000 later recouped through the sale of the old buildings.[63] The scale of this spending, and of the investment undertaken during the 1960s can be judged by the £2.2m valuation placed on the company immediately after the takeover of the *Evening News*, according to the value put on the shares then.[64] In 1969 the *Financial Times* valued YPN's equity at £10m.[65] Even then, the weakness resulting from a limited resource base meant that it this was not enough for a move into the very latest technology. Instead YPN kept its most recent letterpress machinery and married it to web offset presses in hybrid printing units pioneered by Rockwell

Plate 2.8   The Viscount presses made in Leeds by R. W. Crabtree's. Installed in 1963, they were the first phase in the wholesale re-equipment that led to the transformation of the whole company. They are seen here in the old headquarters at Albion Street, but they were later transferred to the new building at Bean Ing and incorporated into the new set-up there. They were updated in 1974 and scrapped in the re-equipment of 1990.

Plate 2.9   The finished product coming off the Viscount presses. The Crabtree nameplate is clearly visible here on the folder, making clear a local linkage that made for swift servicing and the possibility of relatively informal working between the machine room staff and such firms, something that has been lost now that equipment is supplied from all over Europe and North America.

47

Plate 2.10 Advertisements being prepared on computer screens in the pre-press area in 1990, a radical break with earlier practice. By then computer terminals were to be found in nearly all departments, transforming working practices throughout the company and bringing sharp reductions in staffing.

Graphic Systems (Goss). There were features of letterpress printing which were still preferable to the modern alternative so this was an acceptable compromise.

On Saturday 26 September 1970 at six o'clock in the evening the presses in the old building were closed down for the last time, and on Sunday the new system had to be ready to print Monday's *Yorkshire Post*. Hundreds of tons of machinery therefore had to be moved across the city centre in a matter of hours.[66] The finished system was the largest of its type then in use in the world, and it could produce 65,000 copies an hour of a 40-page paper, with four pages in full colour and spot colour on eight others. Again costs were offset by seeking outside work and a subsidiary company, Offset Graphic Arts, was formed to 'offer a highly skilled service in the provision of colour for the lithographic print trade'.[67] Later, in 1975, YPN undertook all the printing required by The Reporter Ltd, a group of weeklies headed by the *Dewsbury Reporter*, and by 1990 this added up to six million newspapers a year.[68] Today the *Observer* and the *Independent* both print on the YPN presses, all of which helps to offset their high price, but also is reminiscent on a different scale of the jobbing printers who started so many local newspapers, the *Leeds Intelligencer* included. Once more the technology is too expensive to allow a single-minded concentration on a company's own newspapers alone.

This must have been a key factor in the decision to consolidate the informal co-operation that existed with Provincial by a merger, which was announced on the 20th of August 1969.[69] Each company placed three directors on the board of the other and guarantees were given that YPN would continue to exercise a high degree of independence within the larger group, something that

Plate 2.11   The editorial room at Wellington Street after the move. Half the size of a football pitch, this allowed an open plan layout that is a complete contrast with conditions at Albion Street, though separate staffs are still maintained for both newspapers. The technology in use has yet to be transformed, but large changes in working practices resulted from the new layout. Thus, the library, in the foreground, has been placed right alongside the reporters for whom it is a vital service, providing background information on a huge range of topics.

concerned traditionalists since Provincial had a Liberal background.[70] Events have proved that the group had no interest in changing the political stance of its new acquisition, in the tradition of British mergers which leave the old units very much as they were under a holding company. With YPN valued at £6.5m, it was generally seen in the financial press as a good deal for their share-holders,[71] especially as it ended the control of YPN's directors over their shareholders' political affiliations and made their shares openly tradeable for the first time. They had previously been limited to a fairly notional quotation on the Leeds Stock Exchange. Thus, YPN saved its effective independence by surrendering the actuality, which could probably have been preserved for only a few more years anyway, given the sobering state of the market that fig 2.5 shows. Gains in circulation had been made after the acquisition of the *Evening News*, but they proved very short-lived, and the *Evening Post* has shown a substantial and continuous decline in sales since then. Given the previous reliance on the revenue it brought in, this was very serious. Part of this must have been due to the rise of free newspapers, and as in the past YPN decided

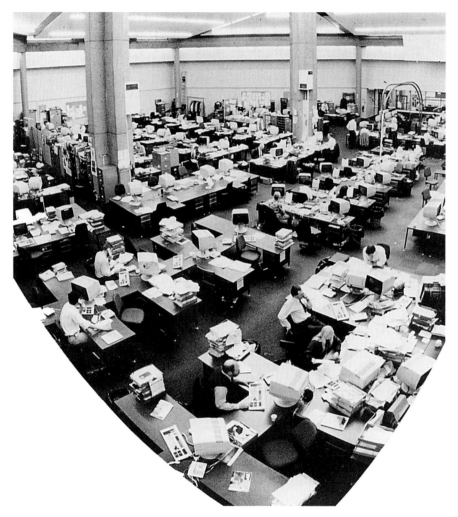

Plate 2.12 The editorial room in the age of the computer. With modern technology far more work is now done directly from desks than was possible even a decade ago. Reporters work over the telephone to a much larger extent, and stories can now be transferred directly to the production department from the reporters' terminals where they are written. Sub-editing and page layouts can all be done simply by calling up material from central memory banks.

its best defence was to get in first. In 1980 it therefore founded the *Leeds Weekly News*, and by 1990 over 212,000 copies were distributed each week.[72] A policy of creating special supplements for each day of the week also helps to bring in advertising revenue.[73]

This has kept the group viable internally, but the value to YPN of being part of a wider grouping was amply demonstrated in 1985 when an even more

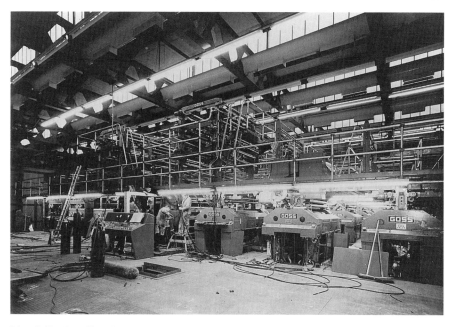

Plate 2.13   Installing the new Goss presses, supplied by Rockwell Graphic Systems of the USA, in the machine room at Wellington Street in preparation for the move from Albion Street.

radical re-equipment was judged essential since the letterpress elements of the printing plant had reached the point where they could only be kept in use at an unjustifiably heavy cost. A move to a new generation of computer controlled presses would offer more colour facilities, greater flexibility, and a lowering of costs. This had been implemented by 1990,[74] at a cost to YPN of £14m, which would have been intolerable alone, and it would have been even higher without the links with United Newspapers in any case, since the group composited this as part of a bigger re-equipment covering many of its other printing centres in a deal worth £100m altogether. Linked to this were dramatic reductions in staffing levels, and a shift in the proportions of the different work groups within the operation.

V

We have thus seen that the apparent continuity of the *Yorkshire Post* masks frequent realignments of strategy, and that this reflects a basic lack of stability in the newspaper industry. Really to stay the same is to court disaster in this environment, and many equally famous names have gone under at different times, or have been so transformed as to be virtually unrecognizable. There

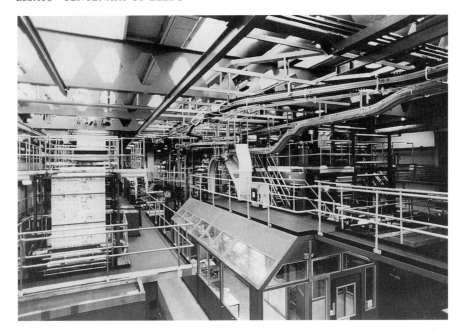

Plate 2.14   The printroom today with its two print lines, each eighty feet long and thirty high. They are controlled from a protected 'sound haven', seen in the centre of the photograph.

is, however, an underlying pattern behind the many different strategies employed by the various owners of the *Yorkshire Post*, stemming from a concern with this title that has nothing to do with its commercial potential. Given this prime commitment, there is then a constant search for some means of providing the stability that is so clearly impossible to any operation whose viability must depend solely upon the commercial success of their newspapers, and especially one with a quality image and a restricted market. The *Yorkshire Post*'s politics have contributed to this difficulty, given its location in Leeds, but it would be very short-sighted to believe that this is the whole story. A multitude of newspapers have been published in and for Leeds since the mid-eighteenth century, espousing all types of ideology, and of them all, only two have survived to the present day, the two *Posts*. However, the morning *Post* has never been the most popular title in Leeds, and often has been in some financial difficulties. Its continuing success, and even its survival, have several times seemed in the balance in its 250 year existence, and it would be quite wrong to suggest that there has been any inevitability about its progress to its present position. Its success seems to rest on two factors.

First, whenever its actual performance has begun to cause concern, it has always been possible to bring in revenue from another source. This may be,

Plate 2.15   One of the two central consoles, each of which gives an operator control over all the functions of one press line from the sound haven. They allow direct control of running speed and of the quality of the finished product.

as it was both originally and now, through establishing linked enterprises to make full use of expensive staff, buildings, and equipment. It may be through direct subsidy, though this has never been available to fund running expenses, simply during particularly difficult patches. It may be through the more subtle type of financial support inherent in having as a chairman the owner or chairman of your bank. It may be through the creation or purchase of other titles which earn revenue, but which paradoxically never really seem to be valued in their own right. It may be through forging co-operative or corporate links with other newspapers and thereby obtaining access to pooled resources. One or more of these strategies has always been in operation, whereas rivals in Leeds relied much more on income from sales and advertising. This could bring great success, especially in the case of the nineteenth-century *Mercury*, but even it lacked staying power in the really long run. In the nineteenth century the extent of local competition made dominance of the market by one firm impossible, but this changed as the costs of running a newspaper mounted and the costs of starting a brand new title became prohibitive. The ability of YCN to maintain itself despite poor results meant that other titles only needed to weaken temporarily to be forced out or bought up, and new titles ceased

Table 2.1 National trends in newspaper circulations, 1957–89.

Years	National mornings	Regional mornings	Regional evenings
1957	16761	2000	7000
1967	15625	1971	6886
1973	14549	2029	6599
1975	14322	2086	6420
1980	14900	2082	5866
1985	14759	2027	5222
1989	14569	1982	4926

Source: The Press Council, *Facts in Figures: Annual Statistical Survey of British Newspapers, 1989*, p. 23.

to take their place. Today it is clear that the local market will barely sustain just one evening and one morning title.

Secondly, while Yorkshire has always had a big enough population to sustain substantial newspapers, it was not attractive enough to tempt the nationals in to produce there, and selling from Manchester weakened their position in Yorkshire. The Leeds industry never dreamed of national glory as Manchester did, and the contrasting fates of the *Birmingham Post*, the *Guardian*, and the *Yorkshire Post* are not accidental. Yorkshire Post Newspapers has successfully used local news without destroying its wider appeal, and has compromised its high status just enough to maintain its commercial viability. However, the process of adaptation goes on. Newspaper readership is generally shrinking as we move into the 1990s, with total sales for mornings down by over a million on 1967 in 1989, and over two million on 1957, as Table 2.1 shows. Regional morning titles have held their own in the long term, but they have lost the substantial gains made in the 1970s, while regional evenings have suffered most of all, losing nearly a third of their 1957 sales in a consistent pattern of decline. This has made the competitive environment even tougher in recent years, as the recent closure of the *Sheffield Telegraph* has shown, and further change will certainly be required. At the same time new technology seems to have made renewed efforts to dispute YPN's dominance in Yorkshire possible. Two separate Sunday titles aimed specifically at the county have been launched recently, one based in Bradford and one in Manchester. This is one type of newspaper YPN has never published, and whether it will be the start of a threat to its titles remains to be seen.

Notes

[1] The archival research at the Yorkshire Post which forms the basis of much of this article was conducted by Graham Sykes, with assistance from Jane Durham. The figures and tables were

prepared from this material by Graham Sykes. The photographs all come from the YPN library, and I am grateful for the help we received in this and the rest of the research from the librarian, Kathleen Rainford.

[2] The Press Council, *Facts in Figures: Annual Statistical Survey of British Newspapers*, 1989, Table 1, p. 7.

[3] John C. Merrill, *The Elite Press: Great Newspapers of the World*, 1968, p. 84.

[4] Alistair Hetherington, *News in the Regions: Plymouth Sound to Moray Firth*, 1989, p. 71.

[5] *Yorkshire Post*, 'Into the 21st Century', supplement, 27/11/1990, p. 10, and also Hetherington, *op cit*, pp. 246–7.

[6] Mildred A. Gibb and Frank Beckwith, *The Yorkshire Post: Two Centuries*, 1954, documents this history and has provided my basic chronological framework up to 1954. Individual references are only given for direct quotations.

[7] *Yorkshire Post* 15/6/67.

[8] *Yorkshire Post*, 'Night and Day: The Story of our Newspapers', supplement, nd (1992?), p. 16.

[9] Political and Economic Planning, *Report on the British Press: a survey of its current operations and problems with special reference to national newspapers and their part in public affairs*, 1938, pp. 53–4. This is a wide-ranging and thorough examination of the pre-war industry which underlies much of the analysis presented here on that period.

[10] BPP, 1947–8, XV, *Royal Commission on the Press, Minutes of Evidence Taken Before the Royal Commission on the Press, 23rd day,* qq 7606.

[11] Andrews, *op cit*, pp. 38–40.

[12] Gibb and Beckwith, *op cit* p. 87.

[13] BPP, 1947–8, XV, qq 7655–9.

[14] Hetherington, *op cit*, p. 18.

[15] Viscount Camrose, *British Newspapers and Their Controllers*, 1947, p. 111, and BPP, 1947–8, XV, qq 7650–9.

[16] Linton Andrews, *The Autobiography of a Journalist*, 1964, pp. 125 and 59.

[17] James Grant, *The History of the Newspaper Press*, III, 1871, p. 379.

[18] Simon Jenkins, *The Market for Glory—Fleet Street Ownership in the 20th Century*, 1986, p. 16. PEP, *op cit*, pp. 91–6 provides a useful short summary of the development of the British Press.

[19] Grant, *op cit*, pp. 371–2 and 376.

[20] Gibb and Beckwith, *op cit*, p. 48.

[21] PEP, *op cit*, chap. 3.

[22] Andrews, *op cit*, p. 227.

[23] PEP, *op cit*, p. 84.

[24] BPP, 1947–8, XV, qq 7499.

[25] PEP, *op cit*, p. 96.

[26] PEP, *op cit*, pp. 81, 83–4, and see also Camrose, *op cit* pp. 30–4.

[27] PEP, *op cit*, p. 84.

[28] *Ibid*, pp. 122–3.

[29] David Ayerst, *Guardian: Biography of a Newspaper* 1971, pp. 591–2. See also PEP, *op cit*, pp. 88–90.

[30] Ayerst, *op cit*, p. 593.

[31] This section is based upon an unpublished article by Dr K. M. Wilson, 'Up To London: the Chairman of the directors of the Yorkshire Post, Conservative Central Office, and the Negotiations for the Purchase of the Morning Post, 1923–1924'.

[32] BPP, 1947–8, XV, q 7478.

[33] This section relies heavily on Andrews, *op cit*, pp. 129–45. See also BPP, 1947–8, XV, qq 7478–7485.

[34] BPP, 1947–8, XV, q 7524 shows Beckett's awareness of the dangers of political commitment.

[35] *Ibid*, qq 7660, 7490–97, 7660–62. See also Camrose, *op cit*, pp. 110–111.

[36] Andrews, *op cit*, p. 150.

[37] *Ibid*, p. 160.

[38] PEP, *op cit*, p. 107.

[39] BPP, 1947–8, XV, q 7877.

[40] Andrews, *op cit*, pp. 162–8. BPP, 1947–8, XV, q 7624–30 shows Beckett's attitude towards the correct line for the *Post* to take, and it is clearly one aimed at a quality market.

[41] BPP, 1947–8, XV, 7567–8, 7572–89.

[42] Andrews, *op cit*, pp. 162–8. See also Camrose, *op cit*, p. 110.

[43] Ayerst, *op cit*, pp. 627–9.

[44] The Press Council, *op cit*, table 1, p. 7.

[45] *Yorkshire Evening Post*, 15/11/63 and 3/12/63, and *The Guardian*, 16/11/63.

[46] *Yorkshire Post*, 18/9/64.

[47] *Yorkshire Post*, 27/11/63.

[48] *Yorkshire Post*, 3/2/66.

[49] Hetherington, *op cit*, p. 18.

[50] *Yorkshire Post*, 22/10/64.

[51] *Yorkshire Post*, 27/6/69.

[52] BPP, 1948–8, XX, pp. 3–5, and BPP, 1961–2 XXI, pp. 30–6 and 57–60, esp paras 225–45. This was also the motivation behind Camrose, *op cit*.

[53] Jenkins, *op cit*, pp. 62–5.

[54] Ms answers by YCN to questionnaire A (General Economic Questions) of the Royal Commission on the Press, 1961, submitted mid-1961, ans 36, 38.

[55] *Ibid*, 1 and 2.

[56] *Ibid*, 11–15.

[57] *Ibid*, 19–30.

[58] *Yorkshire Post*, 2/7/63 and 5/7/63.

[59] 'Night and Day', pp. 8–9.

[60] 'Night and Day', p. 20.

[61] 'Into the 21st Century', p. 14, *Yorkshire Post*, 17/3/67.

[62] 'Night and Day', throughout.

[63] *Yorkshire Evening Post*, 26/5/70.

[64] *The Times*, 16/11/63.

[65] *Financial Times*, 21/8/69.

[66] 'Into the 21st Century', p. 6, see also *Yorkshire Post*, 28/9/70.

[67] *Yorkshire Evening Post*, 17/2/69.

[68] 'Into the 21st Century', p. 21.

[69] *Yorkshire Post*, 21/8/69.

[70] *Daily Telegraph*, 21/8/69.

[71] *Financial Times*, 21/8/69.

[72] 'Into the 21st Century', p. 21, 'Night and Day', p. 21.

[73] 'Into the 21st Century', p. 17.

[74] 'Into the 21st Century', throughout, but esp pp. 2–3.

CHAPTER 3

The History of the Leeds Permanent Building Society, 1893–1993[1]

Michael Collins

THE STORY of the Leeds Permanent Building Society is a story of expansion, of the transformation of a locally-based organization into a national leader in its field. From its foundation in 1848 until the First World War the business of The Leeds was largely confined to the geographical area around the city of its origin[2] but during the twentieth century it developed into one of the nation's leading financial institutions.

In order to make sense of the history that follows, two aspects of the society's growth need to be emphasized. First—as with many other financial institutions where public confidence was of the essence—from the outset The Leeds adopted and maintained a prudent, cautious approach to the conduct of business. Throughout the period legislation has closely defined the activities permitted to building societies—and so constrained the potential for innovation—but, even within these constraints, The Leeds proudly adopted a closely regulated approach. Innovations there were, but under controlled conditions. The management of The Leeds often adopted the sensible approach of letting others try out new ideas first and, if they proved successful, then quickly taking them on themselves.

The second feature of the growth of the society which should be stressed is that, unlike most other leading building societies, The Leeds was not, until recently, greatly involved in merger activity. Almost all of the growth of The Leeds came from expansion 'internal' to the society, especially through the extensive growth of its branching network in the twentieth century. As we will see, important mergers with other leading societies were mooted on occasions but none came to fruition. It is perhaps for this reason that while The Leeds retained its status as one of the country's leading societies throughout the last century, the scale of its business does not rival the giants of the industry such as the Halifax and the Abbey National.

I

The early 1890s were eventful years for all the country's building societies. Most dramatic of all, a number of societies were forced to close down, with two of the largest societies in the country involved in fraudulent scandals entailing major losses for shareholders. Public concern followed on the publicity given to the abuses committed by a small group of officers at the Portsea Island Society (closed December 1891) and at the Liberator Society which at that time was the largest society in the country (at least on paper!) and which was wound up in scandalous circumstances in October 1892. In the short term the collapse of these two adversely affected confidence in other societies and temporarily checked growth in the movement as a whole. Ultimately, however, the outcome of the scandals was favourable to the better-run societies such as the Leeds Permanent because the failures added impetus to those who were pressing for reforms to improve managerial accountability and external supervision. The main reform came with the passing of the 1894 Building Societies Act. This was, in effect, Parliament's attempt to put right some of the major weaknesses in building society law exposed by the failures of the Portsea and Liberator. The Act tightened up regulations governing societies' rules on advances and on officers' powers; enhanced the supervisory powers of the Registrar; required that greater publicity be given to information on arrears and re-possessions; stipulated that accounts be more formally audited by accountants; and created opportunities for shareholders to verify the accounts. In this manner, the new legislation successfully established the framework necessary for a restoration of public confidence and for a return to less turbulent times.

The legislation had followed lengthy deliberations conducted in a parliamentary inquiry. One of the key witnesses before the Select Committee on Building Societies in 1893 was Thomas Fatkin, manager and secretary of the Leeds Permanent Benefit Building Society. His evidence provides a revealing insight into the nature of The Leeds at this time. Fatkin was in no doubt that his society was among the best and most efficiently run. He told the committee, 'I think we are perfect ourselves...' and that it would benefit others to adopt The Leeds' methods of doing business.[3] This high opinion was based on the experience of a half-century during which the society had lent 'some seven millions of money on our Leeds estates, and that certainly we have not lost £100 during the 50 years on all that money advanced in Leeds.'[4] In fact, in 1894 payment on only twenty-three properties was in arrears. The secret of success, according to Fatkin, were the sound, conservative principles upon which the society's business was conducted. In particular, he highlighted how since its inception the society had used formal actuarial tables (developed by

Theodore Jones in the 1840s) to regulate the calculation of borrowers' repayments, depending on the rate of interest and the repayment period (at that time, the rate was 4 per cent and the normal repayment periods were 13, 17, and 24 years).

It was also stressed that at The Leeds, directors were actively involved in the regular vetting and assessing of everyday business, which had not been the case in the less well-managed societies where one or two officers had full control and had, thus, been exposed to temptation. Supervision was much greater at The Leeds where, for instance, details of business were reported to the regular board meetings and even small arrears were discussed with the directors. In addition, the society employed a full-time specialist to evaluate properties and it was his job to ensure that mortgages were well secured. Mr Fatkin held these principles up as a model for other societies to follow and, in fact, claimed that societies from as far afield as Cardiff, Manchester, Liverpool, and Bristol had gone to Leeds for the purpose of discovering and applying the business principles employed there. He also boasted that other societies in Leeds took the Leeds Permanent as their model. In fact, the Leeds & Holbeck—which he described as '…without exception one of the best managed and safest building societies in the Kingdom'[5]—made no secret of the fact that it copied The Leeds' system in every respect.

Certainly by the early 1890s The Leeds was amongst the biggest and most respected of the societies in England. The 'Leeds Building and Investment Society' had been launched in 1848, and by 1893 it had total assets of some £1.5 million, with a membership of 14,328 plus some 6000 deposit accounts. Stability rested on the cautious, regulated approach to business, and on the wide spread of risks. Members were drawn from a broad range of society although most were described by Fatkin as 'operatives'. In other words, the backbone of the society's membership was the small saver. Thus, of the society's resources, £700,000 had been accumulated by the weekly subscribing members who on average had been paying less than 3s. 6d. per week. As with other early Yorkshire societies, The Leeds had established branches or agencies in other towns in the north such as Sheffield and Hartlepool, but the approach of the management was generally conservative. In those days no banking facilities such as cheques or the remittance of funds were offered. All deposits were subject to a notice of withdrawal and this was routinely applied (e.g. six months for sums above £100, and a month for sums of £5). The Leeds would not countenance the introduction of such innovations as preference shares and the society refused to compete actively in the London money markets by more frequently altering interest rates or through the opening of branches in the south of the country.

The new legislation of 1894, in fact, did little to alter the nature of The

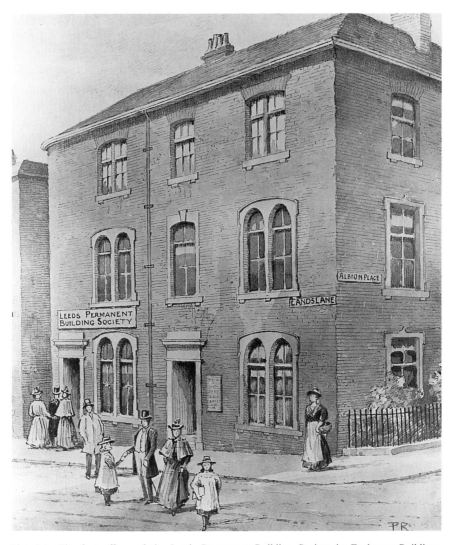

Plate 3.1 The first offices of the Leeds Permanent Building Society in Exchange Buildings, Lands Lane.

Leeds' business. The main change noticeable from the accounts is that the society abandoned its practice of holding virtually no reserve fund and by 1914 had accumulated a reserve equivalent to about 6 per cent of total assets. The question of reserves had been a point of some discussion in the debate over the 1894 legislation and the society's management may have felt it prudent to amass a reserve rather than continue its established practice of redistributing all surpluses as bonuses to investors. In general, then, the society had been

Table 3.1   The Building Society Industry in the Twentieth Century

Date	1 No. of Societies	2 No. of Branches	3 No. of Shareholders 000s	4 No. of Depositors 000s	5 No. of Borrowers 000s	6 Share Balances £m	7 Deposit Balances £m	8 Mortgage Balances £m	9 Total Assets £m	10 Average Annual Growth of Total Assets in Previous Decade % compound
1900	2286		585					46	60	—
1910	1723		626					60	76	2.4
1920	1271		748			64	19	69	87	1.4
1930	1026		1449	428	720	303	45	316	371	15.6
1940	952		2088	771	1503	552	142	678	756	7.4
1950	819		2256	654	1508	962	205	1060	1256	5.2
1960	726		3910	571	2349	2721	222	2647	3166	9.7
1970	481	2016	10265	618	3655	9788	382	8752	10819	13.1
1980	273	5684	30636	915	5383	48915	1742	42437	53793	17.4
1990	117	6051	36948	4299	6724	160588	40695*	175745	216848	15.0

Source: BSA, *Building Society Fact Book*, 1985.
*including loan balances

well-run before 1894, and this continued to be the case after the furore of the 1890s had died away. As can be seen from Table 3.1, during the following twenty years to the First World War the building society movement as a whole experienced a steady, if unspectacular expansion. Table 3.2 reveals that this was also true at The Leeds where total assets had reached just under £2 million in 1914 (from £1.4 million in 1894) and membership had grown to 20,035 (14,328).

II

The inter-war years were to experience much more rapid expansion and The Leeds shared fully in this. The rate of expansion was unprecedented: 'Over the fifty years from 1870 to 1920 the total assets of the movement grew to about three-and-a-half times the 1870 figure. In less than twenty years after 1920 they increased to more than ten times the 1920 total'.[6] One underlying reason for this phenomenal increase was the decline in private investment in houses to let and the corresponding sharp rise in owner-occupation that occurred at that time. Before 1914 only some 10–15 per cent of dwellings were owner-occupied but after the war, rent controls on existing dwellings and Treasury subsidies to local authority housing, combined to make investment in houses to let less attractive. With the continued growth in real income and an increase in the number of families in the country, a shortage of rented accommodation developed and there was increased demand for houses to purchase. The building societies, of course, gained directly from this because the great bulk of their loans was granted for owner-occupation not on dwellings to let. On the other side of their balance sheets building societies were finding that more people were attracted to make investments with them. This arose partly from tax changes. After the war tax rates were higher and, thus, the gains from having tax on building society interest deducted at a fixed rate were subsequently greater, especially for the more wealthy. Difficulties in the stock market in 1929 may also have encouraged funds to flow into building societies. So, too, must the increasing difficulties experienced with overseas investments during these troubled times in the world economy. Also important was the general fall in money market interest rates during the 1930s (including yields on government securities) which made building society rates more attractive to investors.

Table 3.2 shows that between 1920 and 1940, The Leeds increased total assets thirteen fold to £40 million. In 1914 they had been less than £2 million. Membership had grown somewhat more, rising from 23,195 to 251,642, in the same period. In 1914 the number of members had been 20,035. The Leeds was thus participating fully in the expansion of the movement as a whole between

Table 3.2 Growth of The Leeds Since 1893

Date	1 No. of Branches	2 No. of Shareholders 000s	3 No. of Depositors 000s	4 No. of Borrowers 000s	5 Share Balances £m	6 Deposit Balances £m	7 Mortgage Balances £m	8 Total Assets £m	9 Average Annual Growth of Total Assets in Previous Decade % compound
1893								1.4	
1900		6.7	5.6	3.1				2.0	5.2
1910		8.8	6.5	3.7				2.0	0
1920	15							3.0	4.1
1930	33	45.9	38.8	27.9		13		14.0	16.7
1940	43	87.5	65.7	93.8		38		40.0	11.1
1950	37	76.5	37.3	75.7		51		55	3.2
1960	37	124.9	27.7	100.8		130		138	9.6
1970	91	535.5	20.2	186.0		531		556	15.0
1980	351	1637.6	18.2	317.7		2958		3080	18.7
1990	424	–	–	–		11029	11925	14649	16.9

Source: Building Society Association, *Building Society Fact Book*, 1985.

Plate 3.2   The Leeds' Offices in Park Lane, 1878–1930.

the wars; and it was in this period that its business moved significantly beyond the confines of a local—largely one-town—society. An important part of this expansion was the opening of more offices. In 1920 there were just 15 branches, but many new ones were opened up in the second half of the 1920s (with 33 in operation in 1930), followed by yet more in the 1930s (with the number peaking at 48 branches in 1936). These new offices added directly to the volume of the society's business, of course, and thus provided some gains from economies of scale. They brought in more business, acting as an advertisement of the society's name in every High Street in which they were opened.

Such growth was essential if The Leeds was to maintain its status amongst the biggest societies in the country. As we have seen, the movement as a whole was growing rapidly in the period—with total assets growing at an average annual rate of 15.6 per cent in the 1920s and 7.4 per cent during the 1930s (Table 3.1). Some societies were particularly aggressive in increasing their market share. In the 1920s especially, some of the London-based societies such as the Abbey Road, Co-operative, and Westbourne Park gained relative to the societies based in the north. This took a number of forms: vigorous branch expansion; much more competition on interest rates for shares, deposits and loans; the greater use of commission payments to agents and others who secured new mortgages; and—the means of most rapid expansion—amalgamations amongst societies. The largest northern societies responded in like form and by the end of the inter-war period they had succeeded in re-capturing some of the lost ground. The Leeds was amongst those that began to exhibit greater flexibility and imagination with regard to interest payments. Traditionally all deposits had received the same rate but now preferential rates were introduced for larger and longer-term deposits. In May 1920, for instance, the board agreed to pay 4.5 per cent on deposits over £1,000, 4.75 per cent over £2,500 deposited for a minimum of three years and 5 per cent on sums of £5,000 or more left for five years.[7]

The Leeds also fully participated in various innovative schemes that provided finance for builders of new houses. This was a significant source of growth in the inter-war period, especially in the 1930s when there was a sharp expansion in the housing stock, the bulk of which was constructed by the private sector. The method employed, the 'builder's pool', emerged in the 1920s, and was greatly extended in the following decade. The pool arrangements served to improve the terms of borrowing for the purchaser by reducing the amount of deposit needed, while continuing to safeguard the societies' interests. *The Economist* explained: 'The builder's pool has the dual object of enabling a house purchaser to acquire property on a modest initial payment... [usually 5 per cent of its valuation]... and also of covering the building society for the excess of its advance over the normal proportion of 75 or 80 per cent of valuation. The builder usually makes a cash deposit with the society equivalent to the excess advance (15 or 20 per cent of the valuation) on the first batch of houses built. On the basis of its initial experience with the builder and the new estate, the society may subsequently accept cash deposits in respect of only part of the excess advances, but it protects itself for the remainder by obtaining the builder's personal guarantee and also retains the right to draw upon the pool in the event of default. When an estate scheme is in full operation this cash proportion may vary between one-quarter and one-third of the excess advances. Finally as the loan on a given property is reduced and the excess advance is recovered, the due proportion of the builder's cash deposit is released...'.[8] From the building society's point of view, therefore, the pool of cash deposited by the builder and any other collateral such as personal guarantees, provided an insurance reserve against default. Certainly such new business was important to The Leeds and the society was actively engaged in some such schemes throughout the 1930s as the private housing estates in Leeds and other cities expanded rapidly in the decade before the war.[9]

At the beginning of the period The Leeds was also involved in a number of merger negotiations with other societies. Some of these possible partners were amongst the leaders of the movement but, as it turned out, all proposals were aborted. In 1920, for instance, the boards of The Leeds and of the Leeds Provincial agreed on a merger and on the form of constitution for the combined society. If it had gone through it would have marked a major geographical consolidation for The Leeds but, in the event, a special general meeting of the Leeds Provincial failed to ratify the deal. In 1945, the Leeds Provincial was to combine with the Bradford Third Equitable to form the Provincial Building Society. Also in 1920 The Leeds spurned an approach from the small Leeds Equitable Building Society—in this case, because it was considered that the small size of the Equitable did not justify the effort. In 1921 an approach from the Darlington Building Society also came to nought. However, the most dramatic aborted merger talks came during the Second World War. During 1943 The Leeds entered into exploratory talks with the Halifax and the (London-based) Westbourne Park societies.[10] These three, in turn, invited the Woolwich to join the talks in December 1943 with a view to forming a national building society. The negotiations involving all four societies failed, partly because of the ill-feeling created by the Halifax's unilateral decision to push down interest rates. Nevertheless, the Woolwich and The Leeds persisted with their bilateral talks and their respective boards agreed on an amalgamation between the two to form the 'British Building Society'. A postal vote of members approved. However, at the subsequent general meeting of The Leeds in 1944 the proposal failed to attain the necessary three-quarters vote of shareholders present (335). Again, The Leeds had come close to amalgamation but had not succeeded in carrying it through.

Although outright merger evaded The Leeds in the inter-war years, as with most of the large societies from the late 1920s it was increasingly involved in trying other means of regulating market conditions and modifying competition. This largely revolved around the Building Society Association's so-called 'Code of Ethics'. This code laid down a number of largely non-controversial guidelines as to the conduct of member societies with respect to one another and to the movement as a whole but, critically, it also sought to reduce competition amongst members. In particular, it tried to impose on members '...standard conditions in regard to interest rates, maximum duration of mortgages, maximum percentage of normal advances, minimum personal stakes for borrowers, acceptance of collateral security, and payment of commission'.[11] This new code was strongly endorsed at the BSA's conference of 1934, and subsequent postal ballots favoured acceptance. However, acceptance was far from unanimous and The Leeds was one of a number of societies to express serious reservations.

According to Cleary, opposition came from three groups. The first consisted of those societies such as the Temperance which remained loyal to a conservative approach to lending and which had subsequently lost market share. The Temperance felt that its conduct was beyond reproach and certainly did not need a code of ethics to offer guidance and correction. The second area of opposition came from the small, local societies which felt that the large societies dominated the BSA and that they were using their position to impose rules less applicable to the more personal business of a local society. In particular, local societies prized their autonomy and flexibility when it came to negotiating terms on individual accounts. Even though sheer size means that The Leeds cannot be considered to be in this category there was, nevertheless, some empathy with the position of the smaller societies. Although large by contemporary standards, the business of The Leeds at this time was still largely concentrated into the locality. Besides, the traditional ethos of The Leeds had been one of commitment to small, local savers, and investors. Thus, J. P. Herbert Brown (a future President of The Leeds) was amongst those who publicly defended the smaller societies. In his view: 'The big societies of this country have been wanting to rule the movement with an iron hand and too little attention has been paid to the smaller societies'.[12]

The third group of opponents was more important and more directly relevant to The Leeds' own position. As has already been mentioned, a number of the large northern societies had been rather slow off the mark in facing up to London competition. In the 1930s, just as their response was becoming more commercially effective, the BSA was now proposing to curb the means by which they could compete and win back market share. The suggestion was even more galling to these societies because it was those very activities that the Association was proposing to control (such as payment of agents' commission and variation of deposit requirements for borrowers) which had been so successfully used since the end of the war by a number of the southern societies. It was these same societies which, as leading members of the BSA, were now championing acceptance of a Code which would prevent others from fully exploiting similar competitive practices. To the northerners it looked as if the BSA code was trying to safeguard the new status quo, one in which their relative importance had already registered a decline.

It was within this atmosphere of mutual suspicion that negotiations over acceptance of the new code had to be conducted during 1933–36, and it is perhaps not surprising that differences between societies were to lead to a serious rift within the BSA. Negotiations were fraught with difficulties as the BSA tried to reconcile ambivalent attitudes of member societies to reducing competition in general at the same time as maintaining or improving individual market share. This is clear from an episode in 1935 when negotiations were in their final stages and it had been agreed to introduce the new code in April.

Plate 3.3 'Permanent House': the imposing Headquarters of The Leeds, as viewed from Park Lane. Opened in 1930, it was the first building to be completed in the reconstructed Headrow, and served as the Head Offices of the Society until 1992.

In March, however, just as The Leeds adopted the same policy as the other leading societies and agreed to observe the new code, a price war broke out. This involved a reduction in rates below the recommended rate and involved a number of large provincial and London societies, including the Abbey Road whose manager, Harold Bellman, was actually chairman of the BSA. Those societies such as the Halifax that were adhering to the BSA's recommended rate were not amused and, in turn, these threatened to meet fully any rate reductions. It was to take another year or so to smooth ruffled feathers.

Even at the last there was a major hitch, in that the BSA's legal advice was that the Association's current constitution did not permit the expulsion of members (such as the Temperance) who refused to accept the Code of Practice. In the event the BSA dissolved and reconstituted itself in 1936 in such a way as to oblige all, now 'new', members to ratify the Code. The bulk of existing members accepted the change but a significant minority did not. Some, mainly small societies, set up their own rival National Federation of Building Societies. Some large societies such as the Bradford Third Equitable joined neither of the national associations. The Leeds—which on an earlier occasion in 1928 had considered leaving the Association—initially kept within the BSA but then (at the close of 1936) withdrew and decided to stay aloof from both associations. The following message was sent to the BSA in November 1936:

'We...wish to intimate that we feel we are bound to reserve our rights to exercise our discretion in regard to any business that may be submitted to us, at any rate for the present'.[13]

The Leeds was, of course, facing competition from societies such as the Bradford Third Equitable not covered by the Code. But the main complaint was that the Code 'was not being strictly complied with by several of the assenting societies.' The Leeds could not afford to cramp its own freedom of action while others established a competitive edge. It was not long before compromises were being sought and modification of the BSA's constitution and of the Code followed. An important legal case (the Borders case) was also to induce greater co-operation amongst the societies as the interests of all of them came under threat. Even so it was to be 1940 before the rift in the movement was repaired, with the National Federation being finally wound up in 1941.

III

The Second World War brought a halt to the long-term expansion of the building society sector. The years of conflict and immediate post-war years proved to be extremely difficult times for The Leeds. Conditions were unfavourable on all sides. During the war few new houses were built and afterwards severe shortages of construction material persisted. Moreover, the government gave strong priority to public sector house building at that time. Thus, the major source of building society business remained very depressed until the 1950s. Financial constraints also worked against the expansion of private sector mortgage business. Real income growth was poor and in the money markets government retained tight control. One important impact of the war had been the sharp expansion of public sector debt and the building societies were amongst those financial institutions to increase their holdings of government securities far beyond their normal peacetime proportions. The corollary of this increase in public sector assets was, of course, a decline in loans on mortgage to the private sector.

For the industry as a whole the ratio of liquid reserves (overwhelmingly government liabilities) had rarely been above 7 per cent before the war but it was to reach an abnormal peak of 28 per cent by the end of 1944, from which time it only gradually receded.[14] Rent and price controls also adversely affected the attractiveness of investment in housing, whereas various government initiatives helped promote different types of savings schemes and these, too, rivalled those of the building societies. As can be seen from Table 3.2, the impact on The Leeds of these adverse conditions was to cause a sharp fall in the number of depositors, shareholders and borrowers. Between 1940 and 1950 these were down 28,000 to (37,296), 11,000 (to 76,489), and 18,000 (to 74,694) respectively, representing a marked reversal of the strong upward trend established during the inter-war period. Total assets stagnated (and even fell if the value is adjusted for inflation), with the society's business largely marking time until the end of the 1940s. Moreover, The Leeds did worse than many other societies. This period saw a relative decline for The Leeds, and as Table 3.3 shows, the society's share of the industry's total assets fell sharply from 5.3 per cent to 4.4 per cent between 1940 and 1950.

IV

The 1950s marked the beginning of a new phase of expansion, as the relaxtion of wartime controls quickened and money markets returned to more normal conditions. The needs of public sector debt became less pressing, and full employment and rising real incomes provided the means by which an expansion of owner-occupation could be financed. In addition, successive governments were supportive of a growth in private home-ownership.

With hindsight it can be seen that the 1950s marked the beginning of a long-term trend which—allowing for cyclical fluctuations—has continued ever since. It can be seen from Table 3.1 that the number of shareholders rose thirteen-fold from 2.3 million in 1950 to 36.9 million in 1990, and borrowers from 1.5 million to 6.7 million. In the same period, total assets rose from £1.3 billion to £216.8 billion, although allowance must be made for the fact that this was a period of unprecedented inflation, which was particularly pronounced in the 1970s.

Throughout this period the powers and activities of the building societies

Table 3.3 Concentration in the Building Society Industry and the relative size of The Leeds, 1930–1990

Date	1 Total Assets, All Societies, £m (1)	2 Share of Largest Five Societies, % (2)	3 Share of Largest Ten Societies, % (3)	4 Total Assets, Leeds £m (4)	5 Share of Leeds, % [(4)÷(1)] (5)
1930	371	39.1	53.4	14	3.8
1940	756	38.0	50.3	40	5.3
1950	1256	37.3	48.9	55	4.4
1960	3166	45.3	56.9	138	4.4
1970	10819	50.1	64.3	556	5.1
1980	53793	55.4	71.0	3080	5.7
1990	216848	60.0	80.0	14649	6.8

Source: Building Society Association, *Building Society Fact Book*, 1985

have been closely prescribed by law. There have been substantive changes in the legal position, most noticeably in the 1980s, but for the most part societies have remained non-profit making mutual organizations subject to central supervision by the Registrar of Friendly Societies which was superseded by the Building Societies Commission in 1987. The great bulk of their funds have had to be raised from retail sources (deposits and shares) and the overwhelming proportion of their assets held in mortgages on freehold and leasehold property. On the liabilities side, the decades since the 1950s have seen the continued expansion of the societies' traditional role as provider of a safe repository for retail savings from the general public. It should be emphasized, though, that the growing ease with which building society shares and deposits could be transferred has also meant that they have in effect become a major component of the country's retail banking facilities. The clearing banks have retained their pre-eminence within the financial transmission mechanism but the building societies have increasingly been offering alternative services.

On the assets side, two main driving forces have accounted for the tremendous expansion of building society mortgages. The first is inflation. House prices rose and the average mortgage advance grew sharply from just £894 in 1950, to £3131 in 1970, to £30,838 in 1990. This alone has accounted for a great deal of growth in the total value of mortgage business being conducted by the societies. The second factor, the result of more fundamental economic and social change, has been the sharp rise in the proportion of the population owning their own homes. In 1914, just over 10 per cent of the housing stock was in owner-occupation; in 1950, just under 30 per cent; and in the mid-1980s, over 60 per cent. During the post-war period the UK became a property owning nation, especially from 1970s with privatization of the public-sector housing stock in 1980s and the continued favourable treatment of borrowers and savers for tax purposes.

Two other major features of post-war development facing building societies were not always complementary. These were the increasing tendency towards greater competition, at the same time as the continued trend towards greater market concentration within the building society movement itself. Competition became more prominent both among the societies themselves and from 'outside' financial institutions. After the rift between the BSA and NFBS was healed in 1939 the BSA operated a fairly effective cartel, with recommended rates, terms on loans and shares, and the requirement of members to give prior notice of rate changes to the Association (and, thus to their competitors). However, over time the effectiveness of the cartel was called into question as some members found ways of circumventing the controls (such as by offering more competitive rates and terms on 'special' accounts) or as non-members, such as the banks or insurance companies, were able to win more of the business through keener competition.

71

A recurrent problem with all cartels is the retention of member loyalty over time in the face of changing conditions. In the case of a price-fixing cartel such as that operated by the BSA, the pressures are likely to arise when demand and supply get out of equilibrium. This is just what happened with building societies during the 1950s, 1960s and 1970s. On occasions market rates moved down whereas the cartel's rates remained inflexible—so that the societies were faced with an embarrassing inflow of funds which exceeded the demand for mortgages at current rates. More problematic, though, were circumstances in which the demand for mortgages exceeded available funds. If the cartel prevented a rate rise then the societies had to resort to rationing, to 'mortgage queues'. Politically, this was most unpopular. In addition, government macroeconomic policy directly impinged on building society business. Government has frequently acted to influence interest rate levels and general monetary and credit conditions which has inevitably affected the building societies. Here was another element of inflexibility in the societies' pricing policy—even within the constraints of the cartel, national economic considerations did not always make it possible to respond to changing demand and supply.

In reality, of course, the societies found it more difficult to implement a rate rise than a reduction, but in either case there would be pressure on individual member societies to break ranks and respond to market forces and there would be pressure on the BSA as its pricing policy attracted greater attention. Indeed, over time the cartel was exposed to greater public scrutiny as the official vogue for restriction and control of money markets that had been so prominent in the 1930s and 1940s fell out of favour. Moreover, the expansion of home ownership made the question of whether or not the building societies were charging a fair price for mortgages a more sensitive political issue.

It was such considerations that led to the government referring building society interest rates to the Prices and Incomes Board in 1966. The Board was concerned with two inter-connected points: the Association's recommended rates and the size of societies' liquidity reserves. The latter were relevant to the interest rate charged on mortgages. The suspicion was that by the 1960s, public confidence in the societies was so high, reserve ratios based on what the industry had historically considered necessary, were probably excessive. If so, such reserves could safely be drawn down to finance an expansion of mortgages without increasing the interest rate and without endangering the security of the societies. There is an interesting historical contrast here with the position in the 1890s when it was felt that the societies should hold larger reserves in order to maintain public confidence. In the 1960s, the Prices and Incomes Board did not make any firm recommendation with regard to the appropriate level of reserves but the major outcome of its report was the establishment of a committee of the Association whose findings in 1968 were to lead to a general reduction of reserve ratios (on a sliding scale according to a society's size). In the previous year the Prices and Incomes Board report on 'Bank Charges' had also criticized the Association's practice of recommending rates to members.[15] During the following two decades it was to be the generally high and oscillating rate of interest that continued to make the building societies' pricing policy a politically sensitive issue—again, challenging the operation of an effective cartel.

The cartel, in fact, had already begun to fray as a result of the actions of its own members. In 1956, for instance, the largest society (the Halifax) left the Association and was thus free to fix its own rates.[16] The Leeds, too, had its difficulties with the cartel arrangements. By the mid-1950s, for instance, there was increasing frustration over the failure of the Association to ensure full compliance with the agreement. At the beginning of 1955 The Leeds' board recorded that, 'Whilst the Society had up to the present time remained completely loyal to the BSA, and had observed the various recommendations made, the time had now arrived when, in facing continued and ever-growing competition, the Society must, in its own protection, reconsider some of the terms upon which advances could be made'.[17] The Leeds thus announced reductions in mortgage rates and eased other terms governing valuations and period of loans in those areas where it was thought competition was particularly keen.

The recommended rate came under pressure again during the following year, particularly when the Halifax left the Association, and once more The Leeds felt the need to reserve its right to keep in touch with the market. Thus, when considering a request to join with the Abbey National, the Co-operative, and the Woolwich in a joint endeavour to maintain the rates set by the Council of the BSA, The Leeds replied:

> Whilst the Society was desirous of following the recommendations of the Council, and had no intention at the present moment of any alteration in the existing rates, the position was becoming much more difficult in Yorkshire, with other societies increasing their rates, and whilst it would do what it could to assist in joining... the other societies in an effort to maintain existing rates, it could give no guarantee as to how long the present rates could be maintained.[18]

Disagreements and unease amongst the members of the cartel was partly a response to competitive pressures from outsiders. In particular, insurance companies were extending their mortgage business and National Savings, life assurance unit trusts and pension funds were able to compete effectively for small savings and other investment funds, more especially as many of the competitors attracted favourable tax concessions compared to an investment in a building society.[19] In the late 1970s/early 1980s, the commercial banks, too, became serious competitors in the mortgage market—an area of business that they had traditionally ignored. Accepting the reality of these changed circumstances, the BSA cartel was wound up, with 'recommended rates' being replaced with 'advized rates' in October 1983, until these too were withdrawn in November 1984.

At the same time as the small saver and mortgage markets were becoming more competitive, individual institutions operating within the market were growing in size. It can be seen from column 1 of Table 3.1 that the long-term decline in the number of societies continued throughout this period. Thus, whereas there had been just under a thousand societies in 1940, this was down to 273 in 1980, and 117 in 1990. Most of the societies that had disappeared were of a very modest size and many had been absorbed through amalgamation with larger societies. Even so, there were also some notable mergers between large societies. As a result the average society became much larger in the period—in total, by 1980 the industry was operating 5684 branches, employing almost 53,000 staff and had total assets of £53.8 billion. Table 3.3 also shows that the business was heavily concentrated into the hands of the largest societies, with the degree of market concentration increasing in the post-war decades. Thus, the share of the total assets of the sector held by the largest five societies increased markedly from 37.3 per cent to 60.4 per cent, between 1950 and 1990.

As a leading society within the industry, The Leeds was subject to many of the general factors affecting the industry as a whole. As Tables 3.2 and 3.3 show, it is clear that after the poor performance of the 1940s, The Leeds shared in the rapid expansion of the industry. However, it was not until the 1960s that The Leeds regained its successful habit of the inter-war years and began to increase its share of the market—stuck at 4.4 per cent in 1950 and 1960, but rising to 5.7 per cent by 1980 and 6.8 per cent by 1990. (Table 3.3). Throughout, The Leeds was ranked as the fourth or fifth largest society (sixth in 1990 if the Abbey National is included). It was thus large in terms of the typical building society. Nevertheless, as the largest five societies together accounted for 60.4 per cent of the industry's assets in 1990, it is clear that The Leeds' 6.8 per cent meant its business has not been on the same scale as the giants such as the Halifax or the Abbey National.

One major reason for this is that The Leeds had not, until recently, been involved in a large-scale amaglamation, so that the most obvious source of rapid growth did not apply. During the history of the society a number of major mergers have been proposed but none, as yet, has come to fruition. The aborted amalgamation with the Woolwich in 1944 has already been mentioned. This had been partly a reaction to the creation of the Abbey National (with the merger of the Abbey Road and National), and had envisaged further mergers with the (smaller) Liverpool Investment and the Dunfermline which would have created a massive society with truly national coverage.[20] In fact, in this regard The Leeds' next successful merger was a big anti-climax—the mortgage business of the London and North Eastern Railway Building Society (assets of just £130,354) were transferred to The Leeds in 1946.[21] All subsequent take-overs (technically, 'transfers of engagements') have been small—with the Doncaster in 1959, the Aberdeen Property Investment in 1961, the Midlands in 1962, and the Earlestown in 1970.[22] More recently The Leeds has once again been involved in more ambitious merger proposals. In 1985 the management teams of the Leeds Permanent and the Leeds & Holbeck agreed in principle to form the 'Leeds Building Society' and had gone so far as to begin consulting shareholders when the plans were called off.[23] Shortly afterwards— in 1986—the Town & Country, whose business was largely confined to the south-east, approached The Leeds with a merger proposal.[24] The newly-amalgamated society would have had assets of some £9 billion (The Leeds' assets alone were £7.8 billion in 1986) and would have formed the fourth largest in the industry but once again the obstacles proved too great. In the event, the Town & Country transferred its engagements to the Woolwich in May 1992. Thus, since the Second World War The Leeds has been involved in only a small number of successful mergers, all of them of a small scale. It is possible that all this may change in 1993; though the proposed merger of The Leeds with the National Provincial, has yet to be agreed by the shareholders.

In the absence of any significant mergers, the main source of The Leeds' growth has come through the extension of its branch network. It was in this direct way that The Leeds' responded to the expanding market for savings facilities and mortgages, and to the greater freedom granted to all financial institutions as government post-war regulations were eventually relaxed. It was in this way that The Leeds became a truly national institution. Table 3.2 shows how The Leeds' network had languished for two decades after the Second World War, before taking off. From the 1960s there was a sharp expansion which hit a peak rate in the 1970s and early 1980s. In fact, during the 1970s the number of branches rose three-and-a-half times and then doubled in the 1980s (although there had been some rationalization and branch closures by the end of that decade). 'Growth began with opening more branch offices, at first in larger towns, then in smaller ones, in satellites, precincts, suburbs: anywhere and everywhere where demand seemed to justify it, bringing facilities within convenient reach of the public'.[25] A comment made in 1968 by Douglas Crockett, a director, epitomizes the expansionary zeal of that time: 'Our chain of branches must be extended still further. We should be in every big city and in all large centres of population. We are the builders of a great national society'.[26] From the early expansion of the network managerial reorganization had been necessary, with regional offices being formed in 1968 (initially, there were just four, the South, Midlands, North West and South West) each eventually with its own manager. Internally the switch to a more positive branching policy is associated with decisions taken in the later years of Ronald Cowling's term as chief executive (1958–67) though a series of successors has continued the policy.

It was in this manner that for many years in the 1960s and 1970s that The Leeds managed to keep up with the leaders of the industry and, as we have seen, even improve its market share. For the most part the new branches made their major contribution in the attracting small savers. Historically this feature of the business was characteristic of the building society movement as a whole, and considered a particular strength at The Leeds. However, the legacy of large numbers of small-scale balances on inactive accounts is perhaps less of an asset to the multi-purpose financial institution that The Leeds was to become in the 1990s.

In addition to the promotion of an extensive branch network, The Leeds also participated in most of the other innovations and changes common to the other large societies. In particular, over time there has been greater diversification of product, both to meet customer's particular needs and to differentiate The Leeds' savings accounts and mortgages in a market in which price differences were generally minimal. It would be true to say, however, that in general The Leeds for most of its post-war history preferred to wait and see how a particular innovation fared elsewhere before embracing the change itself. As The Leeds President, Ronald Schofield, proudly boasted in 1961, 'We are a conservative, sober, traditional building society, confining our mortgages to homes for the people. We don't like new gimmicks for attracting money. We think people investing in building societies want safety first and a certainty of quick withdrawal as well as a reasonable rate of interest'.[27] Even so, taking the long view of history The Leeds innovated along with the others, for as changes proved beneficial The Leeds did not let rivals steal too clear a lead before adopting them itself. This was true, for instance, of the introduction in 1961 of an attempt to improve the yield on investment accounts by linking them to life assurance policies. This was first used by the Bristol and West Building Society but quickly taken up by others including The Leeds. Similarly in 1973 when many societies began to offer better rates on term shares in which balances were committed for longer periods than normal, The Leeds initially held aloof. Eventually, though The Leeds was to become an important market leader in the provision of such accounts.

Better marketing and advertising have played an important role here. In the first half of the century, The Leeds had published 'advertising booklets' that provided would-be home buyers with basic information on the process of buying a house and on the society's terms. They also tried to attract them with such slogans as: 'We provide the key' or 'Sound as a bell', and informed readers that, 'Here in the sturdy and independent North, it has always been something of a tradition for a man to own his house'. In the 1950s and early 1960s national advertising was 'collective' for the industry as a whole, under the auspices of the Building Society Association.[28] As competition increased, however, the leading societies financed distinctive marketing campaigns. In this respect, The Leeds has been particularly successful in the use of television— beginning with a campaign in 1975 and continuing with the more recent promotion of 'Liquid Gold' accounts using the television character, Arthur Daley.

V

In 1986 the government passed the Building Societies Act which significantly changed the powers and functions of societies such as The Leeds. The main provisions of the legislations were to permit greater commercial freedom over how funds were raised and invested, while at the same time retaining the essential features of societies as mutual institutions (although allowing for the possibility of societies adopting a profit-making corporate structure) substantially engaged in the provisions of loans on mortgage. Thus, societies were permitted to have up to 5 per cent of their assets (15 per cent since January 1993) in the form of unsecured loans for purposes unrelated to property, which allowed not only for an extension of personal loan services but also removed the legal impediment to the use of cheques; they can raise funds in the wholesale money markets (from 1988, up to 40 per cent of funds); and they are allowed to expand their activities to cover a wide range of personal banking and money transmission services. In sum, the new changes have enabled building societies to compete more freely with other financial institutions such as the retail banks, and they have been granted a much greater element of flexibility regarding the raising of funds.

Since the Act The Leeds has rapidly diversified and developed its range of financial services both through 'in-house' initiatives and through various affiliations with other organizations. For the present-day customer, The Leeds more readily resembles a financial/housing supermarket. Thus, The Leeds' main activities now embrace an expert financial advice service (including a share selling service), off-shore banking facilities, an estate agency business and a property development business. Nonetheless, The Leeds—as throughout its history—remains a building society whose chief function is to provide mortgage finance for the purchase of properties which are overwhelmingly for owner-occupation.

VI

The history of The Leeds can only be properly assessed within the context of the building society movement as a whole. As has been emphasized, building societies have always been subjected to close legislative control and central supervision. In fact, they were creatures of the nineteenth-century self-help movement—non-profit seeking, benevolent associations empowered to inculcate the habits of good citizenship appropriate to a democratic society in which property rights were paramount. For the most part, they were not active participants in the commercial money markets, although as the movement grew the secondary impact on other financial institutions obviously became more significant. Even in the post-World War II world the function of the societies as the main suppliers of funds for private house purchase has attracted a political sensitivity that has ensured close central regulation. In turn, this regulation has ensured that the range of possible activities has been carefully circumscribed. For the most part Parliament has allowed extremely little discretion on how the societies could employ their resources (although recent reforms have brought changes here). Until the 1980s, on the asset side of balance sheets the sole function was to provide home loans, taking mortgages as security; on the liability side, societies were to provide an accessible, safe repository for retail savings. Moreover, for much of the last century price competition was non-existent. As a consequence the entrepreneurial skills demanded of the societies' management were also restricted. The scope for innovation was limited.

Within this tight regulatory framework The Leeds has been one of the successes of the movement. Formed in 1848, it gained early prominence not so much by size at that time as through reputation as a soundly managed institution which was run on 'modern' actuarial principles. Over the longer term The Leeds was in the same boat as other societies for most of the twentieth century and was unable to compete on price. In such circumstances it successfully carved out its position as one of the largest societies through competition on services and through differentiation of product. While rarely the first to innovate, the management of The Leeds nevertheless kept abreast of changes elsewhere and, where such changes (say, to the terms of loans or form of share deposits) proved successful, there was a willingness to follow suit. This careful yet not conservative approach to innovation kept The Leeds in touch with the leaders of the movement, whilst avoiding the risks associated with complete novelty. In consequence throughout the twentieth century The Leeds successfully maintained its position as one of the country's largest building societies. Since the 1970s in particular this has been achieved through the rapid extension of the branch network. However, with a share of the market of between 4–6 per cent The Leeds has never rivalled the giants of the movement such as the Halifax and Abbey National—in terms of size, The Leeds is amongst the second order of societies. The main reason is that The Leeds has never yet merged with any other major society, the most potent source of growth for rival societies. A number of mergers have been attempted, but all, so far, have been aborted. Perhaps all this is about to change. At the time of writing, in August 1993, the shareholders of The Leeds are considering the latest proposed merger, with the Bradford-based National Provincial. If the merger goes ahead, the Leeds might move into the Building Societies' Premier League.

Notes

1 I should like to express my gratitude to the present and past staff of the Leeds, especially Alfred Schofield and Howard Briggs who have been extremely tolerant and helpful. I also thank Jane Durham for her work as research assistant on the project.

2 Anon., *Leeds Permanent Building Society. A Survey on One Hundred Years, 1848–1948* (private circulation, 1948?).

3 BPP, 1893–94, IX, *Select Committee on Building societies(no. 2) Bill, Minutes of Evidence*, Q 1294, p. 45.

4 Q. 1281, p. 449.

5 Q. 1204, p. 445.

6 E. J. Cleary, *The Building Society Movement* (Elek Books, London, 1965), p. 184.

7 Leeds Permanent Building Society, Board Minutes, May 1920.

8 *Economist* 18 February 1939, pp. 347–8.

9 Leeds Permanent Building Society, Board Minutes, May 1930; December 1930; February 1934; November 1936.

10 Leeds Permanent Building society, Private Minute Books.

11 Cleary, *Building Society Movement*, p. 212.

12 *Building Society Gazette*, July 1933, p. 533.

13 Leeds Permanent Building Society, Board Minutes, November 1936.

14 *Building Society Association Yearbook*, 1945–9.

15 *Building Society Association Yearbook*, 1968.

16 *Building Society Association Yearbook*, 1956.

17 Leeds Permanent Building Society, Private Minute Books, 24 January 1955, p. 341.

18 Leeds Permanent Building Society, Private Minute Books, 18 June 1956, p. 3.

19 *Building Society Association Yearbook*, 1964.

20 *Building Society Association Yearbook*, 1944.

21 Les Grainger, *A Personal Review of Leeds Permanent Building Society, 1930–1980* (private circulation, Leeds Permanent Building Society, Leeds, 1985), p. 50.

22 *Ibid*, p. 92; Minutes, January 1962.

23 *Building Society Gazette*, January 1985, p. 28; March 1985, p. 288; April 1985, p. 408.

24 *Building Society Gazette*, August 1986, p. 3; September 1986, p. 24.

25 Grainger, *Review*, p. 122.

26 Quoted in Grainger, *Review*, p. 77.

27 *Ibid*, p. 86.

28 Leeds Permanent Building Society, Private Minute Books, 29 April 1957, p. 109; Minute Books, December 1961.

CHAPTER 4

The Public Supply of Gas in Leeds, 1818–1949

Sue Bowden, Ronald Crawford and Graham Sykes

THE PUBLIC supply of gas in Leeds over the 174 years of its existence up to 1993 is best described as one of constant change: in the ownership and structure of the industry, in technology and hence not only manufacturing and distribution techniques, but also in its principal functions and markets. Throughout its long history the overriding priorities and hence policies and strategies of the various managing bodies alternated between profit maximization for the benefit of the rate-payer or the industry and operation for the benefit of all consumers with profits being passed on in the form of lower prices. The performance of the industry whether measured in terms of the number of consumers, the value and sources of revenue or profitability has been characterized by fluctuations. To a large extent, the history of gas in Leeds reflects the ability (and at times the apparent inability) of the industry to adjust to the changing population and industrial structure of the City and to adapt its products to technological change and competition from alternative sources of power.

That story may be broken down into four main periods. Between 1818 and 1870 public supply of gas in Leeds was characterized by small private companies operating over specific localized areas in the manufacture and distribution of gas for lighting purposes. From 1870 to 1914 the industry was operated as a municipal utility, the area of supply was extended to the outer reaches of the City, and the industry's functions grew to incorporate the provision of gas for heating purposes. Although gas remained a municipal utility during the inter-war years, that period witnessed a marked change in the structure and function of the industry. Competition with electricity became acute as gas began to lose its traditional lighting function but extended its activities in the provision of heat to domestic, industrial and commercial users. In 1949 gas entered yet another period in its history as the industry was nationalized and Leeds as a separate functioning entity to all intents and purposes ceased to exist. In 1949, the undertaking was absorbed along with seventy-five other undertakings into the North Eastern Gas Region which itself constituted one of the five regional groups of the nationalized gas industry.

This chapter concentrates on the period prior to 1949 (there are no records relating specifically to Leeds after nationalization) and begins with an overview of the crucial period prior to municipalization in 1870, the legacy of which was to constrain the ability of the municipal gas authority to achieve its stated objectives.

I

Public supply of gas in Leeds dates from 1818 when a small group of the Leeds Tory élite formed a company and raised money to obtain an Act to entitle them to make and sell gas, and break up the streets to lay mains. Although by no means the first such company (that privilege belongs to the Gas Light and Coke Company in London in 1812), the Leeds Gas Light Company was among the early pioneers, following soon after the establishment of gas companies in Bristol, Exeter, Liverpool, and Glasgow in 1816/17. Gas provision for the first century of its existence was essentially a localized affair since technological limitations precluded distribution over any considerable distance and, as its name implies, the Leeds Gas Light Company saw its activities as being restricted to the geographical confines of Leeds. The main function of the company, in common with other companies, was in the provision of light for street lamps, private dwellings, shops and factories through the manufacture and distribution of gas.

For seventeen years the Leeds Gas Light Company enjoyed monopoly status and operated as a purely profit making enterprise. The Act of 1818 contained no clauses restricting the company on either profits or the price of gas. The company's managing committee took full advantage of this. Supply depended on profit potential and areas of Leeds were not lit unless the company was confident there was a clear profit to be made. The price of gas was high and discounts were used to discriminate against smaller consumers to offset potential losses.[1]

Consumer dissatisfaction was high on three counts: high prices, restricted area of supply and, increasingly, the poor quality of gas. Opposition to the practices of the Leeds Gas Light Company was particularly acute among the growing and vocal body of Leeds shopkeepers and small businessmen and culminated in the creation of an alternative gas company in July 1835 backed by the Liberal group in the town. Coal gas was first produced by the new company at its new works in January 1835. Gas in Leeds had thus assumed political overtones with the Leeds Gas Light Company being operated by the

Tory faction and the new opposition from the Leeds New Gas Company supported by the Liberals.

From 1835 to 1895 the two parties were to approach the public provision of gas with radically opposed priorities. Whereas the Leeds Gas Light Company adopted profit maximization as its guiding principle, the stated intention of the new company was to ensure that gas prices were kept at a reasonable level and to spread gas lighting to the southern townships of the borough. Conflict between profit and the extension of supply at low prices was to become acute once the industry came under local government control. The break up of the monopoly position did not, however, realize its anticipated benefits. Reductions in price and improvements in supply and the quality of gas did not materialize. Price reductions were more apparent than real and until the mid-1850s the two companies collaborated on a range of matters and colluded over prices and areas of supply. The outcome of this bi-partite structure was one of duplication of effort with consequent waste and diseconomies in the manufacture and distribution of gas. For the industrial and domestic consumers of Leeds, there was no price advantage in the existence of two so-called competing companies. To make matters worse, there were constant complaints about the quality of gas supplied by both companies. This situation continued for twenty years, interspersed with complaints from the local press, the council and the vestry on the activities of the two companies. It was not until the mid-1850s that gas in Leeds entered a new era as the two companies competed for the market of the rapidly growing industries, retailing and commercial sectors of the town. Competition was particularly acute over gas supply to the railways.

Partly in reaction to the tide of complaints against the two companies, local government ownership and control of gas supply in Leeds had been canvassed as early as 1842. Municipal ownership of gas supply in Leeds however dates from 30 June 1870 when the Council acquired the two companies for £763,225. The delay is explicable in terms of other overriding preoccupations of the Council and the opposition of the two companies. In 1842, an Improvement Bill was drawn up which contained powers to enable the Council to manufacture gas but the bill was abandoned in the face of fierce opposition from the two companies.[2] Twenty years later, the town Council petitioned against the New Gas Company Bill with the object of purchasing the works and making the gas for sale. Again, the two companies co-operated in opposing the Bill and, in exchange for the petition not being presented, agreed to their gas being tested by a council representative. The Council moreover had more pressing problems on their hands in the mid-nineteenth century, namely the sewerage system and the water supply, both of which had prior claims on its budget.[3] Municipal ownership of gas only became a matter for serious consideration once the problems of sewerage and water supply had been resolved.

The opposition of the gas companies and the more urgent problems of the Council go part way to explaining the delay in municipal ownership. They do not explain why by the late 1860s the Council had become so concerned about the state of gas supply in Leeds that they were prepared to buy out the two companies and run the industry. According to Millward, by the middle of the century there was widespread dissatisfaction throughout the country with both water and gas services as a result of prices and the reluctance of the companies to extend supplies in both quantity and quality into profitable areas. Despite the increasing regulation of the gas companies throughout the century, dissatisfaction grew: not least because the regulatory systems proved ineffective. The incentive to municipal ownership thus came out of frustration on the part of local authorities with their inability to control, through market transactions with private companies, the supply of gas in their areas.[4]

Leeds appears to be a classic example of this phenomenon. Complaints by the Council date back to the early 1840s and the agreement of 1862 between the Council and the companies to the gas being tested by a council representative was an attempt by the Council to achieve a measure of control over price and quantity. The need to control the quality and quantity of public supply was made more urgent by the Council's statutory responsibility for the highways of the town; by 1868 the Council had absorbed the functions of the highway surveyors and was buying out the bridge and turnpike trusts to establish an absolute control over the highways.[5] The quantity, quality, and price of gas thus became of importance to the Council through its responsibility for street lighting.[6] By 1870 the failure of the regulatory systems, the increased importance of the council's responsibility for street lighting and the resolution of the problems of sewerage systems and water supply added to the momentum in favour of municipal ownership. The final factor in Leeds as elsewhere was that of profits.[7] As early as the late 1840s it was proposed that Leeds should follow Manchester's example in subsidizing municipal services out of the profits of municipal gasworks.[8] Financial considerations may not have been the main factor in the decision but they were highly significant. Public ownership of remunerative activities became an increasingly attractive option and was finally realized in June 1870.

II

The legacy of this inheritance was to compromise the Council's activities for the rest of the century. Three issues in particular acted to constrain the Council's declared intention of turning the undertaking into a profitable venture to relieve the ratepayers of the City, namely the excessive amount it paid for the New Gas Company, the capital expenditure required to rectify the disrepair of much of the works, mains and services of the New Gas Company, and the sums needed to rationalize the two systems. The Council was thus constrained both by heavy capital costs, much of which could have been avoided, and heavy expenditure costs which resulted both from its legacy and the strategy it pursued in the ensuing years.

All the evidence indicates that the Council paid far more for the Leeds New Gas Company than was necessary. Although in the years leading up to municipalization the works of the Company had been allowed to fall into a state of disrepair no allowance was made for this in the calculation of the purchase price. Indeed, the Council appears not to have sent assessors in to value the Companies prior to purchase: an expensive mistake as later events were to show.[9] Not only were the capital costs of purchase excessive, but the Council had to meet the capital expenditure costs of rectifying the disrepair of the works of the Leeds New Gas Company. The subsidy out of the rates for the Meadow Lane works alone totalled £14,000 in 1873 and 1874;[10] by 1900 the capital expenditure on the Meadow Lane works had reached £151,934, twenty per cent of the original purchase costs of the two companies in 1870. The capital account of the new undertaking was burdened from the beginning with the high purchase price paid for the New Gas Company whilst the revenue account and hence profitability was undermined for years by the cost of repairing the works.

The revenues of the new undertaking were further constrained by the inevitable problems and costs involved in rationalizing the works, mains, and services of the two companies into one composite whole. To some extent this problem was alleviated by the collusion practised in the preceding years whereby the companies had divided Leeds between themselves and had effectively operated exclusive areas of supply. Some instances remained, however, of replication of mains and services which drew the Council into inevitable expenditure costs. Likewise, the reluctance of the companies to extend supply into areas of doubted profitability necessitated heavy expenditure on laying new mains and extensions. Not all of this expenditure, however, can be attributed to the private gas companies. The premium set on extending supply was to a large part the result of decisions made on the basis of political rather than economic rationale.

From 1870 public supply of gas in Leeds underwent a major structural change as ownership shifted out of the hands of two private companies into the hands of a single, local authority, undertaking. Conflict, change and competition still however characterized the industry after 1870, albeit in different guises. Conflict was marked by the opposing interests and hence strategies of the two main political parties in Leeds who viewed the role of the undertaking in very distinct but different ways. In the initial two years of existence the undertaking was viewed by the Conservative majority as a profit making enterprise to subsidize other municipal services and hence the ratepayers of Leeds. From 1872 to 1895, when the Liberals were in control, the undertaking was operated for the benefit of the consumer rather than the rate-payer.[11] In this period the aim was to extend gas at the cheapest price to consumers; the resultant strategy was to pass on profits in the form of lower prices and to extend supplies. The return of the Conservatives to power in 1895 saw the resurgence of the profit maxim. Although the Liberals were vociferous opponents of this policy at the time, they did not interfere with the arrangement when they later returned to power.[12] No consistent long term strategy as such was devised and followed through for the undertaking in its first twenty-five years. This was compounded and undermined by the legacy of the need for structural repairs and the inability of the undertaking to control manufacturing costs and the market for its by-products with serious implications for the long run performance of gas supply in Leeds.

The two key areas of strategy were the supply and price of gas. In terms of the former, the policy appears to have been to extend supply and to rectify the infrastructure deficiencies of the undertaking's inheritance. Again, however, the policy does not appear to have been applied consistently (Table 4.1). Gas mains were not extended at a constant rate. If overall, up to the end of the century, the length of mains laid in the City grew quite remarkably, the record is interspersed with periods of decline (for example in 1889 and 1894) and periods of substantial growth (most notably from 1898 to 1900). Nevertheless the strategy of extending gas mains appears to have been realized. In 1886 there were 660 miles of gas mains in Leeds; by 1900 the figure had increased to 840 miles. Although the rate of growth declined after the turn of the century, just before the outbreak of the First World War there were 1008 miles of gas mains in Leeds.[13]

The exercise was costly. By 1900, £213,320 had been spent on mains and services, fourteen per cent of the total net capital expenditure of the gas undertaking up to that year. By 1910 the figure had increased to £369,364.[14] Self evidently the undertaking honoured its declared policy between 1872 and 1895 of extending gas supply in Leeds. The cost of the exercise was high: not only in terms of the burden on the capital account but also in terms of the failure to realize potential sales revenue from the extended supply area.

The declared strategy of extending supply necessarily entailed additional pressure on the existing works of the undertaking. This, together with the state of disrepair of the works inherited from the New Gas Light Company, led to high capital expenditure on extending works in the first twenty five years of the undertaking's existence. Up to 1897 the undertaking was spending roughly

Table 4.1   The extension of Gas Supply in Leeds, 1886–1914

Date	Length of Gas Mains Laid During Year miles	Total Length of Gas Mains miles
1886	5.9	660
1887	7.4	670
1888	10.1	678
1889	5.8	686
1890	6.0	692
1891	7.3	702
1892	9.0	710
1893	10.2	720
1894	7.0	730
1895	8.8	737
1896	11.8	746
1897	10.9	758
1898	24.0	782
1899	29.2	810
1900	28.1	840
1901	24.0	884
1902	24.7	908
1903	26.7	935
1904	13.1	948
1905	10.6	958
1906	10.2	969
1907	7.1	976
1908	5.4	981
1909	6.9	988
1910	3.5	996
1911	3.8	1001
1912	5.6	1004
1913	1.4	1008
1914	1.0	1014

Source: City of Leeds, *Annual Report and Accounts of the Gas Committee*, 1886–1914.

similar amounts on works and mains and service. From 1897 however the expenditure on works soared. By 1900, £152,948 had been spent on the New Wortley works, £151,934 on the Meadow Lane works and £16,647 on the York Street works, a total of £321,529 or forty two per cent of the original cost of the enterprise. In the next ten years an additional £67,982 was spent on New Wortley, £21,782 on Meadow Lane and £24,767 on York Street.[15]

The pricing strategy of the gas undertaking swung between periods of rapid and marked reductions up to 1881, to price increase and stabilization after 1895. Between 1835 and 1870 the price of gas in Leeds was more than halved from 8s. to 3s. 6d. per 1000 cu. ft.[16] From 1877 the price was progressively reduced under Liberal hegemony until it had reached 1s. 10d. per 1000 cubic feet by 1881.[17] In 1890 the price was increased to 2s. 2d. per 1000 cubic feet

Plate 4.1 The last years of Town Gas: the principal gasworks of Leeds, Wellington Road, New Wortley, undated [1960s?], with surrounding space from slum clearance, and Wortley Junction to bottom right.

and then again in 1893 to 2s. 4d. From 1895 to the end of the period it never fell below 2s. 2d., even increasing to 2s. 3d. between 1900 and 1904.[18] The swing back to price increases after a long period of price reductions, coupled with the reluctance of the undertaking to improve the quality of the gas supplied, were to have serious repercussions on the performance of the undertaking and to make it less robust in the face of competition from electricity.

Although competition from within the industry terminated after 1870, a new and, in the event, far more damaging form of competition emerged in the late nineteenth century with the advent of the electricity industry. In 1882 the first electric lighting act was passed; seven years later the first municipal power station was opened at Bradford. In 1893 Blackpool, Bristol, Burnley, Derby, Dundee, Glasgow, Huddersfield, Hull, Kingston-upon-Thames, Manchester, Whitehaven, and Woolwich started electricity supply. In Leeds public supply of electricity was initially given into the hands of a private company, the Yorkshire House-to-House Electricity Company, the Council being unsure (unwisely as it turned out) as to the viability of this new form of supply. For the first twenty-eight years of its existence the Leeds gas undertaking was thus subjected to competition from the private electricity undertaking for the domestic, industrial, and commercial lighting market in Leeds. For most of this period the gas industry enjoyed a comparative cost and supply advantage. In its early years, electricity proved to be considerably more expensive than gas for lighting. The Town Clerk of Leeds reflected the views of many on the council when he claimed in 1886 that it was impossible, from a commercial point of view, for electricity to compete successfully with gas as an illuminant.[19] The same financial considerations deterred would-be domestic and industrial consumers from switching to electricity.

Gas however chose not to compete with electricity on the grounds of quality of supply. According to Poulter, Leeds had the reputation (among its townsfolk at least) of having the worst gas in Britain. Complaints were levelled throughout the late nineteenth century at the gas undertaking for the quality of the gas supplied and reached crisis levels in 1879, 1885, and 1886. Gas, it was claimed, was not only extremely dirty but pressure was low and the illuminating power was poor; 'wretched' was one term used to describe the quality of supply in the town.[20] The gas industry chose to compete on cost rather than quality, taking the short term view that its market was safe so long as there was little economic incentive for its consumers to switch to electricity. Such a strategy was to cost the gas industry highly. As electricity prices started to decline as the result of technological changes, gas slowly and surely began to lose the market not only for new consumers but from its existing ones as well.

From the end of the century the competition between gas and electricity underwent a further change as electricity was transferred to municipal ownership. From 1898 the competition was between two rival undertakings owned and operated by the local authority. The electricity undertaking was purchased from the Yorkshire House-to-House Co Ltd on 31 August 1898 for the sum of £217,420. The late transfer of electricity to local authority ownership and control in Leeds reflected not only doubts based on relative costs but also concern with its own by now heavy investment in the gas industry. If the Council had initiated electric light supplies they would have detracted from their own gas undertaking and put at risk the heavy investment they had made in the gas works and it was not until the end of the century, when the financial viability of electricity was firmly established, that electricity in Leeds was transferred to municipal control and competition was between two rival undertakings owned and run by the same local authority.[21]

The full force of that competition was not however to manifest itself until the inter-war period. Competition for the lighting market was initially blunted by the comparative cost advantage enjoyed by the gas undertaking: an advantage which was to be increased as a result of technological developments. In 1894 the invention of the Welsbach incandescent gas mantle gave gas lighting a new lease of life. The new gas mantle had greater illuminating powers (it gave a light source eight times brighter than that of a gas flame) and thus required about a quarter of the gas consumption for a given degree of illumination.[22] It also had significant cost effects since it made possible the production of gas of lower illuminating power, thus increasing the yield of gas per ton of coal carbonized.[23] Of more long term significance was the advance in techniques in the use of gas for heat.[24] Change in structure in the period after 1870 was thus accompanied by change in product emanating from technological change and a gradual transition in the principal function of gas supply away from the manufacture and distribution of gas for lighting to the manufacture and distribution of gas for heating.

Given the change in the structure, product, priorities and hence strategies of its managing bodies, it is not altogether surprising that the profit record of the gas undertaking was one of fluctuation rather than any sustained growth in profits (Fig 4.1). Fluctuations in profit performance and the decline into negative profits, appear to be the result of endogenous rather than exogenous

Figure 4.1   Net profits of the Gas Undertaking of Leeds 1886–1914

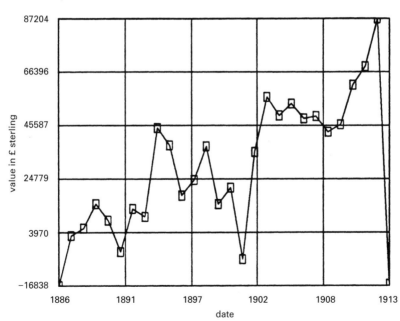

Source: City of Leeds, *Annual Report and Accounts of the Gas Committee, 1885–1914*

factors in Leeds. The profit performance follows a pattern in Leeds which was not replicated in other areas. The following paragraphs set the record for Leeds against that for Manchester and Sheffield; the former was one of the first municipal undertakings in the country; the latter one of the most long-lived private gas supply companies. Manchester did not incur the repair and rationalization costs which constrained the Leeds municipal undertaking, whilst Sheffield was not constrained by the need to redistribute profits for relief of rates. The erratic nature of the growth of profits for Leeds were shadowed by the municipal gas undertaking in Manchester and the Sheffield Gas Light Company. However, neither Manchester or Sheffield experienced a deficit, unlike the Leeds undertaking which recorded negative profits three times in this twenty-seven year period (1886, 1891 and 1901). The evidence thus suggests that the strategy of profit maximization with a view to relief of rates from 1895 was not necessarily successful—at least before 1901.

Explanations for the somewhat erratic and, in terms of declared strategy, disappointing performance relate to both the revenue and expenditure of the gas undertaking between 1885 and 1914.[25] The income of the gas undertaking depended on sales of gas to consumers and sales of by-products. The former was dependent on both the number of consumers and the amount of gas used by each consumer. The performance of Leeds, in relation to consumers was one of sustained upwards growth with a marked increase after 1896 and some tailing off towards the end of the period and, as such, it could be argued that the revenue of the Leeds gas undertaking was not constrained by any failure to attract new consumers (Fig 4.2).

More surprising was the marked increase in the number of consumers after 1897, a period which coincided with the period of Tory control when the extension of supply assumed less priority. It was in this period that the number of consumers soared. The increase in the number of consumers would appear to vindicate the amount of time, effort and money the undertaking spent on extending supply in terms of extending and laying new mains and improving its works. The success of that policy depended, however, not only on the number of consumers but on the amount of gas they used and, in this respect, the evidence indicates that the policy was not successful.

In Manchester, sales of gas grew rapidly throughout the period. Although there were periods of relative stagnation, the overall trend in that undertaking was one of strong upward growth. In 1886, just over 2,560,000 cubic feet of gas were sold in Manchester. By 1900 sales were just under five million.[26] In Leeds, the growth rate in the late nineteenth century was markedly lower than that of Manchester and, despite a period of initial growth up to 1900, the record thereafter was one of decline up to the turn of the century, stagnation up to 1908 and decline again until the outbreak of war. The value of gas sales in Leeds was noticeably less than that of either Sheffield or Manchester.

90

Figure 4.2   Total number of gas consumers, Leeds 1886–1913

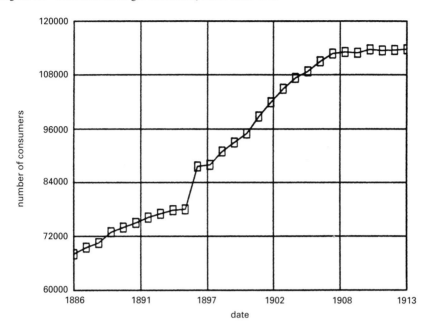

Source: Board of Trade, *Authorized Returns of the Gas Undertakings, 1886–1914*

Although the number of consumers continued to grow, the indications are that consumers were beginning to curtail their use of gas. Sales per head of gas in Leeds (Fig 4.3) increased up to 1895 but the overall trend was then downwards until 1913. Consumers in Leeds were not extending their use of gas. The Leeds gas undertaking did not therefore realize its potential revenue in terms of the amount of gas used by consumers. The level of sales per consumer actually declined. This would seem, given the timing, to coincide with the period when the Council reverted away from its cheap pricing policy.[27] Not only was there no sustained reduction in gas prices in Leeds: the price of gas actually increased. It is therefore not altogether surprising that consumers began to curtail their use of gas: both in the home and in the factory.

The decline in the use of gas was the culmination of several factors, including the pricing policy and the quality of gas. Given a combination of rising prices and low quality supply, it was not surprising that domestic and industrial consumers increasingly turned to electricity. A final factor was the repercussions of industrial change in Leeds. Crawford has suggested that the decline in gas consumption in Leeds could also be the result of the decline in the older power-intensive industries, such as the textile industries of cloth, flax and worsted spinning and the rise of new industries such as mechancial engin-

Table 4.2   Value of Sales of Gas 1886–1913

Date	Manchester £000's	Sheffield £000's	Leeds £000's
1886	470	209.6	158.8
1887	476.4	209.0	166.7
1888	499.6	224.9	233.5
1889	522.8	269.8	199.4
1890	543.3	292.8	227.7
1891	572.4	274.7	277.7
1892	580.4	256.5	244.2
1893	573.7	230.2	236.3
1894	496.0	221.1	256.8
1895	510.7	219.1	262.1
1896	601.6	224.0	258.3
1897	621.7	226.3	258.4
1898	607.0	234.6	271.4
1899	617.2	246.5	272.2
1900	613.0	259.2	311.1
1901	620.4	262.0	308.7
1902	578.2	277.1	311.2
1903	na	286.1	312.5
1904	676.3	355.7	301.1
1905	681.8	438.3	307.9
1906	809.2	468.2	297.2
1907	858.0	599.2	297.1
1908	1016.9	844.5	300.2
1909	1183.0	912.7	287.5
1910	1299.2	833.3	282.8
1911	1150.7	693.1	278.8
1912	1068.5	632.8	289.4
1913	1002.1	618.8	287.9

Source: Annual Report and Accounts of the Leeds, Manchester and Sheffield Gas Undertakings, 1886–1914.

eering, leather, chemical, clothing footwear and printing which were less dependent on heavy gas supplies.[28] The net outcome was a decline in the industrial market for gas supply. The decline in sales however was also a reflection of a conscious decision to switch from gas to electricity. Some of the newer industries opted for electricity both as a form of lighting and to drive their machinery.[29]

The gas industry suffered as a result of the general decline in demand resulting from industrial change and from the exercise of consumer choice on the part of the newer industries in favour of electricity. The undertaking had no control over the former; it did however have some control over the latter. Given the rising tide of complaints about the quality and price of gas and its apparent inability to rectify the latter it is not surprising that many consumers turned away from gas. Whereas from 1898 gas entered a period of relative

Figure 4.3   Value of gas sales per consumer–Leeds 1886–1914

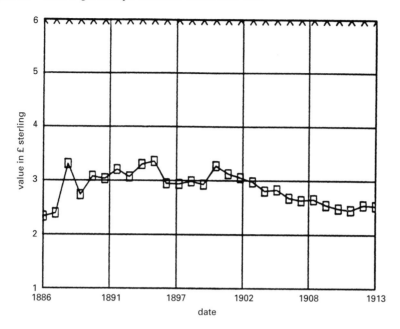

Source: City of Leeds, *Annual Report and Accounts of the Gas Committee, 1885–1914*

stagnation and even decline in sales revenue, the electricity undertaking, with the exception of a small dip around 1908, enjoyed a period of relative growth and expansion (Fig 4.4).

An important source of additional income for many gas undertakings was the sale of by-products derived in the manufacture of gas.[30] The principal by-products, or residuals, at this time were coke, ammoniachal liquor, and tar. For Leeds income from this source was never more than thirty per cent of its total income. Revenue from residuals moreover was never a reliable source of income (Fig 4.5). The record is one of fluctuation throughout the period, although from the turn of the century the level of income from by-products did increase.

Deficiencies in revenue from sales of gas were never, in the case of Leeds, compensated for by revenue from the sale of by-products. The market for such products was unstable both in the immediate and longer term. Most of the ammoniachal liquor, tar, and coke were sold on the local market. Fluctuations in trade could and did have adverse effects on sales. In the longer term, sales of the residuals of gas manufacture were undermined by the rise of the chemical industry which increasingly produced synthetic versions. Both problems were to become particularly acute in the inter-war period.

Figure 4.4   Value of sales of gas and electricity, Leeds 1898–1913

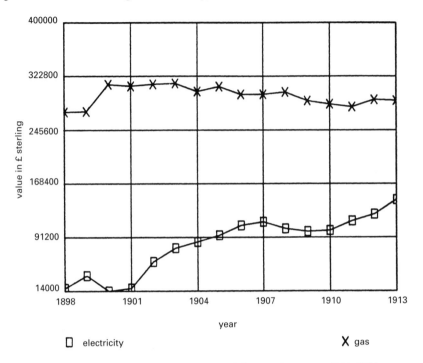

Source: City of Leeds, *Annual Report and Accounts of the Gas Committee, 1898–1914*

The profit performance of the gas undertaking in Leeds was thus undermined by its failure to boost revenue which, in turn, was the outcome of both the uncertainty in the by-product market and by the decline in demand for gas. The latter was a reflection of external factors over which the industry had no control, namely the rise of the electricity industry and industrial change in Leeds, but also of factors over which it did have control, namely its strategy after 1895 of failing to improve the quality of supply of gas and the decision to increase prices. Excessive expenditure on manufacturing and distribution compounded the problem. The bulk of the expenditure of the undertaking was on the manufacture rather than distribution of gas. Distribution costs increased up to 1900/1 but then showed a steady decline (Table 4.3).

Up to the turn of the century, expenditure on mains and services accounted for the bulk of the expenditure on distribution, reflecting the premium on infrastructure improvements needed as a result of the undertaking's legacy, particularly in relation to the state of disrepair of the mains and services of the New Gas Light Company.

The expenditure was not entirely, however, the outcome of this dubious

94

Figure 4.5   Value of sales of gas and residuals, Leeds 1886–1913

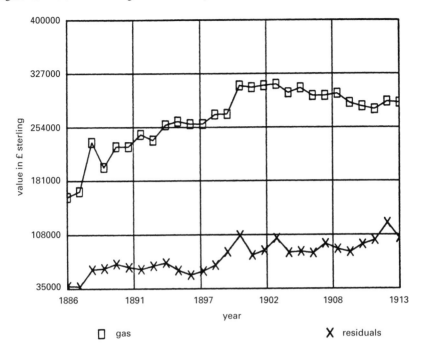

Source: City of Leeds, *Annual Report and Accounts of the Gas Committee, 1886–1913*

legacy. It also reflects the premium placed on extending and improving the supply of gas throughout the City. By the turn of the century, the bulk of the repairs had been carried out and the initial state of disrepair rectified, thus giving Leeds a relatively modern gas infrastructure. The policy does appear to have been successful insofar as expenditure on distribution fell after the turn of the century.

Manufacturing costs on the other hand fluctuated quite markedly over the period, alternating between periods of substantial increases (up to 1890, between 1897 and 1901, and after 1907) and decreases (notably between 1901 and 1907) (Fig 4.6). The cost of manufacturing does not indicate the realization of any economies of scale. The record, yet again, was one of erratic performance with periods of substantial cost increases; periods of increase moreover do not appear to coincide with either the number of consumers or sales of gas but appear to be quite independent of the demand for gas.

One explanation for this is the high cost of coal (Fig 4.7) as the undertaking appears to have experienced problems in controlling both the cost and supply of coal. Another explanation is, at worst, fraud and, at best, financial inefficiency. According to Poulter, in 1881 the Gas Committee was accused of

Table 4.3   Distribution Costs of Gas in Leeds, 1891–1910

Date	Total Distribution Costs £000's	Expenditure on Repairs and Extension of Supply £000's
1891	199.8	145.1
1892	202.8	143.7
1893	231.2	170.4
1894	249.8	191.5
1895	212.9	150.6
1896	278.1	206.2
1897	238.3	163.5
1898	249.3	168.4
1899	295.7	179.6
1900	359.6	279.1
1901	363.8	257.7
1902	336.9	231.2
1903	384.9	259.3
1904	372.8	212.5
1905	360.3	188.9
1906	362.6	193.7
1907	340.5	203.3
1908	351.8	216.7
1909	354.8	194.5
1910	329.5	199.8

Source: City of Leeds, *Annual Accounts of the Gas Undertaking, 1892–1911*.
Note: Data not available prior to 1891 and after 1910.

purchasing, in full knowledge, inferior coal from the collieries and of making no financial adjustment for this. The matter was deemed serious enough for it to be discussed by full Council on 6 March 1889. At that meeting, an analysis of the previous five years figures of coal was presented. The gas committee's own data indicated that 600,000 of the one million tons of coal purchased over that period were below standard. Allegations of corrupt practices were only increased when it was revealed that several of the gas committee members had vested interests in the coal industry as directors and proprietors of the collieries which supplied the coal. The accusations went unproven and the Council opted for the somewhat bizarre 'explanation' that, despite financial loss due to the purchase of inferior coal, there had been a corresponding gain because in years when good coal was purchased, the coal was much higher than standard.[31] The Council obviously decided not to dig too deeply into the financial arrangements of the gas undertaking and its committee and nothing more was heard of the matter. Although fraud was never proved, the explanation as accepted by the Council does reveal a singular inability to control costs on the part of the gas undertaking. Coal accounted for between sixty-five and seventy-five per cent of manufacturing costs and inability to control such an important

96

Figure 4.6   Manufacturing costs of gas, Leeds 1886–1914

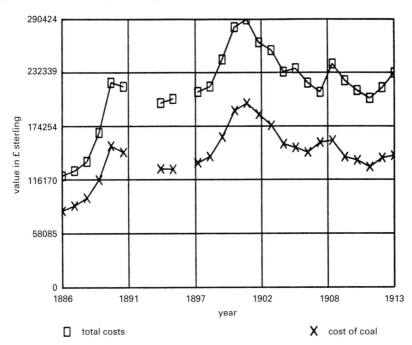

Source; City of Leeds, *Annual Accounts and Reports of the Gas Committee, 1886–1913*

aspect of the undertaking's expenditure implies complacency and inefficiency in the financial management of the undertaking.

This apparent failure to control manufacturing costs had serious consequences for gas supply in Leeds. The financial loss incurred in the years 1881–86 from inferior purchases of coal amounted to £14,744 or nearly £3000 a year.[32] In the financial years ending 1886, 1887, 1888 and 1889 the undertaking had made a net profit/(loss) of (£16,838), £2748, £5543 and £15,132 respectively.[33] All the indications are that the amount spent on coal by the gas undertaking in Leeds was excessive and that large sums of money were being paid for substandard coal. Prior to 1914, the undertaking was unable to increase the yield of gas made per ton of coal which could reflect of the purchase of substandard coal. This, in turn, would have constrained its ability to effect price reductions.

According to Millward, all gas undertakings seem to have been motivated strongly by considerations of profit, with consumer interest not apparently strong.[34] The record of the Leeds undertaking deviates somewhat from this view in the fluctuating priorities of the political groups in Leeds. Profit considerations dominated prior to 1872 and after 1895, but were less important between

97

Figure 4.7   Cost of gas manufacturing in Leeds, per million cu ft of gas made

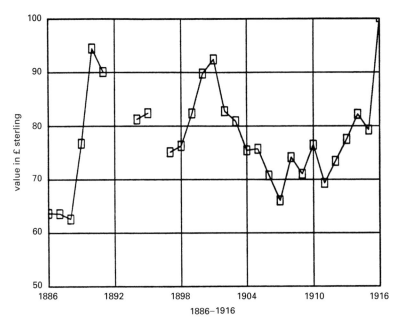

Source: City of Leeds, *Annual Report and Accounts of the Gas Committee, 1886–1914*

1872 and 1895. Consumer interests were strong in price and supply terms between 1872 and 1895. But at no time were consumer interests in terms of the quality of gas supplied afforded high priority. Underlying the profit motive (and certainly a strong consideration in the initial decision to purchase) was the aim of using gas profits to relieve rates. From 1895 there was a shift in policy towards transferring surplus funds from the gas accounts to the City Fund. In 1895, £18,000 (forty-eight per cent of total net profits) were transferred to the City Fund whilst between 1908 and 1912 a total amount of £73,136 was transferred. By 1910 £209,262 had been transferred.[35] This coincides with the period when the gas undertaking was becoming profitable. The intentions of the Conservatives were not realized until after the turn of the century. By contrast, transfer of funds from the electricity undertaking to the City Fund only totalled £162,608 by 1920.[36]

By its own intentions of maximizing profits and relieving rates, the gas undertaking was therefore moderately successful in the medium term. The fact that it took until the end of the century to realize these aims was partly due to its dubious inheritance and the amount it had to spend on infrastructure repairs. For most of that time, Leeds consumers benefited at a time when there was no real alternative power supply for lighting in terms of the extension of supply, at least up to the early 1890s, in terms of the reductions in price if not in terms of the quality of the gas supplied. In the long term however, the gas undertaking in Leeds alienated its consumers by the failure to sustain price reductions (and indeed to increase prices from the early 1890s) and its reluctance to improve the quality of gas. It was then to some extent inevitable that it would begin to lose custom once there was a viable competitor, namely electricity. This in a period when industrial change in the City reduced overall demand for gas supply was to culminate in a new chapter in the history of public supply of gas in Leeds in the inter-war period.

III

From 1918 the gas undertaking entered one of the most problematic periods in its history. The contraction of industrial markets as a result of economic depression was to have serious effects on revenue from sales of both gas and residuals. Although the wide industrial base and the commercial interests of the City insulated Leeds to some extent from the ravages experienced in those parts of the country dependent on the worst affected industries, the City and its surrounding area were not immune from industrial depression and unemployment. Leeds did not become a centre for any of the 'new' industries of the period such as motor vehicles, chemicals, and electrical engineering and therefore did not experience the industrial restructuring which might have alleviated the effects of the economic problems of the period.

This had serious effects on demand for industrial and domestic gas and for the residual by-products. As industries collapsed or tried to cut costs, the undertaking was faced with declining sales. Unemployment and the fear of unemployment acted to constrain domestic demand. In the case of by-products, the problem was compounded by the commercial production of synthetic products by the chemical industry which replaced some of the traditional by-products of the gas undertaking. A collapse in the industrial market was to some extent inevitable given the economic climate, and beyond the immediate control of the gas undertaking.

The undertaking, however, also faced additional problems in the domestic sector which were not purely a reflection of the effects of the depression on the purchasing power of consumers. The decline in gas sales was largely the result of the exercise of consumer choice in favour of electricity. In many respects, the history of public supply of gas in Leeds between the wars is best understood in terms of the seemingly inexorable rise of competition from the electricity undertaking. The performance of the gas undertaking in the inter-war years was thus again characterized by change in structure and in market demand. The combination of economic depression with its consequent effects on industrial demand for power, heat and the by-products of gas manufacture together with the apparently unstoppable rise of the electricity industry, culminated in two decades of low and negative profit growth, declining sales revenue, and falling consumption.

The combination of economic depression and the rise of the electricity industry in turn encouraged a switch in strategy away from the pre-war concern with extending mains and services and an apparent lack of consumer awareness. From 1918, extension of supply was ceded a very low priority as the undertaking adopted an aggressive marketing approach designed to persuade consumers of the relative benefits of gas—both in the home and in the workplace. The success of the approach can be gleaned from its overall failure to boost consumption of gas and to stem the tide of the growth of electricity usage in Leeds.

This change in strategy was encouraged by technological change, notably the application of nineteenth-century innovations in the use of gas for heating purposes to commercial use and, on the manufacturing side, in improvements in technique which raised the average yield of gas from 64 to 75 therms per ton of coal.[37] Prior to the First World War the industry had seen its main function as the manufacture and distribution of gas for lighting purposes. In the inter-war period, as electricity increasingly took over the lighting market, gas concentrated almost exclusively on the heating market. From 1918, there was a marked switch of emphasis to the manufacture and distribution of gas for heating purposes, symbolized in 1920 when the industry sought and obtained from Parliament the right to charge for gas on its heating value and not on its volume. After 1920 gas consumers bought heat as gas was charged 'per therm' and not 'per 1000 cubic feet'.[38] Technological change also underpinned the post-war sales strategy of encouraging an extension in the use of gas for heating. The efficiency and appearance of domestic gas appliances, including automatic control, higher thermal efficiencies as well as aesthetically better design and finishing placed gas in a potentially sound position to capture the market for heating appliances.[39] In the event, that potential was not realized in Leeds. Strategy was therefore largely defensive and, in the event, relatively unsuccessful. In some respects the strategy and performance of the undertaking was governed less by its own actions than those of the electricity undertaking.

Competition from electricity was not, however, the only exogenous factor which constrained the gas undertaking in the period since the decline in consumption and hence revenue were also the result of strategy imposed on the gas undertaking by the Council. Increasingly, in the inter-war period the undertaking was subjected to a more interventionist approach as its policies were tied to the wider aims of the Council. In 1921, for example, it was instructed to carry out a number of building, repairs and reconstruction works in order to relieve local unemployment.[40] Shortly afterwards, the Council opted to supply gas in new local authority housing, despite the undertaking's reservations that the revenue from the resultant sale of gas would be totally inadequate to recompense the department for the capital expenditure.[41] In the 1930s, the undertaking became involved in the Council's slum clearance programme, laying forty-two miles of gas mains in 1937[42]. Extension of supply to poorer areas of the City, where consumption of gas was likely to be low, not only had limited benefits in terms of the marginal return on increased supply, but also had negative effects in the consequent capital and expenditure costs. This, however, was a policy over which the gas undertaking had little or no control. At a time when it was faced with fierce competition from electricity, the gas undertaking increasingly found its room to manoeuvre constrained by an interventionist Council.

In the long term, however, the apparent willingness with which domestic and industrial consumers embraced electricity in Leeds in this period can be traced back to consumer dissatisfaction prior to the War and the apparent complacency of the undertaking in the face of the rising tide of complaints. In many respects, the problems of the gas undertaking can be seen as the culmination of its policies and performance in the pre-war period. The growth in electricity consumption in the inter-war decades was largely a function of rational decision making by consumers based on the relative prices and quality of the two sources of supply.[43] The history of public supply of gas in Leeds in the inter-war years would appear to confirm this view.

In 1918 just under 3000 million cubic feet of gas was sold in Leeds. The undertaking however was barely able to maintain this level of sales in the inter-war period. The average volume of sales for the twenty years was 2984 million cubic feet. The undertaking was never able to exceed its sales peak in 1927 of 3197 million cubic feet. Between 1931 and 1939 the volume of sales of gas grew by only six per cent.[44] The decline was not the result of a general fall-off in demand for power. It was the result of a transfer of demand away from gas to electricity.

Since its advent in 1880, electricity had always provided an intrinsically more efficient method of converting coal energy into light.[45] In the inter-war period, technological change leading to cost cutting innovations and the rationalization of supply following the establishment of the National Grid, coupled with electricity's accepted advantage in safety, convenience, and cleanliness, shifted public opinion in favour of electricity initially in favour of lighting and later for heating. The rapid growth in electricity usage in Leeds, as elsewhere in the country, was largely the result of product market changes and specialization of function as gas lost its traditional lighting market to electricity. In

1918, 62,387 kilowatts of electricity were sold in Leeds; within ten years, sales had reached 135,498 kilowatts. Between 1931 and 1939 electricity sales grew by forty-five per cent and by 1938 electricity sales were in excess of 250 million kilowatts a year.[46]

The decline was not the result of any fall in the number of consumers. In 1921 there were 117,480 gas consumers. By 1938 the number had risen to 153,682; a net gain of 36,202 consumers. The decline was the result of a continuation of the pre war trend of a fall in gas consumption (Fig 4.8).

In these terms, the undertaking never bettered its 1900 performance when the average consumer used 33.06 cubic feet of gas. From then onwards consumption declined. An initial boost in the post-war boom proved short-lived. From 1927 consumption collapsed, reaching an all time low of 19.62 cubic feet in 1935. The enthusiasm with which consumers adopted electric power in Leeds (Fig 4.9) reflects, in part, the revolution in lighting which took place in the inter-war period. Between 1926 and 1938 electricity consumers in England and Wales grew by eighty-five per cent.[47] The upsurge in Leeds, at seventy-two per cent was, if anything, low by national standards.

Figure 4.8   Value of sales of gas and electricity, Leeds 1918–38

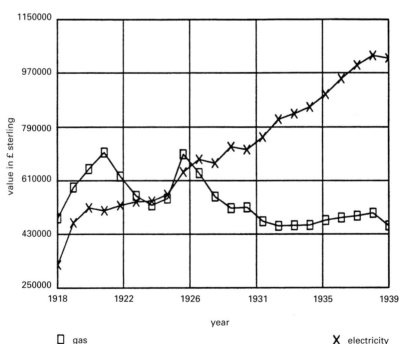

year

□ gas   X electricity

Source: Board of Trade, *Authorized Returns of the Gas Undertakings, 1886–1939*

Figure 4.9   Number of gas and electricity consumers, Leeds 1914–38

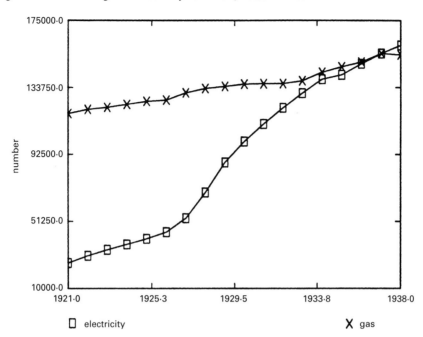

□ electricity   X gas

Source: City of Leeds, *Annual Reports and Accounts of the Gas and Electricity Committees, 1918–39*

The steady decline in sales was largely the result of the collapse in consumption of gas for lighting and heating, (Table 4.4), which became particularly marked from 1926. The evidence indicates that, despite its aggressive marketing and advertising campaigns, the gas undertaking was unable to boost gas consumption in industry. Nor did the rise in prepayment sales compensate for the decline in demand for gas power and lighting. Sales of gas to works and offices declined steadily up to 1932, although economic recovery from that date did reverse the trend. The only source of comfort, discussed below, was the increase in public lighting sales.

By contrast, the electricity industry recorded substantial increases in sales of power and bulk supplies from 1921 and residential bulk supplies from 1925. In 1918, the undertaking sold 6739 kilowatts of electricity for private lighting. By 1938, sales from this source had reached just under 34,000 excluding prepayment consumers (Table 4.5).

The 'take-off' of electricity consumers in Leeds after 1927 was, as elsewhere in the country, largely the result of the introduction of assisted wiring schemes. Although costs fell, electricity installation was an expensive exercise at this time. In 1919 the cost of installing a modest system was between £11 and £20.

103

Table 4.4   Sales of Gas by Type in Leeds, 1918–1938

Date	Power & Light	Central Heating	Prepayment	Public Lighting	Works & Offices	Total
	Million cubic feet					
1918	2160.3		600.7	52.0	48.6	2863.3
1919	2012.7		624.2	82.1	42.3	2761.4
1920	2012.7		618.0	140.7	39.1	2715.7
1921	1917.9		720.6	169.5	34.0	2843.5
1922	1919.7		681.6	236.8	27.8	2822.1
1923	1875.5		717.5	254.3	29.5	2964.1
1924	1962.8		804.8	272.8	26.4	3069.9
1925	1928.3		885.3	295.4	27.5	3136.5
1926	1996.7		1056.5	224.6	25.2	3302.9
1927	1883.1		1022.6	268.5	22.6	3196.8
1928	1852.8		1039.9	278.8	21.8	3192.9
1929	1789.5		885.6	291.6	21.8	2988.5
1930	1755.4		927.2	297.8	21.3	3001.7
1931	1661.2	3.1	902.2	311.7	22.7	2900.9
1932	1622.2	21.1	854.8	327.8	24.1	2851.7
1933	1585.9	52.8	869.4	338.9	24.1	2871.1
1934	1591.0	50.1	854.1	352.4	25.2	2872.8
1935	1668.8	64.1	872.7	365.0	28.2	2998.9
1936	1688.3	75.8	884.5	378.0	30.7	3057.3
1937	1693.7	84.1	928.3	392.9	29.9	3128.8
1938	1626.7	133.3	986.9	411.2	28.7	3186.8

Source: City of Leeds, *Annual Report and Accounts of the Gas Committee, 1918–1939.*

By 1938 although the cost had fallen to £5 to £6 this was still beyond the means of the majority of the population who had a weekly income of £5 or less.[48] Assisted wiring schemes were introduced to allow potential consumers to acquire installations on hire purchase terms. In Leeds, the electricity undertaking introduced such a scheme in May 1927 which, by national standards, was progressive. The take-up of such schemes was generally associated with the 1930s rather than the 1920s in the country in general. The upsurge in electricity consumers and electricity consumption was to a large extent associated with the introduction of such schemes.[49] Leeds was no exception to this general rule. By March 1928, 7901 orders for assisted wiring schemes had been placed and within four years, 41,470 consumers in Leeds had availed themselves of this scheme.[50] At the end of the decade, 58,145 households had electricity installed by an assisted wiring scheme.[51]

By comparison, the success of the gas undertaking in the 1920s was limited to the retailing sector, notably fish and chip shops, bakers and confectioners and, in the 1930s, the local hotels and hospitals. The existence of 157 gas-fired fish-fryers in the City not surprisingly made little impact on industrial sales

Table 4.5   Sales of Electricity by Type in Leeds, 1918–1938

Date	Power & Bulk	Private Lighting	Prepayment	Street Lighting	Heating
	Thousand Kilowatts				
1918	46991	6739		159	1178
1919	42485	8367		235	1706
1920	43061	9551		265	1995
1921	36797	9857		311	2471
1922	43099	11898		434	2573
1923	51626	13953		479	3263
1924	54903	15774		558	3103
1925	58481	16776		617	3482
1926	57397	16137		592	4099
1927	67209	18841		761	4049
1928	72665	19850	1394	853	5302
1929	71601	21248	2796	885	5224
1930	68224	21983	3890	914	6091
1931	66807	23059	4983	953	6157
1932	69411	24427	5573	1014	6787
1933	79608	26121	6110	1045	6783
1934	86440	28337	6732	1073	7485
1935	96209	30804	6921	1118	9334
1936	104983	32776	6948	1191	9535
1937	108250	34000	7016	1468	9750
1938	114647	33596	5803	1835	9428

Source: City of Leeds, Annual Report and Accounts of the Electricity Committee, 1918–1938.

and revenue.[52] Nor did the undertaking's efforts to persuade the commercial sector to expand its use of gas meet with much success; gas consumption in works and offices remained stagnant at a very low level throughout the period. Given Leeds' wide and important commercial base, this was a significant blow to the gas undertaking. A similar pattern was repeated in the domestic sector. Although the undertaking boosted consumption via the introduction of prepayment meters, the initial increase was not sustained. Domestic use of gas from this source stagnated after 1929.[53] The one small area of comfort for the undertaking lay in public lighting. The small but sustained increase in this market and the lack of any sizeable increase in electric public lighting at a time when the nation trend was away from gas is somewhat surprising and was probably the result of the undertaking's coup in 1918 when, as a result of a rationalization of the committee structure by the Council, the Gas Committee took over control of the Street Lighting Committee. Given the demand side problems the undertaking experienced in the inter-war period, the gas committee had a vested interest in ensuring that public lighting in Leeds continued to be gas-based. By 1938 there were 20,760 gas lamps in Leeds, but only 1677 electric lamps. Continued sales of gas for public lighting were, however, insufficient to compensate for the problems in the industrial, commercial and domestic markets.

Not surprisingly, this had serious effects on the sales revenue of the gas undertaking (Fig 4.10). The structural break can be dated from 1927 after which time sales of electricity soared whilst those of gas effectively collapsed. By the end of the inter-war period, the value of gas sales was forty-nine per cent that of electricity. Between 1886 and 1913 the average value of sales of gas per consumer was £2.87. Although there was a slight increase during the inter-war period (the average value was £4), the performance of the gas undertaking compared unfavourably with that of electricity. In 1938 the average value of gas sales per consumer was £5.99; the average value of sales of electricity per consumer was £6.41.[54]

To compound the problem, the gas undertaking was faced with a collapse in the market for its by-products (Fig 4.11). The post-war boom in sales of residuals was short-lived. From 1920, the market declined, although there was a slight revival after 1934. The inter-war period witnessed the culmination of

Figure 4.10   Value of sales of gas and electricity, Leeds 1918–39

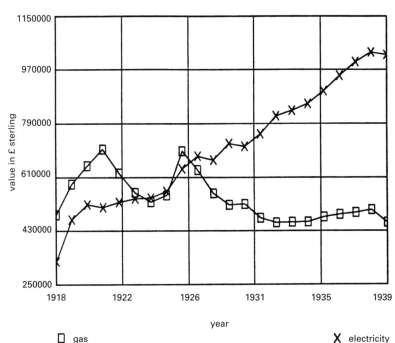

gas   electricity

Source: City of Leeds, *Annual Report and Accounts of the Gas and Electricity Committees, 1918–38*

Figure 4.11   Value of sales of residuals by type, Leeds 1918–38

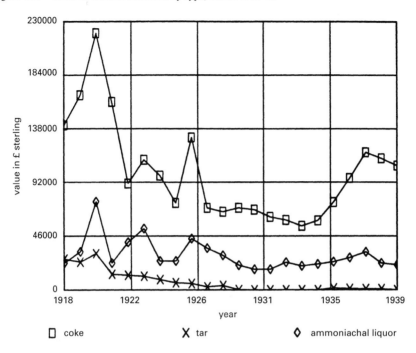

□ coke   X tar   ◊ ammoniachal liquor

Source: City of Leeds, *Annual Report and Accounts of the Gas Committee, 1918–38*

the pre-war trend of competition from synthetic substitutes compounded by falling demand in the depressed economic climate. Sales of ammoniachal liquor evaporated as 'the price at which sulphate of ammonia was offered for sale abroad by our competitors was below the cost of production in this country'.[55] By 1929, the undertaking was gloomily forecasting that it was doubtful that it would obtain any revenue from this source in the future.[56] From the late 1920s, revenue from tar declined 'due to the continued fall in the prices of nearly all tar products'.[57] Revenue from benzole was adversely affected by the decline in raw material prices, notably petrol and the undertaking's revenue from this source was reduced despite its increased output.[58] In the case of coke, the decline in sales was the result of the collapse in demand during the depressed local trading conditions of the period. Demand for coke did not recover until 1936 as a result of the larger quantity of coal carbonized, the increase in the yard price and the higher price for coke shipped abroad.[59]

The many problems of the gas undertaking were manifested in its relative profit performance, with the profits of electricity exceeding those of gas by a large margin in every year in the period and the gas undertaking recording nine years of negative profits (Fig 4.12). Average profit for gas in these

107

Figure 4.12   Profits of gas and electricity undertakings, Leeds 1918–1938

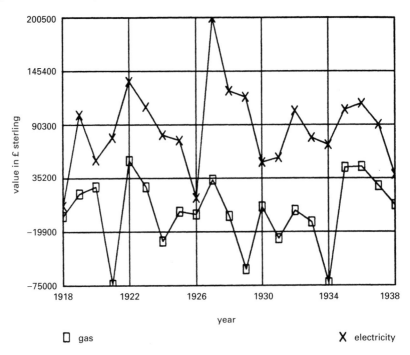

year

☐ gas   ✗ electricity

Source: City of Leeds, *Annual Report and Accounts of the Gas and Electricity Committee, 1918–38*

years was £698 as against an average profit of £85,816 for electricity.[60] The outcome was a vicious circle in which the gas undertaking, faced with declining profits was unable to effect price reductions. The gas undertaking did try to compete on prices in the 1920s.

Between 1919 and 1930 gas prices were changed every year, save 1921, 1925, 1928 and 1931. The changes were not, however, always reductions. On four occasions (1 July 1920, 1 October 1926, 1 January 1927, and March 1927) the price of gas for cooking, heating and lighting was increased.[61] Between 1931 and 1938 there was no change in the price of gas; cooking, heating and lighting prices remained at 2.98*d*. to 9.57*d*. per therm. The take-off in electricity consumption in the 1930s was heavily influenced by gas prices as consumers switched from gas to electricity on the basis of relative prices.[62] The evidence would suggest that Leeds was no exception to this rule.

By contrast, the profit performance of the electricity undertaking was strong enough to withstand price reductions. Between 1918 and 1938, the average price of electricity in Leeds fell for all power uses (Table 4.6), but was particu-larly marked in the crucial domestic market of private lighting where the unit

Table 4.6   Average Electricity Net Price Per Unit in Pence 1918–38

Date	A	B	C	D	E	F
1918	0.98	3.89		1.36	1.28	1.54
1919	1.36	5.17		1.74	1.69	1.73
1920	1.46	5.29		1.80	1.66	1.73
1921	1.51	5.43		1.80	1.71	1.90
1922	1.20	5.00		1.67	1.57	1.91
1923	0.97	4.43		1.51	1.45	1.62
1924	0.85	4.15		1.28	1.25	1.32
1925	0.80	4.08		1.25	1.19	1.14
1926	0.93	4.29		1.42	1.36	1.20
1927	0.85	4.09		1.28	1.21	1.12
1928	0.79	3.16		1.25	1.13	0.99
1929	0.78	3.11	4.75	1.25	1.13	1.03
1930	0.77	2.84	4.34	1.25	0.95	0.91
1931	0.78	2.79	4.25	1.25	0.95	0.93
1932	0.78	2.68	4.25	1.25	0.95	0.95
1933	0.74	2.32	3.91	1.25	0.90	0.92
1934	0.70	2.16	3.58	1.25	0.88	0.92
1935	0.70	2.16	3.58	1.25	0.88	0.92
1936	0.65	2.06	3.50	1.25	0.84	0.90
1937	0.64	2.03	3.50	1.25	0.83	0.92
1938	0.62	2.02	3.50	1.25	0.79	0.96

Key:
A Power and Bulk Supplies
B Private Lighting—Ordinary Tariff
C Private Lighting—Prepayment Tariff
D Street Lighting
E Heating
F Residential Bulk Supplies
Source: City of Leeds, *Annual Report and Accounts of the Electricity Committee, 1918–1939.*

price on the ordinary tariff halved between 1919 and 1933. In Leeds, the decision to change from gas to electricity was entirely rational given the fall in electricity prices against fluctuations in gas prices in the 1920s and stagnation in the 1930s. The gas undertaking was thus trapped in a low profit, high price situation with little immediate prospect of gaining domestic and industrial consumers.

IV

In 1949, the gas undertaking in Leeds ceased to exist as a separate entity. From this period, its activities were amalgamated within the nationalized gas industry. There are no records with which to trace the fortunes of Leeds within the manifold changes which took place in the industry after 1949 and this chapter therefore by definition ends in 1949.

Over a period of 131 years, the supply of gas in Leeds was dominated by fluctuation: in the structure, in the aims and strategy, and finally in the performance of the industry. If there is one constant characteristic it is that of change. The ability of the industry to deal with change, both in the wider economic environment and in competition, be it from other gas companies or from electricity, met with varying degrees of success. To some extent, the ability of the undertaking to realize its goals was constrained by the legacy of its inheritance prior to 1870, by changes in party political policy and, notably in the inter-war period, by other council preoccupations. To a large extent, the undertaking in these matters was constrained by factors beyond its immediate control and, in the circumstances, was successful in extending gas to the city of Leeds. The troubled fortunes of the industry from the late nineteenth century, however, owed less to these exogenous factors than to its disregard for consumer concern and its apparent inability to rectify complaints on the quality of gas.

Notes

[1] R. Crawford, 'The Gas Industry in Leeds in the Nineteenth Century', MPhil., Leeds, 1986, p. 198.

[2] B. J. Barber, 'Aspects of Municipal Government, 1835–1914' in D. Fraser (ed), *A History of Modern Leeds*, Manchester, 1980, p. 318.

[3] *ibid*, 319.

[4] R. Millward, 'Emergence of Gas and Water Monopolies in Nineteenth Century Britain: Contested Markets and Public Control' in J. Foreman-Peck (ed), *New Perspectives on the Late Victorian Economy; Essays in Quantitative Economic History*, Cambridge, 1991, pp. 96–124.

[5] Barber, 1980, p. 319.

[6] *ibid*, p. 318.

[7] R. Millward and R. Ward, 'From Private to Public Ownership of Gas Undertakings in England and Wales, 1851–1947: Chronology, Incidence and Causes', *Business History*, 35, 1993, 1–21.

[8] Barber, 1980, p. 318.

[9] Crawford, 1986, pp. 203–4.

[10] Crawford, 1986, p. 204.

[11] Barber, 1980, p. 324.

[12] *ibid*, pp. 324–5.

[13] Board of Trade, Authorised Returns of the Gas Undertakings, 1887, 1899 and 1914.

[14] City of Leeds, Annual Report and Accounts of the Gas Committee, 1885–1914; City of Leeds, Annual Accounts, Finance Committee, 1885–1914.

[15] City of Leeds, Annual Report and Accounts of the Gas Committee, 1885–1914.

[16] Crawford, 1986, p. 201.

[17] Barber, 1980, p. 20.

[18] City of Leeds, Annual Report and Accounts of the Gas Committee, 1885–1914.

[19] I. C. Byatt, *The British Electrical Industry 1875–1914, The Economic Returns of a New Technology*, 1979, Oxford, p. 22.

[20] J. D. Poulter, *An Early History of Electricity Supply; The Story of Electric Light in Victorian Leeds*, 1986, p. 44.

[21] *ibid*, p. 49.

[22] Frank Heath and A. L. Hetherington, *Industrial Research and Development in the United Kingdom; A Survey*, 1946, p. 66; Political and Economic Planning, *Report on the Gas Industry in Great Britain*, 1939, p. 42.

[23] Political and Economic Planning, 1939, p. 42.

[24] *ibid*, pp. 3–4, 44.

[25] Records for the period prior to 1885 are not available.

[26] City of Manchester, Annual Report and Accounts of the Gas Committee, 1886–1914.

[27] The price of gas was increased from 1*s*. 10*d*. to 2*s*. 2*d*. in 1890 and 2*s*. 4*d*. in 1893. Although there was a small reduction in 1895 the price was increased again to its 1893 level in 1900. City of Leeds, Annual Report and Accounts of the Gas Committee, 1885–1914.

[28] Crawford, 1986, pp. 216–219.

[29] Crawford, 1986, pp. 216–219.

[30] Millward and Ward, 1993.

[31] Poulter, 1986, p. 46.

[32] *ibid*, p. 46.

[33] City of Leeds, Annual Report and Accounts of the Gas Committee, 1885–1889.

[34] R. Millward, 'The Market Behaviour of Local Utilities in Pre-World War I Britain: The Case of Gas', *Economic History Review*, 2nd ser, XLIV, 1991, 1, 122.

[35] City of Leeds, Annual Report and Accounts of the Gas Committee, 1885–1889.

[36] *ibid*.

[37] Political and Economic Planning, 1939, p. 43.

[38] *ibid*, p. 43.

[39] *ibid*, p. 44.

[40] City of Leeds, Annual Report of the Gas Committee, 1922, p. 8.

[41] *ibid*, p. 9.

[42] City of Leeds, Annual Report of the Gas Committee, 1938.

[43] S. M. Bowden, 'The Consumer Durables Revolution in England 1932–1938; A Regional Analysis', *Explorations in Economic History*, 25, 1, 1988, 42–59.

[44] City of Leeds, Annual Report of the Gas Committee, 1918–1939.

[45] Political and Economic Planning, 1939, p. 49.

[46] City of Leeds, Annual Report and Accounts of the Gas and Electricity Committees, 1918–1938.

[47] Electricity Council, 1980.

[48] S. M. Bowden, 'Credit Facilities and the Growth of Consumer Demand for Electric Appliances in England in the 1930s', *Business History*, 1990, 32, 1, pp. 61–2.

[49] Bowden, 1988.

[50] City of Leeds, Annual Report of the Electricity Committee, 1928, p. 5; City of Leeds, Annual Report of the Electricity Committee, 1932, p. 4.

[51] City of Leeds, Annual Report of the Electricity Committee, 1938, p. 3.

[52] City of Leeds, Annual Report of the Gas Undertaking, 1927, p. 8.

[53] *ibid*, 1921–1939.

[54] City of Leeds, Annual Reports of the Gas and Electricity Committees, 1918–1938.

[55] City of Leeds, Annual Report of the Gas Committee, 1922, p. 4.

[56] *ibid*, 1930, p. 3.

[57] *ibid*, 1930, p. 3.

[58] *ibid*, 1932, p. 4.

[59] *ibid*, 1937.

[60] City of Leeds, Annual Accounts of the Finance Committee, 1918–1939.

[61] *ibid*.

[62] Bowden, 1988, p. 57.

CHAPTER 5

Joshua Tetley & Son, 1890s to 1990s: a century in the tied trade

John Chartres

JOSHUA TETLEY & SON, the Leeds brewer has recently become a part of the Carlsberg-Tetley PLC group, with an national beer marketing brief. In the process of this recent reorganization, the brewery has become separated from the tied public houses, which had been a fundamental feature of the business. The large-scale restructuring of the industry, with new and separate brewing and retail divisions being established by all of the 'big six' national brewers, has been the consequence of regulation, the outcome of the 1989 Monopolies and Mergers' Commission report, *The Supply of Beer*, and its subsequent partial implementation. For Tetley, late entrants to the tied house trade, this has brought an end to a link that began in 1890, although the former Joshua Tetley & Son pubs remain part of the Tetley Pub Company Ltd, a division of Allied-Lyons Retailing.[1]

Tetley was already a long-established name in Leeds brewing in the early 1890s. The family had bought into the brewing trade in 1822. Joshua, the third son of William Tetley, maltster, wine and spirit dealer, of Armley, had purchased the brewing business of William Sykes, at Salem Place, Hunslet Lane in October 1822 for £409. He carried on his father's malting trade after his death in 1834, the two brothers engaged with the business having died in 1829 and 1831, and the firm continued to deal in malt until the 1860s. Thereafter, Tetley's concentrated entirely on brewing.

The firm was therefore older still in its origins. William Sykes had opened his new brewery at Salem Place in 1792, opposite the coal staith, where Brandling's waggonway delivered coal from Middleton. It joined a limited number of other common breweries in the town: the first had opened in 1756, in Meadow Lane, built and owned by the Denisons, and taken by Thomas Jacques from 1758; a second, Robert Arthington's brewhouse was open by 1769, in Hunslet Lane; and during the early 1790s, four others are listed in

Plate 5.1   Joshua Tetley, from Souvenir Beermat of 1993.

directories, Thomas Appleyard in the Calls, Humble at Belle Isle and Green elsewhere in Hunslet, and George Sawyer in Sheepscar. The Sykes/Tetley enterprise was one of six common breweries in Leeds in 1817 and 1822, one of seven in 1830, and one of ten in 1834, but brewing for retail remained largely the concern of the brewing publican, and there was very little continuity among the common brewers. By the late 1830s, only the Jacques, Arthington, and Tetley, enterprises remained from the eighteenth-century firms, and the first two disappeared by 1860: Jacques became Jacques and Nell, but disappeared in 1857; and Robert Arthington spectacularly converted to teetotalism during a Quaker meeting in 1850, closed the brewery, and sent his million to missionary work overseas. Tetley's thus distinguished themselves first by longevity.[1]

Tetley's were thus the sole representatives of the long-established Leeds breweries by the third quarter of the nineteenth century, and the same period saw the firm's consolidation as the largest enterprise not only in Leeds, but probably also in the county as a whole. The scale of its output can only be estimated crudely, but using the evidence of the malt brewed, the years 1859–75 saw Tetley established as the dominant force in Leeds brewing. Some indication of their share of Leeds output is provided in Table 5.1 below:

113

Table 5.1   Tetley in the Leeds Brewing Trade, 1859–75

Year	Leeds Brewers			Joshua Tetley			
	Number	Malt (000Q)	Barrels (000B)	Malt (000Q)	Barrels (000B)	% Share of Brewers	% Share of All Leeds
1859	22	39.9	175.4	9.8	43.1	24.6	11
1871	20	67.6	297.6	20.0	88.0	29.6	15
1874	22	83.6	368.0	33.0	145.0	39.4	20
1875	25	90.4	397.8	39.0	171.5	43.1	23

The figures presented here are broad indicators of Tetley's position, and should not be regarded as precise estimates, having been produced from Excise data—PP, 1860, LXIII, p. 451; 1872, LIV, p. 1; 1875, LXXi, p. 1; LXVIII, p. 25—using the method adopted by Sigsworth, *Brewing Trade*, and additional data from Lackey, *Quality Pays...*, pp. 54, 64. The conversion rate of malt to beer, at four barrels the quarter, implies too high a rate of extraction for 'standard barrels', and the figures are best treated as 'bulk barrels'. Percentage share of 'all Leeds' is estimated on the basis of the output of common brewers, brewing victuallers, and beerhouses. I am indebted to Dr R. G. Wilson for advice on these points.

This striking pattern of growth is confirmed by that of increasing employment. In 1851, Tetley employed only thirty-two men, plus two coopers, four clerks, and Mr Firth, the cashier; this number had grown to eighty, plus twenty-one coopers, eight clerks and the cashier by January 1856, strongly pointing to growth, and, in the figure for coopers, to increasing labour productivity in the production work. By 1889, when Alfred Barnard visited, the brewery employed 400 men, and eighty-five clerks besides, roughly two-thirds of the total employment in Leeds breweries recorded in the 1891 Census. The malt consumption of brewing can no longer be used to estimate market shares by the late 1880s with even this degree of confidence, but the Tetley workforce indicates an output in excess of 200,000 barrels per annum, which represented around half of the total output of Leeds breweries in 1889/90, and perhaps two-fifths of total beer production.[2]

This growth had been in large part attributable to the superior quality of the Tetley product, Joshua's commitment from 1822, but it was aided by the extensive capital investment made at the brewery during the growth of the 1850s, 1860s, and 1870s, and reinforced by the impact of the railways. Their facilities permitted wider distribution of beer in barrels, and by 1889 the firm had storage capacity for over 20,000 barrels beneath the Midland (Wellington Street) and North-Eastern (New) Railway stations. To these technical sources of scale economies were added those of effective self-promotion, aided by the advertised testimony of academic experts. One of Tetley's first recorded advertisements, from 1859, cited the scientific analysis of Dr Sheridan Muspratt, professor at the College of Chemistry, Liverpool, in support of the quality of its beers and East India Pale Ale. By the early 1890s, then, the firm had

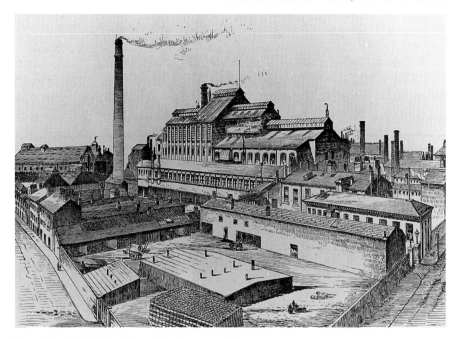

Plate 5.2   A Bird's Eye View of the Brewery, 1889.

survived and prospered, and had established its dominance within the Leeds
Excise division over all other brewers, and, in its increasing share of the total
market for beer, over all other producers. Although it was of modest scale by
comparison with such giants as Bass, by far the largest in the country, with a
barrellage of 1.5 million in 1890, and some of the London brewers, Tetley was
established, with John Smith's at Tadcaster, as a regional leader. There were
few others half its size in the other Yorkshire towns, and employment in
Tetley's alone dwarfed that in the breweries of Sheffield, and exceeded that of
Bradford, Halifax, and Hull added together.[3] They had established themselves
as the major brewing business of Yorkshire.

I

What kind of retail drink trade did Tetley's serve in the 1890s? In several ways
Leeds was also unusual in this, again reflecting the position of the regional
capital vis-à-vis the other industrial towns of the county. As background to
the great changes of the 1890s, it is important first to set the city's drink trades
into context.

Leeds in the 1890s stands out from most of the rest of England in the

115

Plate 5.3   Grains Courtyard and Brewhouse, 1889.

relatively small proportion of malt converted into beer by its common brewers.
There were four categories of producer: the common brewer, like Tetley; the
brewing victualler, the traditional fully-licensed publican who brewed for sale;
the beerhouses, smaller-scale home brewers; and the small group of beersellers
who brewed only for off-premises' sales. The last three had been all but

116

Plate 5.4   Yard, Showing Loading Stage and Drays, 1889.

eliminated in the London market by or before 1831, when over 95 per cent of output was produced by the common brewers, whereas the brewing victualler produced over 34 per cent of the national brew, and 60 per cent in Yorkshire. What differentiated Leeds most clearly, however, was that whereas by 1892, for the county as a whole, victuallers and beersellers used only one-eighth of the malt brewed, in Leeds they accounted for more than a third, and the contrast is still more striking when the comparisons are confined to the country's principal towns (Table 5.2).

This adds further emphasis to the extraordinary dominance of Tetley's position: the other thirty-six Leeds brewers shared less than a quarter of the entire market. The reasons for the comparative resilience of the brewing victualler and the relatively unassertive position of the common brewers in Leeds are not entirely clear. Sigsworth suggested that distributional problems inland in comparatively hilly districts protected the position of the victualler, but if this held good for both Leeds and Sheffield in the earlier part of the century, the divergent experience of the two over the century as a whole demands a different explanation. Small and dispersed 'breweries' and independent brewing victuallers clearly survived in the outlying parts of the Leeds district, outside the influence of the giant city brewery, but, to a greater or

Table 5.2   Common Brewers and Share of Malt Brewed in Yorkshire Towns, 1892

Town	Number of Breweries	Percentage Share of Total
Leeds	37	64.4
Sheffield	52	99.3
Bradford	58	96.5
Hull	33	93.5
York	47	89.3

Source: Sigsworth, Brewing Trade, Table 3, pp. 4–5. Towns are ranked by the aggregate size of the brewing industry. The figures relate to 'Excise Collections', areas which comprise the town and a substantial hinterland, and are therefore not comparable with data on the number of breweries cited by Sigsworth for these core towns, which for c1891, were as follows: Leeds, 22; Sheffield, 23; Bradford, 11; Hull and York, no data. Even so, the figures for 'common brewers' seem consistently high by comparison with the directories.

lesser degree, the other Yorkshire towns, particularly Sheffield and Bradford, also had hilly outlying districts, which might have protected the independent operators. This strongly suggests that the coincidence of the high survival rate of brewing victuallers with the county's only giant brewery were related: Tetley's dominance may have inhibited the expansion of other brewers at the expense of the victuallers, and, in supplying a premium quality product, provided the supply of light and bright beers the customers of all pubs were beginning to demand.[4]

It was also the case that by the 1890s there were proportionately fewer drink outlets per thousand of population in Leeds than in any of the other major towns of the county, and Leeds was indeed used as the standard of reference by other benches of licensing magistrates. On average, therefore, the scale of business of each of its victuallers and beerhouses was significantly greater than that of the other Yorkshire towns, and this may also help to account for the remarkable structural differences observed in the 1890s. Clearly, to comprehend Tetley's position, a clear appreciation of the comparative structure of the retail trade is essential.

Taking all licensed premises, including off-licences, the average catchment in Leeds in the mid-1890s was significantly greater than that of the principal Yorkshire towns, and that of Liverpool and Manchester, as shown in the figures of Table 5.3. The contrast was magnified when confined to on-licences. Leeds had only one per 578 persons, far below the 200–250 ratio characteristic of the other towns, with the exception of Hull, which averaged one to 442. It strongly suggests that the strict licensing policy of the magistracy proved an effective control on access to drink, hence the approbation of other benches, but also had two other effects: it reinforced the comparative scale of the publican businesses; and it added considerably greater commodity value to the licence itself.

Table 5.3   Population and Licensed Premises in Major Northern Towns, *c*1895

Town	Population	Licences	People per Licence
Leeds	402,500	1167	345
Sheffield	347,278	1754	198
Bradford	228,809	1272	180
Hull	212,000	876	242
Huddersfield	97,552	346	282
Liverpool	631,384	2078	304
Manchester	505,368	3000	168

Source: Royal Commission on Liquor Licensing Laws, 1897, PP 1897, XXXIV, XXXV; 1898, XXXVI, XXXVII; 1899, XXXV. The main comparative evidence was that of W. E. Clegg, solicitor and alderman of Sheffield, PP 1897, XXXV, pp. 227–39.

Having set the licensed premises of Leeds into this wider context, we can focus briefly upon the structure of the trade as a whole within the Leeds division. The 1167 licensed premises comprised 353 fully-licensed public houses, 410 beershops, and 404 shops, principally off-licences. They had diminished significantly in proportion to population since 1873, from 1:252 to 1:345, with both public houses and beershops slightly falling in numbers, and off-licences increasing from 247 in 1873 to 404 in 1896, of which only 300 were regarded as 'bona fide' off-licences, the rest being chemists' shops.[5] The outdoor retail trade was in Leeds, as elsewhere, an important and rapidly growing segment of the beer trade, and one in the supply of which the commercial brewer had no real rival. The general pattern of changing consumer taste which produced this reorganization in the retailing of drink was thus a further force favouring the Tetley business in the last quarter of the century.

There was a final new element to the profile of the drink trade in the period, one that had seen considerable growth since the 1870s, the clubs. Nationally, numbers grew by 85 per cent in the decade before 1896, and Leeds shared fully in this growth, with thirty-seven of its seventy-nine clubs founded after 1895. The numbers, set out in Table 5.4, were insufficient in any way to correct the relative deficiency of licensed premises in the city. Most of the recent growth was of working-men's, Irish, and political clubs, and nearly all of those declared 'badly conducted' by the police Superintendents came from this group.

Tetley's were thus operating as the single and dominant brewer in a city in which the brewing victualler remained an important element of the trade. Elsewhere, by the 1890s, the brewing publican had retreated to a minor role in the brewing industry, but in Leeds they took second place, behind Tetley's, and collectively ahead of the other thirty-six breweries of the city. The reasons for this unusual structure are unclear, but suggest that Tetley, were selling a premium quality product across the whole market, much of it, of course,

Table 5.4   Clubs in Leeds, 1896

Division	Number	Licensed	Membership	Number Unruly
A: City and East Leeds	23	23	8329	11
B: Holbeck and Hunslet	15	15	2702	0
C: Woodhouse and North-east	11	11	1956	1
D: Burley, Kirkstall, and West	20	11	3180	3
West Riding:	10	6	1084	0
Leeds Total	79	66	17521	15

Source: PP, 1898, XXXVII, pp. 87, 119–22.

outside the immediate Leeds district, and that the remainder of the brewers were unable significantly to interpose themselves between this 'giant' and the strong brewing victualler. In the growth of the off-licence and club trade, Leeds shared common features with other major towns in the period, but it remained, in the mid-1890s, far less heavily endowed with drink outlets than them. Tetley was thus able to distribute its premium beers with greater economy to a large free trade, in which much of the beer retailed was home produced.

II

There was a second aspect in which the Leeds beer trade was unusual in the 1890s, the relative absence of 'tied' public houses. By this time, the bulk of the brewing trade had already seen control of retail outlets, both pubs and off-licences, shifting into the hands of the brewers, as they sought to guarantee markets through territorial control. Until 1890, Tetley owned no public house property, and this decade saw a decisive shift in policy, affecting both the firm and the trade in the city as a whole. This change in company strategy took some time to achieve full implementation, but the years after 1890 represent a watershed, the point at which Tetley adopted policy already characteristic of many other major brewers.

The growth of the tied trade as a whole was a major issue in public debate after the restriction of licensing in 1869. The easy entry to the retail trade in beer that had characterized the period 1830–69 had been felt to protect the consumer against brewer monopoly, and the renewed control made the licence, because of its scarcity, a commodity of increased value to the producer. To this, there was added a permissive factor in the growth of the tied trade, the growth of limited liability in the brewing trade, through which funds raised on the stock market greatly helped in the finance of public house acquisitions. Between 1886 and 1892, eighty-five firms incorporated, and a further 149, including Tetley, did so by 1900.[6] The third element in this shift lay in wider market conditions, in the secular fall in consumption of beer. Its timing fitted the trend towards the tied house very closely: from a peak in 1873/4 (year ending 31 March), beer consumption per head fell by over 20 per cent to calendar year 1886, and subsequent recovery failed to approach that peak.[7] From the mid-1870s, therefore, pub licences became more valuable, as supply became constricted and the level of demand for beer fell, and the public company offered new means for the finance of their acquisition.

The rate at which this acquisition took place varied a great deal regionally. London had early been characterized by tied houses, from the later eighteenth century, but their proportion of total outlets remained relatively low until the 1890s, and in 1892 brewers owned no more than 30 per cent of licensed houses.[8] Elsewhere, ties had started somewhat later but grown but more rapidly, with the result that the Royal Commission of 1897 put the share of tied houses at 75 per cent. The evidence of their own witnesses suggested that this 'rough calculation' may have been exaggerated. In Manchester the extent of tied property was certainly put at 90 per cent, but without hard figures being provided; 78 per cent of pubs and beerhouses in Sheffield were tied, as were 72 per cent in Lancashire, and 61 per cent in Liverpool; but in other major areas, proportions were lower, around 55 per cent in Staffordshire and Cheshire, and as low as 37 per cent in Leeds. The trend towards the tied house from the 1880s was very clear, but uneven and far from complete by the 1890s.

The tied house was at the same time a matter of increasing public concern. General considerations of consumer satisfaction were there, with concern about price and quality, and the extent to which the tie was exploitative of the customer. It was also held, in a context of the increasing advance of the temperance movement, to promote greater sales of drink: public houses were compelled to stay open by the brewer proprietors; the 'long pull', provision of overmeasure, was used by tied publicans to enhance sales; and devious devices such as 'high kickers' and 'female pianists' were employed to attract custom. Modern concerns for the risks of brewer monopoly were also visible, with the comprehensive nature of some tied contracts: in Hull, it was said that publicans were tied for 'everything but sawdust'.[9] There was was also the worry about public order and the quality of publicans: tied houses in many cities were shown to have a much more rapid turnover in licensees, and this was taken as indicative of a lower level of respectability and reliability of such pub-licans.[10] Given the high share of the licensed victualler in the Leeds beer trade, and the high standards for which its licensing bench was known, it is not surprising to find the city lagging behind others in the spread of the tied house.

The evidence of ownership of on-licences for 1891 indicates the relatively small degree of concentration of public houses into brewery hands in Leeds, but placed Tetley (Table 5.5) towards the bottom of that distribution, behind a significant number of their competitors. Of the top eight owners listed, six were breweries of significance; at least seven more breweries can be identified among the multiple owners. Significantly, of those listed, several stemmed from outside the city: two from Tadcaster, and three from Bradford. By comparison with other major towns within the area, by virtue of the relatively low level of the tied trade, and the continuing presence of the brewing victualler, Leeds represented an open door to external competition. The comparative figures for other major Yorkshire towns emphasizes the point: in Bradford, the brewers held over a quarter of the licences, and in Halifax and Huddersfield over 40 per cent, with comparable levels in Hull and Sheffield. The three main Tadcaster brewers, John Smith (Riley Smith), Samuel Smith, and Hotham & Co (The Tadcaster Tower Brewery Co), had all built up substantial tied estates in the county by 1891, respectively of 62, 30, and 118 pubs.[11] In addition, the agencies of major Burton and London brewers were already in Leeds by the 1870s and 1880s, and represented a further threat to Tetley's premium trade, among them Allsopp, Bass, and Ind Coope. In comparative terms, therefore, at the beginning of the 1890s, the Leeds brewers, including Tetley, were vulnerable.

This was exactly the expressed motive for Tetley's first purchases of pub property, in 1890. They were being squeezed outside Leeds by the general expansion of the tied trade, and feared for their local markets, as noted by Charles Francis Tetley in 1923:

> There was a veritable orgy of buying bricks and mortar in order to provide markets and outlets for the ale of this or that firm. House after house whose cellars hitherto Tetley's had supplied was sold to one or other of these wealthy companies and

Table 5.5 Concentration of Ownership of Licensed Houses in Leeds, 1891

Owner	Number	Percentage of Total
Albion Brewery Company	20	2.5
F & H H Riley Smith	19	2.4
Henry Bentley	13	1.6
Kirkstall Brewery Co	13	1.6
J S Tempest	13	1.6
Pious Use Trust	12	1.5
Samuel Smith	11	1.4
Joshua Tetley and Son	9	1.1
Sub-total	110	13.8
Other 45 Multiple Owners	212	26.5
Total Houses	799	100.0

Source: Return of the Number of On-Licenses [sic], 1891, PP 1892, LXVIII, pp. 77f.

became 'tied'. In sheer self-defence the firm had to adopt the policy of other breweries, or else suffer severe diminution of its trade and fortunes. How very regretfully and reluctantly was the decision made is clearly revealed by the fact that at the end of 1890, the year in which the firm commenced buying licensed property, only two 'tied' houses were in its possession.[12]

Those two pubs were the Duke William, now in the brewery yard and forming part of the brewery tour, linked to the new visitor attraction 'Tetley's Brewery Wharf', and the Fleece, Farsley, each purchased for sums around £2200.

Profit levels around this period confirm the motivation, and point to the difficulties to experienced in financing the purchases. Tetley's profits had peaked at around £70,000 in the mid-1870s, but fell sharply in the late 1880s and early 1890s, to a low point of just under £28,000 in 1891, but recovered as the impact of the new policy and wider revival in the brewing trade took place, rising to £37,631 in 1892, and nearing £70,000 in 1896.[13] Profits clearly suffered initially from the impact of this investment, as the tied house estate was rapidly built up in the early 1890s. The two purchases of 1890 were followed by seventeen in 1891; fourteen in 1892; eight in 1893; thirteen in 1894, and six in 1895, by which time the capital account showed tied house assets of over £150,000.

These purchases appear to have been made with urgency, rather than panic, and the scrutiny given by the company prior to the purchase of a freehold or a lease was rigorous. The decision to purchase the Fleece at Farsley was taken as the result of a detailed report on its location, on two roads, in a growing village, with further new housebuilding imminent, and was itself in good condition. The purchases of 1891 confirm this approach, with a clear spread of the Tetley net into eight other houses in Leeds, to a leading off-licence in Ilkley, Brooksbank's, and to public houses in Shipley, Dewsbury, Morley, Wakefield, York, Brighouse, Ossett, and Castleford. The most substantial was the purchase of the Pack Horse, Woodhouse Lane, Leeds, for over £8000. Clearly these were not the simple acquisitions of property around the brewery, designed for easy local delivery, but were rather carefully targeted purchases of good or potentially good trading houses, across the wider Tetley 'territory'. The company's entry to the tied trade was making a statement in more ways than one.

The build-up of tied property, once started, continued rapidly, and the years up to and including the First World War saw the creation of a very substantial tied estate (Fig 5.1). This dramatic growth was further stimulated and sustained by the continuing rapid purchases by other breweries, and, like them, was concentrated into the years up to 1904/5.

This investment boom in public house property had a number of adverse effects, notably the extraordinary inflation of pub prices. The *Country Brewers'*

Figure 5.1   The growth of Joshua Tetley's Public House Estates, 1891–1920.

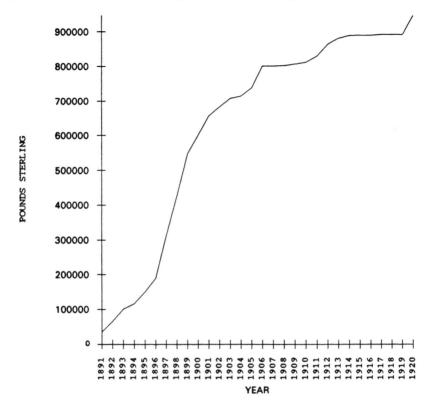

Gazette for 1897 published a complaint that prices had increased by 200 or 300 per cent.[14] It was coupled with the rapid growth of the public company in the industry, and the practice, in such flotations, of raising the new capital by debentures and preference shares. These attracted great public interest, and correspondingly provided very cheap funding and helped to fuel the inflation. From 1899–1900 there was a sustained downturn in beer sales and consumption per head, associated with stagnant or falling real wages, and the strong attachment of working-class consumers to the normal consumption of other goods, of which tobacco and the new cigarettes were the most prominent.[15] The outcome was a general depression of profit levels in the trade, and for many breweries severe financial difficulties, and this helps to account for the general slowing of pub purchasing, in which Tetley's shared the experiences of other brewers.

From 1904 onward, other factors intensified this effect. The new Licensing Act of that year confirmed the right of JPs, established by *Sharp v Wakefield*, to remove licences on the grounds that they were unnecessary, but levied a fund upon the remaining public houses to compensate the displaced publicans. At once, therefore, the costs of the tied estate were increased, and for some brewers at least, assets were being written off. Nationally, over 9800 licences were removed between 1905 and 1914, and compensation of nearly £9m was paid out, most of it to the brewer owners of tied property.[16] The distribution of licensed houses in England and Wales fell from an average of one per 285 persons in 1896, to one per 416 by 1915.[17] The one countervailing trend of the period was the sustained growth of clubs, for which both numbers and membership more than doubled over the same period, and over half the 'loss' of public houses was offset by the appearance of new clubs in England and Wales as a whole.[18]

For various reasons, Tetley's seem to have avoided the worst of these reverses. Profits dipped in real terms, but held up reasonably well to the eve of the War in money terms, at around the £65,000 level. The company had gone public in July 1897 on a pattern familiar from many of the larger concerns. The assets of the company had been assessed at over £570,000 in the share prospectus, and authority was given for the issue of £450,000 in 3½ per cent first mortgage debentures. Only £200,000 of this was offered for sale, at £95 per cent, and the offer was oversubscribed within hours. Tetley's had thus secured a relatively cheap increment to their capital, while retaining the whole of the ordinary share capital, and the 5 per cent preference shares, in the hands of the vendors, the seven members of the Tetley and Ryder families.[19] They seem to have judged the levels of issue with some skill, and largely avoided the substantial writing down of capital experienced by many of the largest brewers.[20]

The other reasons for this may lie in the nature of the region and market within which they had operated. As we have seen, the Leeds JPs had long been tough on licence renewals, and the legal decision in the case *Sharp v Wakefield* (1891) confirmed their stance, despite successful appeals to the West Riding Quarter Sessions in two cases, relating to the Lloyds Arms and the Hope Inn, Lands Lane. The average distribution of on-licences in Leeds in 1896 was far above the national level of 1914. In addition, Tetley's had targeted their early purchases with care, and continued to do so, as the share prospectus of 1897 made clear. By July 1897, the tied properties were valued at over £310,000, and consisted of 58 'fully licensed hotels and inns' and 27 Beerhouses, all bar four freehold, 17 off-licences (one leasehold), and 100 other shops and dwelling houses. More important was the strategic disposition of the licensed houses, which was in the better quality and more 'necessary' houses across the wide geographical territory displayed in Fig 5.2.

Tetley, in their expansion to the First World War, had acquired a tied estate and one that provided a better spread than that of many of the London

Figure 5.2   The Tetley Tied Estate in 1897.

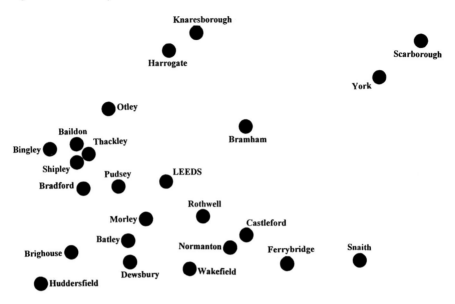

brewers, such as Watney, Combe, Reid, and correspondingly reduced the impact of the pre-war depression. Substantial investments had been made before 'going public' in 1897, but this move, in permitting the raising of cheap capital, enabled Tetley to continue public house purchase at the boom prices that characterized the years before 1904. They did so while continuing to sell predominantly to the free trade on the basis of premium quality, and developments such as the growth of clubs helped to sustain this. In the 1880s they had been one of the country's largest brewers, but were miniscule in terms of the tied estate that could bring secure sales; by 1914, they had yet to join the giants, but had established their territorial presence in property as well as sales area.

III

Although the tied estate had been the critical new development of the years from 1890, and one with long term impact upon the Tetley business, other changes too pre-date the public company of 1897, and have continuing significance through the inter-war years. The entry to the tied trade after 1890 had been a forced response to changing market conditions, and this was the principal motive for the other great change initiated in that decade, bottling. In addition, more general improvements were made in the physical plant, and the quality strategy maintained, all of which provided long-term benefits in the years after 1914.

That the adoption of bottling in 1892 was in some senses a forced response is clear from the increasing presence of the Burton, Tadcaster, and other major brewers in the Tetley territory. Many of these had long-standing positions in the bottled-beer trade—Bass and William Younger were notable examples— which was particularly important to the two new and growing sectors of the market, off-licence shops and clubs. C. F. Tetley noted that bottled beer 'especially was the form found to be suitable for the family trade'.[22] Not to have entered the bottled trade would have been to sacrifice a competitive edge to outsiders in home territory. Tetley's began experiments in 1892, and were ready for marketing and production from December of that year, building sales of their bottled beers from the very modest £3000 in the first nine months of 1893, to and annual average of £50,000 on the eve of the war.

This growth led to consequential further improvement and investment in the plant. 1894 saw the removal of some of the last remaining buildings of the Sykes brewery, the old gate and the buildings in the yard (visible in Plate 5.3), for the erection of the four-storey bottling store, and sustained growth in the trade required further investment, facilitated by the capital injection generated by the share issues of 1897. Extensions to the central block of the brewery building were made in 1905, and continuing expansion of the demand for bottled 'Tetley's Special' led to the clearance of the old book store for a further extension to the bottling plant in 1913.

At the same time, improvements were made to the stone, 'Yorkshire Square' fermenting vessels used in the brewery, partly as a result of the external monitoring of the quality of their products. The report of Horace Brown, the distinguished brewing chemist and consultant with the firm of Moritz and Morris, in September 1896, questioned the use of stone for the squares, because of its porosity and consequent difficulty in cleaning, and this initiated their replacement with slate. His report was otherwise generally favourable, commenting upon the good practice of keeping stocks low, that the bitter and pale ales were 'excellent in every respect', but suggesting improvement to the bottled special, a blend of the two, by ensuring that the bitter employed was not too old.[23] Around the First World War Tetley's began the first experiments with stainless steel and aluminium squares, a significant innovation later adopted by other brewers in the region.

Their experience during the First World War was broadly that of the other major brewers. The volume of bulk barrels of beer produced plummeted, falling nationally to less than 40 per cent of the 1914 level by 1918, and from 1915 controls on the opening hours of public houses were introduced, long to survive the war. Sharp tax increases raised the duty per standard barrel by over 200 per cent between 1914 and April 1917, and later that year further restrictions were made to reduce permitted gravity. The net effect was to increase the dilution of beer, and by 1918–19 the bulk barrellage actually brewed was almost double the level of the 'standard barrels' authorized.[24] The impact was further contraction among the smaller brewing plant, almost a fifth closing during the war, coupled with generally enhanced profit levels, dramatically summarized by Wilson as follows: 'Then came the war, and out of its holocaust of horrors the brewing trade arose phoenix-like to hitherto undreamed of heights of wealth'.[25] Wilson's estimates of profit levels confirmed his comments: nationally, brewers' profit levels increased from an index of 100 in 1913 to 143 in 1917, and to 303 in 1919; Tetley's shared in this growth, though performed less spectacularly, increasing from 100 to 127, and then to 205.

The war, however, also enhanced trends visible in the years before 1914. Numbers of public houses continued to decline gradually in number throughout the 1920s and 1930s, showing a modest fall of 10 per cent between 1919 and 1936, while the off-licences increased, by around 6 per cent over the same period. Club numbers, by contrast, soared, doubling over the same period, and in Yorkshire numbers had increased by 620 in 1896, to 1166 in 1905, and to 2213 by 1935, and national membership rose almost fivefold between 1896 and 1930. By the mid 1930s, clubs were accounting for an estimated 7 per cent of national sales of drink, and in Yorkshire clubs over £1.3 million per annum was being spent.[26] Their growth offset much of the fall in the number of pubs, and did so under freer licensing terms. The Royal Commission of 1929–31 confirmed this: 'we are satisfied that there are many clubs in all parts of the country which have been brought into existence solely for the purpose of supplying intoxicants'.[27] The national total of breweries, however, fell spectacularly, from just under 3000 in 1919 to under 1100 in 1936, and the brewing publican all but disappeared, as economies of scale in production, packaging, and distribution were expressed, and the big brewers continued their policy of acquisitions and mergers at the expense of the small. All of these developments favoured large plant, with effective bottling capacity, and argued for the continuing build-up of the tied trade.

Tetley's were exceptions to this pattern in only one respect: they did not have a significant acquisition of another brewery during the inter-war years, although, as we shall see, this became a marked feature of the development of the business after 1946. They did, however, benefit from the broad market trends, and the growth in the club and off-licence trades was reflected in the substantial development of their bottled beer business. From 1920, the old family small-cask trade had ended, replaced by bottled supplies, and the turnover in Tetley's bottled beers reflected their strong performance in this sector. From around £50,000 in 1913, turnover of bottled beers had risen to over £230,000 by 1935, and reached £283,000 in 1939, roughly 13 per cent by value of total beer sales. Although this was well below the 25 per cent cited by Vaizey for the industry as a whole, that figure was inflated by the low value of the bulk of production, and the relatively high prices of the leading national branded producers, Guinness, Ind Coope, Whitbread, Bass, and Worthington, and represents a reasonable performance for the primarily regional base on which Tetley operated.[28]

That region had been very much east of Pennines before the First World War, and encapsulated in the advertisement for Tetley in 1889 (Plate 5.5), which identified the region as twenty miles radius of Leeds, for direct delivery by dray, and further afield by agencies for beer despatched by train. The company had adopted mixed delivery systems for towns such as Harrogate, despatching the dray and horses at the beginning of the week from the stables in Leeds, to deliver from the railway station, returning home at the end of the week. Tetley's was a significant employer of the horselads, who left the East Riding on marriage, and brought their horse skills into the city: two members of the firm who served in the First World War (one killed, one a POW), S. and F. Goodwill, were from one such Malton family, one a drayman and the other in the 'transport department', where the next generation also worked.[29]

Even before the war, Tetley's had purchased their first steam lorry, in 1912, and after the war moved quickly into petrol lorries for distribution over a wider area. This was coupled with a marketing initiative after 1920, designed to revive Tetley's sales in Lancashire, which had suffered as a result of the growth of tied houses, and under Seymour Clayton, working on commission, sales improved, and were followed by the acquisition of public houses and off-licences during the 1930s. Deliveries were made, traditionally, by train to a depot at London Road Station in Manchester, and to parts of east Lancashire, direct by lorry. From 1928, such had been the improvement in beer transport, that Tetley's were able to become sole suppliers to the 119 Whitaker pubs in and around Bradford.[30] Tetley's had offices in Deansgate, and this base was used to spread their free trade supply into north Wales, Cheshire, and the Lake District.[31] The introduction of the lorry increasingly aided the spread of the Tetley 'territory', and laid the basis for increased westward expansion after 1945.

By 1939, these developments, the growth of the tied trade, and expansion of bottled supplies to pubs, off-licences, and to clubs, and improved distribution, had been reflected in broadly satisfactory profit performances, and in the substantial incremental growth of the tied house estate. The value of the tied estate had more than doubled between 1920 and 1943, reflecting its increased size, and the improvement of many houses to meet rising consumers'

JOSHUA TETLEY & SON,
THE BREWERY, LEEDS.

STORES:

LONDON . . . . 83, Pancras Road.
Agent—A. F. EVANS.

LIVERPOOL . . . 7, Slater Street, Bold Street.
Agent—WM. WOODS.

MANCHESTER . . Jackson's Row, South Street.
Agents—WADDELL & HOPE.

YORK . . . . . . Swinegate.
Agent—GEO. MOORE.

YORKSHIRE AGENCIES:

BARNSLEY. . . C. SUGDEN, Eldon Street.
BOSTON SPA . . GEORGE WINTER & SON.
FILEY . . . . SAMUEL TOWSE.
HOLMFIRTH . . WM. HAIGH, Wine & Spirit Merchant, Upperbridge.
HULL . . . . J. J. RIPPON, 62, Prospect Street.
KNARESBRO' . . MRS. MARGERISON, High Street.
RIPON . . . . WM. WELLS & SONS, North Street & Old Market Place.
SALTBURN . . W. MELLISHIP, Milton Street.
SCARBRO' . . . HY. WELLBURN & Co., 55, Newboro' & 6, South Street.
SOWERBY BRIDGE . T. SUTCLIFFE.
SKELMANTHORPE . JOHN JEBSON.
WHITBY . . . FALKINGBRIDGE & SON
YORK . . . . STORES, Swinegate.

DELIVERIES BY DRAY WITHIN 20 MILES OF LEEDS.

Plate 5.5 Tetley's Advertisement in the Reprint of George Barnard's *Noted Breweries*, of 1889.

Plate 5.6 Yard, with Drays, 1920s.

expectations. At the end of the Second World War, including short leasehold property, the tied estate was valued at over £2.5 million. Net profits fluctuated sharply over the period, with troughs in 1921, 1932, and 1933, much as experienced by the trade as a whole, but did show absolute growth, as the scale of the enterprise grew, particularly during the mid-1920s.[32] Although the figures cannot strictly be compared, because of the incremental growth in the size of the Tetley business, profit levels seem to have held up well by comparison with the business as a whole, 1926–38 (Table 5.6).

IV

The 1940s and 1950s can be taken as a whole, and here Tetley's showed the continuity of policies visible before the war, within a changing industrial context. From 1945 to 1960, a number of general changes in the drink market represented the critical background to the Tetley business, and its development. Principal among these were the sustained fall in draught beer consumption, which fell by 14 per cent in the UK, 1945–60; the continued fall in the numbers of public houses; significant increases in the drinking of wines and spirits; the continued growth of the bottled and the beginnings of the canned beer trades;

Plate 5.7   The Tetley 'Huntsman' Trademark, 1920s.[1]

[1]The trademark was produced in the 1920s, by the south-western agency of Causton & Sons, who were also commissioned by the Dorchester brewers, Eldridge Pope to produce a trademark for their own 'Huntsman Ales'. It was some years before the two companies realized that they were both trading under the same mark. Edwin Pope had trained as a Master Brewer at Tetley's, and an agreement was made that neither company would cross the Wash with their emblem. The signs have, of course, raised false hope of Tetley's in the eyes of holidaying Yorkshiremen.

Table 5.6   Comparative Profits, Tetley and UK Brewers, 1926–38[33]

Year	Joshua Tetley & Son		United Kingdom	
	£000	Index (1926 = 100)	£m	Index (1926 = 100)
1926	208.63	100	26.50	100
1927	218.93	105	24.50	92
1928	223.33	107	24.00	91
1929	199.33	96	24.50	92
1930	198.30	95	25.00	94
1931	180.77	87	26.00	98
1932	123.23	59	23.00	87
1933	144.76	117	16.00	60
1934	203.01	97	18.00	68
1935	203.21	97	23.00	87
1936	208.10	100	26.00	98
1937	217.63	104	28.50	108
1938	211.10	101	31.50	119

Source: Tetley Annual Accounts; Wilson, *op cit*, p. 89. As indicated in the text, these figures have to be treated as no more than broad indicators of comparative trends.

sustained growth in the off-licence and club trade; and the continued tendency towards the concentration of ownership of public houses in the hands of the major brewers.

The first and last points were, of course, different facets of the same issue, and it set a clear strategic task for major regional brewers such as Tetley. In order to survive and prosper in these post-war years, particularly before beer sales began to revive at the very end of the 1950s, it was necessary to express to the fullest degree such economies of scale as were possessed by larger brewers, such as themselves. Yet, at the end of the war, the industry remained numerically dominated by the smaller, local and often family brewer, who accounted for perhaps three-quarters of the industry, and who was producing perhaps eighty per cent of the volume of beer in the early 1950s. Such small firms were protected from the economies of scale in their larger potential rivals by the bastion of their tied estates, and in some parts of the country, notably the West Riding, the market in this sense remained relatively 'open', at least by comparison with London and Birmingham. Vaizey's assessment presented the picture with great clarity:

> The tied house system has the effect of maintaining many small breweries in operation in markets in which the transport costs of bringing beer from a distance would not protect...a large number of existing breweries, possibly 250 or more, are kept in existence because of a monopolistic practice.[34]

For both the national brewers, such as Whitbread, and major regional brewers like Tetley's, the only route to growth and scale economy lay through the intensification of acquisitions.

Accordingly, they were very active in this, as indicated by the evidence of Table 5.7. The policy was new, representing a breach with their pre-war tenet of 'no mergers, no take-overs', and had a massive impact on what was still, at the beginning of the period, a relatively small tied estate. In 1949, Tetley had only about 400 tied properties, and, as shown in Table 5.7, the acquisitions of the 1950s, this new assertive take-over policy almost trebled that figure. This was a rapid change in scale and relative standing, and took Tetley to about a quarter of the size of the largest brewer at the end of the 1950s, Watney Mann, with 3900 houses.[35]

Much of the finance was internally generated, something the Tetley Chairman reflected on with pride, in 1956: 'Total capital expenditure for next

Plate 5.8   Labels from Companies Acquired by Tetley's, 1950s and 1960s.

Table 5.7   Tetley's Principal Mergers and Acquisitions, 1945–60[37]

Year	Deal	Company	Place	Public Houses	Off-Licences	Price £K
1946	A	Reaney & Greaves	Bradford		unknown	
1949	A	Burtonwood	Burtonwood	23		
1950	A	Boardman	Hulme	6		
1951	A	Cunningham	Warrington	34	18	550
1954	M	Duncan Gilmour	Sheffield	350		
1959	A	William Whitaker	Bradford	119		1128
1960	A	Melbourne	Leeds	245		3500

Source: Based upon Lackey, *Quality Pays...*, pp. 81–4; *Yorkshire Post, passim.*

year will doubtless exceed considerably the amount of our immediate commitments, but we hope to meet this as we have done this year out of our own resources'.[36] Debentures were issued to help in financing the Cunningham purchase of 1951, and a rights issue was needed in 1959 to meet expenditures on bottling stores in Leeds, and stores and offices in Sheffield, the Whitaker purchase, and, perhaps, strategic planning for the acquisitions of 1960. Not all of this expenditure was on assets for retention, however, and the astute Tetley judgement that had characterized the first purchases of public houses was reflected in the sale of the Gilmour brewery to Sheffield Corporation for the building of the new magistrates' court (already agreed before the takeover), and in the acquisition of a very valuable city-centre site with the Melbourne Brewery, later sold for development.[38]

Profits had been sustained remarkably well during these years of high capital expenditure. They rose from around £250,000 in the later 1940s, to £500,000 plus in the early 1950s, after some significant acquisitions, and exceeded £1 million for the first time in 1956. Returns on capital are notoriously hard to judge in this industry, but ordinary dividend payments and bonuses ran at 10–12.5 per cent over the same period.[39] This certainly represented a competitive level of performance for a major regional brewer in the period, but even these measures were felt insufficient to provide continuing autonomy and security. The 1960s were to see even more startling changes in the business.

V

That growth was insufficient to need in the context of 1960 was the outcome of rapid changes in what had been until very recently a 'genteel' industry. The years 1959–61 saw the old culture of the industry shaken and changed by three related factors: the acrimonious Charles Clore [Sears Holdings] bid for Watney Mann in 1959; E. P. Taylor's alien Canadian influence, and the transition from free sales of his *Carling Black Label* into the creation of a tied house chain, United Breweries, which brought him into direct conflict with significant members of the British 'beerage', and the more general appreciation by the stock market that breweries were very traditional and conservative, and had largely failed to revalue their property assets in line with the inflation of their value, and hence asset values were often far higher, by two or three times, than the book value of companies. With new and often ungentlemanly predators around, these years initiated a merger wave that was largely defensive in its motivation.[40]

That was the principal motive for the second great event affecting Tetley in 1960, for which negotiations were being conducted as the Melbourne Brewery acquisition was being completed, the merger with Walker Cain, of Liverpool and Warrington, and the creation in October 1960, of a new parent company, Tetley Walker Ltd. This created a new business of great strength, particularly in Yorkshire and Lancashire, where, as noted earlier, the level of concentration in the brewing industry had been historically low, and where, in the context of the early 1960s, both parents felt vulnerable to predators. The merger created a new company with 2771 tied properties, and with an issued share capital of over £16.6 million, and a firm and focused regional base, which offered apparent security. It was to last less than a year, before the second major merger took place, the effective creator of the modern company.

While the Tetley Walker merger of 1960 had established a stronger regional company, it had not fully secured the firm against rivals within its two regions— Hammonds, of Bradford, for example, had 950 West Riding pubs—nor was it invulnerable to the acquisitive outsider, looking for basic asset value and lacking the appropriate brewing mission. With appropriate dramatic effect, Clifford Lackey described the events that created the cumbersome but powerful Ind Coope Tetley Ansell Ltd in May 1961. In February 1961, Brigadier Noel Tetley, deputy chairman of Tetley Walker met with the representatives of Ind Coope and Ansells on the moors near Kinder Scout, and began the negotiation over a picnic lunch that was sealed on 17 March. The motivation was explicitly defensive against the risks of entry by outside financial interests, and the Chairman of the new company, Edward Thompson [formerly of Ind Coope] captured its spirit, by calling the new firm 'a Commonwealth of Brewers'.[41] The merged company, renamed Allied Breweries in 1962, and which evolved into Allied-Lyons in 1981, created the biggest national brewer of the time, with 9500 licensed houses, and capital of £126 million.

It possessed great regional strength, with Ind Coope established in the midlands and south; Ansells in the midlands; and Tetley Walker in Yorkshire

Plate 5.9   Deliveries in the early 1960s to the Queen's Arms, Harrogate Road, Leeds.

and Lancashire; and, in Ind Coope's *Double Diamond*, one of the strongest national brands of bottled and keg beer. Further acquisitions during the 1960s reinforced this position, as each unit in the 'commonwealth' continued to trade with a high degree of regional autonomy. Tetley Walker thus acquired a further 270 or more public houses, a further bottling store, and numerous breweries, off-licences, and hotels in the take-overs of Ramsden's of Halifax, Roses of Malton, Hemingway of Leeds, and Jackson of Sunderland, between 1964 and 1967. As with the Melbourne Brewery in 1960, these acquisitions brought valuable urban property under the redundant breweries and other plant, and thus provided several sites for sale to developers. Property, rather than beer, was in many senses the economic core of the business.[42]

The new organization of course also made investments in the brewing operation, and continued the Tetley policy of the 1950s in the large-scale improvement of the tied estate. The new brewhouse with capacity of around 1.25 million barrels was opened in 1967 at a cost of £650,000; two new Yorkshire square fermenting rooms entered production in 1961 and 1964, the first nicknamed and subsequently formally titled 'Quality Street', and the

Plate 5.10   'Quality Street', the Yorkshire Square Fermenting Room.

second 'Coronation Street'; the new office block, 'Huntsman House', in 1968; and the keg and packaging plant, for Tetley and other products such as *Skol* lager, started operations in 1975. All of this helped to place Tetley at or near the optimal scale for new brewery plant to gain maximum economies of scale in production, in distribution, and through the wider group to secure such small gains as were to be achieved in other costs, such as marketing.[43]

From the mid-1970s, the economics of the industry shifted, principally under the impact of oil price inspired inflation, from 1973. Distribution costs for UK breweries had averaged 7.1 per cent in 1965, and although the oil price rise increased these only by 1 to 2 per cent for the furthest points, they came near to the scale economies achieved by large brewery plants. To this was added the impact of the consumer reaction to keg beers, and the heightened esteem in which cask-conditioned traditional local and regional beers came to be held, and the long-term shift in the profile of drinkers towards the young, and with them towards 'lager'. The outcomes have been mixed: there has been some shrinkage in the scale of the market for traditional beers, reflected in the 1978 rationalization of Allied into brewing divisions, clearly focused upon their traditional regional bases—the recreation of Tetley but as a real territorial giant. In addition, the huge scale of plant and organization has increased the

138

ability of companies such as Allied to promote brands, such as *Skol* lager, on a national scale.[44]

Many of these policies paid off and offered continuity through the 1980s,

Plate 5.11   The Garden Gate, Hunslet, a Tetley 'Heritage Inn'.

139

Plate 5.12   Interior of The Fox, Holgate, York, a Tetley 'Heritage Inn'.

up to the coming of the brewers' Armageddon, in the early months of 1989, the report of the Monopolies and Mergers Commission. The first development began in 1978, with the designation of pubs with particular historic or architectural merit as Tetley 'Heritage Inns', and marked by a blue plaque, and overall by sympathetic restoration. This was but a specific dimension of the long-established Tetley policy of investment in their tied estate to reinforce their 'quality' marketing approach, and other segmentation of the estate followed, principally the 'Cavalier' chain of pub restaurants; the Tetley family inns (named as such in 1984), with family rooms away from the bars, such as the famous Dick Hudson's at High Eldwick; and from 1982 the American diners, which started in the metamorphosis of the St Ann's, Headingley, into the Boston Diner. In September 1982 Tetley's experimented with their first 'brew-pub', The Station, Guiseley, selling *Guiseley Gyle*, as their reaction to changing consumer taste, just about a century after they had started to make real inroads into the number and market share of the former brewing victuallers. Along with this development of the tied house stock, and its careful targeting onto segments of the leisure market, went the continuing process of acquisition, particularly of good free houses, new pub building, and selective disposals.

The other principal feature of the decade was the continuing investment in the site and the plant, leading to new products and new marketing approaches. By August 1985, some £10 million had been expended on a comprehensive redevelopment of the Leeds site, in Tetley's terms fitting the brewery for the next century, and with it the development of some new processes. From October 1982, the famous Tetley bitter and mild began to be marketed in 16 oz cans. The logical marketing outcome of this and of the Allied-Lyons group as a whole came with the formal launch of Tetley bitter as a national brand in August 1988, with a £4.5 million Saatchi and Saatchi advertising campaign, the bulk of it targeted on the midlands and the south. Significantly, in view of Tetley's long history as a major regional brewer, the campaign emphasized the Yorkshire base in the locations of its television advertising.[45]

As suggested in the opening paragraph of this short study, the events following the MMC report of 1989 superficially recall the position of a century earlier. The principal recommendations of the report were designed to increase competition within the industry, and measures were proposed to restrict the extent of the tied estate to a ceiling of 2000 pubs, to introduce 'guest beers' and expand the free trade, give greater legal protection for the position of tenants, and concede to them the right to buy non-alcoholic or low-alcohol

Plate 5.13   The Modern Brewery by Night.

Plate 5.14   Artist's Impression of 'Tetley's Brewery Wharf'.

beers, wines, spirits, cider, soft drinks, and mineral waters from any source. The report was vigorously disputed by the Brewers' Society, and by individual firms and divisions, such as Tetley, but it has already affected this business. Faced with the possible mandatory separation of brewery from the more profitable public house estate, Allied recreated 'Tetley' as the name for its half of a pure brewery joint venture, Carlsberg-Tetley plc, which brought a cluster of national and international brands together from January 1993, in a larger and better-balanced brewing business, notably *Carlsberg, Castlemaine XXXX*, and *Skol* lagers, *Tetley Bitter* and *Burton Ale*, the first two, with Tetley, described in the current Annual Report as the group's 'core brands'.[46] The public house and other properties, meanwhile, were integrated into Allied-Lyons Retailing Limited. 1993, just over a century after the acquisition of the first Tetley tied houses, thus saw the formal severance of the tie. The tie came to the rescue of Tetley's waning free trade in the 1890s: the challenge of the later 1990s will be to see whether a new era of 'free trade' is viable.

Notes

[1] I am indebted to Graham Sykes for research assistance in the preparation of this chapter, and to Dr Richard Wilson and Mr Colin Waite for advice.

[2] This section is based upon the work of Eric Sigsworth, *The Brewing Trade during the Industrial Revolution: the Case of Yorkshire*, Borthwick Papers, York, 31, 1967; *Tetley's, a Review of a Hundred Years*, Leeds, 1923; Clifford Lackey, *Quality pays...the Story of Joshua Tetley & Son*, Ascot, 1985; and Leeds directories. The events leading to Arthington's closure of the brewery are covered by A. M. Chirgwin, *Arthington's Million: the Romance of the Arthington Trust*, 1935, pp. 12–15.

[3] Barnard, *Noted Breweries*, p. 40. From 1880, the mash tun had been freed to use sugars and other raw materials in addition to malt, and malt figures therefore represent less accurate indicators. No attempt has been made here to allow for the substantial quantities of sugar recorded as being used, but the effect may well be relatively to understate Tetley's share of total output, and to do likewise for all breweries.

[4] Based on employment figures estimated by Sigsworth, *Brewing Trade*, p. 9. John Smith's, at Tadcaster, were probably as large, and brewed as much beer by the 1890s: information from Dr R. G. Wilson.

[5] This is my speculation, but the shift in taste towards the light and bright beers was noted by many of the witnesses appearing before the Royal Commission on Liquor Licensing of 1897.

[6] *RC Liquor Licensing*, PP, 1897, XXXV, Appendix IV, p. 507, and other evidence of Mr John Thornton, Clerk to the Justices of the City, pp. 71f. Chemists' shops required the licence because most of the 'medicines' they sold at this time consisted of alcohols in various coloured and flavoured forms.

[7] K. H. Hawkins and C. L. Pass, *The Brewing Industry: a Study in Industrial Organisation and Public Policy*, 1979, pp. 28–9.

[8] PP, 1899, XXXV, Appendix I; D. M. Knox, 'The Development of the Tied House System in London', *Oxford Economic Papers*, new series, X, 1958, 68–9. To some extent the official figures may overstate the extent of the fall, since they are couched in terms of official bulk barrels, and watering could have offset the decline. However, since the brewers sharply perceived this decline, and took it as the basis for a strategic reaction, this may not matter. Later figures cited by George B. Wilson, *Alcohol and the Nation (A Contribution to the study of the Liquor Problem in the United Kingdom from 1800 to 1935)*, 1940, p. 332, put the peak at 34.4 gallons in 1875/6. These should perhaps be preferred, although the order of magnitude of the fall remains the same.

[9] Knox, *art cit*, p. 75.

[10] Evidence of Mr Shackles, Clerk to the Hull JPs, PP 1897, XXIV, p. 327.

[11] *Royal Commission on Liquor Licensing*, 1897, *passim*.

[12] Based upon the analysis of the Return of the Number of On-Licenses, 17 June 1892, PP 1892, LXVIII, 147 ff.

[13] *Tetley's: a review...*, p. 18.

[14] Lackey, *Quality Pays...*, pp. 64–7.

[15] Wilson, *Alcohol and the Nation*, p. 86.

[16] A. E. Dingle, 'Drink and Working-Class Living Standards in Britain, 1870–1914', *Economic History Review*, 2nd ser, XXV, 1972, 608–22.

[17] This is the inescapable inference to be drawn from the figures produced by Dingle, *op cit*, Table 20, p. 381. 87 per cent of compensation was paid to others than the licensee, and with the tied trade taking at least 80 per cent of the total, around three quarters of compensation must have been paid to them.

[18] *Ibid*, Table 19, p. 380.

[19] *Ibid*, Table 22, p. 384.

[20] Lackey, *op cit*, pp. 68–9.

[21] Wilson, *op cit*, pp. 85–8.

[22] Drawn from listing in the share prospectus of 1897.

[23] *Tetley's: a review*, p. 20.

[24] Lackey, *Quality Pays...*, pp. 69–70. I am indebted to Dr R. G. Wilson for further information on Horace Brown.

[25] Standard barrels were notionally brewed at full strength, the basis for Excise duty, and differed

from the 'bulk barrels', reduced in strength by watering (always called 'liquor' in the drink trades) from the standard original gravity of 1055°.

[26] Wilson, *op cit*, p. 88; for details of the war regulations, pp. 127–33.

[27] *Ibid*, pp. 140–7.

[28] *Royal Commission on Licensing (England and Wales) 1929–31*, PP, 1931–2, XI, p. 106.

[29] J Vaizey, *The Brewing Industry 1886–1952*, 1960, p. 68.

[30] Lackey, *op cit*, pp. 72f; Stephen Caunce, *Amongst Farm Horses: the Horselads of East Yorkshire*, Stroud, 1991, p. 223; personal communication from Mr William Goodwill, who began in the transport department in the 1920s, and was one of the early drivers for Tetley's trans-Pennine lorries.

[31] See below, p. 18.

[32] Lackey, *op cit*, pp. 76–7, and information from William Goodwill.

[33] Figures are not wholly comparable, but were £113,061 in 1924, and jumped to £208,632 in 1926, reflecting much if the gain in the 'Lancashire' trade.

[34] Tetley Annual Accounts; Wilson, *op cit*, p. 89. As indicated in the text, these figures have to be treated as no more than broad indicators of comparative trends.

[35] Vaizey, *op cit*, cited by Hawkins and Pass, *op cit*, p. 98.

[36] Hawkins and Pass, *op cit*, p. 66.

[37] Col. F Eric Tetley, December, 1956, reported in the *Yorkshire Post*.

[38] Based upon Lackey, *Quality Pays...*, pp. 81–4; *Yorkshire Post, passim*.

[39] I am indebted for information on this point to my colleagues, K. N. Field and A. R. Cooper, and to Barrie Pepper.

[40] Annual Accounts; Lackey, *op cit; Yorkshire Post, passim*. On the difficulty of judging returns, see Hawkins and Pass, *op cit*, pp. 107–115.

[41] Based largely upon *Ibid*, esp pp. 60–78. I suspect that this picture will be significantly modified in the forthcoming study of the industry by Terry Gourvish and Richard Wilson.

[42] Lackey, *op cit*, pp. 88–9.

[43] This is true of most UK brewers—I am grateful to Sir Bryan Askew for making the point to me with great clarity.

[44] The consensus among industrial economists is clearly that scale economies in production were smaller in brewing than in much of the rest of manufacturing: the huge proportion of revenue taken by tax helped to damp down the impact of scale economies on final price: based upon the findings of C. F. Pratten, *Economies of Scale in Manufacturing Industry*, Cambridge, 1971, pp. 73–6; the unpublished 1975 study by Tony Cockerill and my colleague George Rainnie, 'Concentration and economies of scale in the brewing industry'; and S. J. Prais, *Productivity and Industrial Structure: a Statistical Study of Manufacturing Industry in Britain, Germany, and the United States*, Cambridge, 1981, pp. 110–121.

[45] Prais, *op cit*, p. 13.

[46] This and the previous paragraph based largely on *Tetley's Open Line*, the internal company newsletter, with some additional detail from Lackey, *op cit*.

[47] *Report and Accounts*, 1993, p. 20.

CHAPTER 6

John Waddington PLC, 1890s to 1990s: a strategy of quality and innovation[1]

John Chartres

JOHN WADDINGTON PLC is a company almost synonymous with Leeds. Though now but a small part of the total business, its games division, containing such global brands as *Monopoly, Cluedo*, and *Subbuteo*, has helped link the names of company and city for over half a century. It was therefore very fitting that Waddingtons' special contribution to the Lord Mayor's Christmas charity appeal in 1989, was the production of a limited special edition of *Monopoly*, with Leeds locations replacing the familiar London streets of their British edition, and the Atlantic City grid of the Parker Brothers' original.

This popular association is wholly appropriate. The company was founded in Leeds in the 1890s, and the bulk of its plant is located in this city a century later. Other places have featured in the company history—Keighley, Covent Garden, Stoke Newington, and Gateshead for example—but none has been so enduringly linked with it as Leeds, predominantly south Leeds, the company's continuing headquarters. Over this period, the company has grown on its Leeds base from a small and distinctly wobbly firm, producing playbills and other theatrical printing before 1900, refounded from an insolvent position in 1905, and effectively bankrupt again by 1913, to a very substantial business by 1993, at the retirement of the second Victor Watson from the Chairmanship, with a turnover in excess of £220 million, and a workforce of almost 2700.[2]

The principal themes revealed by the growth of Waddingtons from the theatrical ragamuffins of the 1890s, to the modern packaging, financial printing, and games business, are those of innovation, the drive for quality, strategic and tactical alliances, and of a strong corporate vision. Some of these have also contributed to the more than normal share of ups and downs experienced in the company history. Waddingtons have incorporated many larger-than-life characters in and with its business, and its history is one almost worthy of the board games for which the company is justly famed. Stalking that board, over the last century, in greater or lesser roles, are such characters as Fred Karno and Wilson Barrett, the actor/manager of the Leeds Grand Theatre; John Waddington himself, and three generations of the Watson family; the shadowy figures of MI9, the wartime escape branch of the British secret service; and a range of other home and overseas businessmen, from the Parker brothers in Salem, Massachusetts, to Edward Martell and Robert Maxwell. These themes and characters appear all too briefly in this outline survey of the development of the company, in which the principal recurring themes are those of our title, quality and innovation.

I

The origins of the company are not wholly clear, and records for many of its first years totally deficient. Internal notes from the company, and accounts published in the in-house magazine in the 1920s can however, be combined with the imprecise evidence of the trade directories to provide a general outline. The origins of the firm appear to lie with the theatrical printing business started by Wilson Barrett, the actor/manager of the Leeds Grand Theatre, and his two sons. The earliest reference to such a firm appears to be that in *Kelly's Directory* for 1897, the latest copy date of which was November-December 1896, when Wilson Barrett, 'general printer' was running a business from 13

Plate 6.1   John Waddington.

146

Wade Street.[3] John Waddington probably joined this firm, and had bought into the business by 1897, since by the latter year, Wilson Barrett had disappeared as a printing name, and 'Waddingtons, printers' were established at 59 Wade Lane. The hearsay evidence of longer-standing employees recounted by Victor Watson I in a memoir of 1927, indicated that this had indeed been a fairly primitive business, despite the financial backing of Robert Courtneidge,[4] and the assets of the Waddington firm established around 1897 had consisted of 'a hand cart with sundry quoins, type, and chases, bought very cheaply, and dumped down in an office in Wade Lane'. Waddington and Wilson Barrett, they recalled, chased round the customers each week to secure the cash to pay the wages.[5]

The two did not, however, collaborate for long, and by the first half of 1902, John Waddington had decamped to new premises, south of the river at 38 Great Wilson Street, where he was established as 'John Waddington, Theatrical Printer', leaving, very confusingly, 'Waddingtons Ltd' at 59 Wade Lane.[6] The two firms, probably seeking both to trade upon the name and theatrical linkage, coexisted in the directories until 1920, when John Waddington purchased their rival, and thus reunited the two.[7] Waddingtons, the original firm, continued to produce the theatrical printing for the Grand, producing the programme and the 'book' for the its pantomine in 1897, and two playbills survive from July that year. The earliest surviving records at the Theatre Museum are programmes for the Theatre Royal, 8 December 1913, and for the 'Robinson Crusoe' pantomime at the Grand Theatre and Opera House, December 1914; both come from the Wade Lane/Camp Road firm.[8]

Not surprisingly, the new firm soon found itself in financial difficulties, and a cash flow crisis early in 1905 brought the reorganization that created the modern company. Liquidity problems brought Mr Eley, John Waddington's bank manager, into the picture, and though his agency, and that of the National Provincial Bank he managed, the firm was re-established as a private limited company, John Waddington Ltd, as from 31 January 1905. John Waddington and H. M. Carter, a company promoter, were the first directors, and the capital provided by the Bank and Eley himself. William Peacock, and in 1907, Edgar Lupton, a member of a leading Leeds merchant and textiles family, later joined the board, and Lupton became Chairman. R. B. Stephens, a Leeds stockbroker, later to become Managing Director, replaced Peacock on the board in 1908, when Arthur Copson Peake, solicitor also joined. John Martin Harvey, later a London actor/manager and knighted for his services to the theatre, and Fred Karno, music hall impresario, were among the early shareholders of what was clearly an ambitious company.

Performance, however, did not match ambition, and in the words of Victor Watson I, 'the fact that the Company was formed did not stop the steady drift

147

Plate 6.2 Waddington Play Bills from 1897 and 1922.

downhill, and the capital gradually disappeared'.[9] John Waddington's personal drive was clearly not matched by the quality of business practice, what modern management theory might classify as a 'proactive ad hoc' style,[10] and the years

1908–13 saw the snakes of debt repeatedly countering the ladders of innovation. There were, however, two significant developments in these years, one technical, and a consequential one in personnel. The company had established itself, like its parent, on a letterpress base, and in 1908 was said to possess the finest collection of wooden type in the country. Colour work requiring lithography, however, was sent out to others, and Waddington persuaded the board to invest in new machinery to bring this back into the firm. Thus entering lithographic printing, the firm required specialist staff, and Victor Hugo Watson was recruited as the new lithographic foreman.

Watson proved a critical appointment. Born in Brixton in 1878, he had come to Leeds when his father, a commercial traveller, came north. He had been a sporty and adventurous lad, more inclined to riding butcher's cattle bare-back in Roundhay than to study at school, and the necessary corrective was provided by apprenticeship, around 1890, to the firm of Goodhall & Suddick.[11] By 1901, he appeared in the directories as 'lithographer, 5 Bellevue Place', and was working for Harrison and Townshend, when his brother-in-law, Walter E. Turner, persuaded Victor to join him at Waddingtons, as lithographic foreman. This fresh face was not wholly welcomed. The existing foreman was dying of consumption, and his replacement became the natural focus of retributive dirty tricks: putting acid in water, loosening screws, and other devices were used to impair his supervision of the two machines, and Watson doubted whether he would have survived in the post beyond the first few weeks, had he not been given a twelve-month contract.

The new blood helped to improve turnover, which rose from around £5000 to £16,000 over the five years, 1908 to 1913, but was insufficient to counteract the fundamentals of Waddington's bad management, exemplified above all in weak or non-existent financial control. Though hardly a disinterested witness, Victor Watson's own account of these years perfectly describes a roller-coaster business headed inexorably for bankruptcy:

> ...Things went along and we were doing nothing else but theatrical work. Sometimes the customers paid, more often they didn't... We used to work very hard in those days, each man was doing his very best to kept the firm above water, but slowly and surely we were sinking. This was not because the workpeople were not doing their part: the office was wrong, the management was wrong, and we did not get paid for above half the work we turned out.[12]

That destiny was achieved on 7 March 1913. John Waddington resigned, having been caught with his hand in the till. He admitted the irregularities, given two weeks' pay in lieu of notice, and was allowed to keep his one-month rail pass.[13] He was not required to repay the losses, and the directors proposed to cut their losses and close down the firm.

Plate 6.3   Victor H Watson I.

II

Instead, Watson sought and secured six months to attempt to turn the firm round. Survival seemed improbable, given the bank overdraft of £4000, plus other debts, and the fact that a large proportion of the turnover of £16,000 was illusory, and had to be written off as bad debt. In a later memoir he put the net worth of the company in March 1913, with its then twenty-three employees, at 'minus £10,000'. Supplies were desperately difficult to obtain in these parlous circumstances, and Watson summarized the position in a later report to the board:

> In the Summer of that year, our credit was very bad. Commercial travellers would not come near the place and with the exception of one isolated firm, we could not get credit for paper...We had practically no material to work with and we were compelled to buy week by week.[14]

Immediate steps were taken to try to ensure survival The wage bill was reduced, with many of the employees being dismissed, and grossly over-valued stock written down, but without the support of suppliers, secured through the personal persuasiveness of the new manager, nothing would have been achieved. The business remained predominantly in theatrical posters, and Watson persuaded his primary supplier of paper, Olive & Partington Ltd, and of ink, Frank Horsell & Co Ltd, to grant six months' credit. More surprising was his success in winning a printing contract for *Toby* magazine, for which, even more helpfully, the publishers paid in advance. Survival was achieved— in retrospect, Watson was not sure how—and the first year of operation, to March 1914, showed an increased turnover, to £27,000, and the writing off of bad debts to the tune of £1400.[15]

The immediate crisis of survival over, war soon provided a further threat. Events during the war were to prove the quality of the managerial changes that had already been made. In 1913, a new plant with one machine had been established at Elland Road, itself testimony to recovery through expansion; this Quad Crown machine, producing 40″ × 30″ work, was replaced in January 1914 by Eight Crown machinery, capable of producing commercial posters at 60″ × 40″, and thus supplementing the risky theatrical work. The move towards commercial poster work represented the first clear signs of a strategic repositioning by the new management, a conscious attempt to diversify and to shift to a better quality market.

The resilience achieved by the reorganized Waddingtons was proven by the experiences of the war. All staff were put onto two-thirds pay as a precautionary measure in August 1914, but the volume of business held up well, and both hours and pay restored. On the night of 1–2 April 1915, Good Friday, the Elland Road factory burnt down, destroying the entire stock of paper and print; one or two machines were subsequently found to be usable. By 10 am on Good Friday, Victor Watson had heard that the business of Charles Russell, lithographers and colour printers at Union Mills, Dewsbury Road, was for sale on the death of the proprietor; by noon he and Ralph Stephens, the financial director, had made tentative arrangements to purchase the business; and the deal was concluded in Harrogate that afternoon. The next morning, the plant was running, and Waddingtons' lithographic staff worked through the Leeds Easter weekend—Saturday to Tuesday inclusive—to replace lost orders and stock. The returning Russell staff were astonished to find a new workforce installed at Union Mills, but were retained in employment, as recovery from disaster was treated as the basis for expansion.[16]

A further critical development took place during the war: the establishment in 1916 and 1917 of first an office, and then printing plant in London. The objective, regarded as madness within the Leeds printing community, was to win the printing contracts for tours, and to break into the market then dominated by David Allen & Sons, of Wealdstone. Again, a strong marketing approach was rewarded by good fortune: Waddingtons benefited in 1918, when Allen's became a casualty of war, requisitioned under DORA to print ration books.[17] Victor Watson himself spent a great deal of time in London, talking to West End proprietors and producers, and the establishment of a new printing works in the heart of theatreland, Floral Street, Covent Garden consolidated the strategy. As in other parts of the company history, Victor Watson's personal magnetism and good nose for contacts joined with some good fortune in overcoming adverse conditions. Although the company showed losses in the financial years to March 1919, Floral Street was showing a net profit of around £20 per week by March 1917, and overall profitability was the certain outcome of a greater volume of business. The London base was consolidated further by the purchase of Tribe & Sons, Stoke Newington, in January 1919, which had been deferred during the war. Horace Watson, Victor's brother, was installed as manager.

By March 1919, therefore, the company had survived and consolidated its position, achieving a virtual monopoly of the theatrical and cinema business in the Leeds area, and were 'rapidly killing off the opposition in the West End of London, and if only we continue to give the people what they want instead, as some of our competitors have tried to do, give them what *they* want, I have no fear that we shall lose the position we have attained'.[18] Waddingtons were thus established in London, with new plants at Floral Street and Stoke Newington. It also had Union Mills in Leeds, and had established its markets; and the firm was moving into profitability as turnover had risen from around £16,000 in 1913, to near £200,000 by 1920/1. They had long surpassed the parent company, Waddingtons Ltd, which was losing £50 per week in 1919, but did retain some valuable customers and influential friends—Howard and Wyndhams among them—and had the potential for better performance, and the early history of John Waddington therefore ends with the purchase of the 'very small old lady' of a mother company. Although Waddingtons Ltd was initially run as a wholly owned separate company, reunification was soon complete.[19]

III

By 1920, therefore, the modern company had been established in all significant respects, and critical elements of the corporate strategy established. John Waddington was set on quality; on responsiveness to the demands of its customers, a marketing orientation; on proper costings and minimizing overheads by appropriate expansion of volume; diversification away from its dependence upon theatrical work; and innovation in both markets and products. During the 1920s, this strategy was carried forward significantly by the development of new products, by going public, and through reorganization. Like several of the companies in this study, notably Watson's and Burton's, John Waddington also promoted a strongly paternalistic organizational culture in this period, seeing in teamwork and closer relationships between managers and the rank-and-file, the route to better results.

A successful foundation was established by going public in 1921. Broadening the financial base provided the essential development capital for what was an ambitious firm becoming more so. Relatively little external capital had previously been invested in the company—Victor Watson estimated the cumulative total as £9800 'hard cash'—and had financed most of its improvements and developments by internally generated funds, undoubtedly depressing its dividends. The strain of post-war developments combined with the favourable context of the capital market—1920 and 1921 saw levels of Gross National Product and rate of domestic capital formation unsurpassed before the late 1930s, although the summer of 1921 was to experience a trough in economic activity—led to the flotation of John Waddington as a public limited company in March 1921.

The new company had a familiar board, with Edgar Lupton, 'woollen merchant', as Chairman, and Arthur Copson Peake, solicitor, Ralph Bernard Stephens, stockbroker, and Victor Hugo Watson, Master Printer, as its directors, the last two as joint Managing Directors; registered its office at 36 Great Wilson Street; and issued 35,000 £1 ordinary shares, and 14,250 £1, 10 per cent preference shares. Internal documents for around the same date suggest the total asset value of the company was at least £100,000.[20] Sir Frederick Eley, Bt, who had participated in the first rescue in 1905, now felt sufficiently sure of its prospects to become Chairman, with a personal shareholding of over 12,000 ordinary shares in 1921, and Lupton became his deputy.[21]

The immediate priority was the reorganization of the company's plant. By 1921, Waddingtons' plant, acquired incrementally with the growth of the business, was expensively dispersed. Even in London, where operations were relatively recent, there were three units in operation: Floral Street; Stoke Newington; and Bear Street, newly acquired in 1920 as offices and artistic studio. In Leeds, the business was still more dispersed. There were four principal units—Union Mills, Great Wilson Street, Camp Road, and Hope Mills (Water Lane)—plus the process department and the garage, separately rented in Great Wilson Street, and the new playing card factory [discussed below]. This was costing the firm over £5000 a year in overheads and duplicated effort, arising principally from additional handling of goods because of space shortages; stock rooms in three plants; excess overtime, and managerial and clerical staff; transit costs; and wastage of materials. Above all, this lack of centralization affected the quality of the work: 'the printing trade being so intricate that mistakes creep in where least expected and it is necessary for the various Managers to constantly refer to higher authority in order to prevent them'.[22]

The outcome was the purchase of a seven-acre site at Dewsbury Road for the construction of a new works, but before construction could start, an alternative solution offered itself. The Conqueror Typewriter Co, a venture involving Lord Lascelles, had collapsed, and its Wakefield Road factory (Hunslet) was on the market. This was purchased by Waddingtons, the Great Wilson Street property sold, and the new premises occupied in September 1922. In retrospect, this change of plan may have been unwise, though offering a speedy solution to the company's accommodation problems. The roof at

Wakefield Road was unsound, and after an attempt to bodge it with a bitumen seal, had to be replaced, at a total cost of around £4000. Space needs had also been underestimated, and a warehouse and an artist's studio soon had to be added. Thus 1922 saw the company in Leeds located on a single site, where it remained for the best part of seventy years, and was able to enjoy the operational economies it offered.

By 1921, Waddingtons had begun to diversify away from the theatrical business, and developed their commercial work, with clients such as Birds [custard], the North-Eastern Railway, Boots Cash Chemists, Reckitts, and the Underwood Typewriter Co in their portfolio. The key to continuing and successful diversification lay in technical and design quality: both were developed during the 1920s by the recruitment of critical craftsmen, and reinforced by the entry from 1921 into the playing card business.

Three individuals made critical contributions to the improvement of colour lithography, apart from Victor Watson himself, who was a first class transferor. The first was a lithographic 'machine man', retained when the Russell business was acquired in 1915, Douglas Cameron, who eventually joined the board in 1941. George Spink, the general manager, ran the day-to-day affairs very

Plate 6.4   The Wakefield Road Factory and Head Office in Leeds.

154

efficiently. In 1921, Achille Vauvelle, a Frenchman domiciled in England, traced as the man responsible for the outstanding artwork on a chocolate box job, put out to John Waddington by a fellow printer, and a leading pioneer of the photographic process for lithography, was signed by the company on an exclusive contract. Vauvelle and Cameron made a design and production team that gave the company a significant lead in technique and quality for commercial poster and in art-quality reproduction, another related business development.

Within three years, the company was a leading offset photo-litho printer, and had stamped its quality though the Blue Ribbon of the Royal Academy of British Printing won in 1923 for the prints of Mr Fred Taylor's painting of York Minister, and through its production of the same artist's poster for the British Empire Exhibition at Wembley in 1924. This was reputed to be the largest poster ever printed—twenty-four eight-crown sheets, making in all a poster 10×40 feet—employing ten colours, and with a run of 3000 copies. This demonstrated the great advance from the first commercial poster, some years earlier, in which the child's face in the artwork faded to nothing and the custard changed colour.[23]

Plate 6.5   Waddingtons' Posters, *c.* 1930.

These developments were reinforced by the decision, made in July 1921, to commit £1250 to entering the playing card market. Victor Watson had been studying the process for over a year beforehand, and saw this as a product which would set very high quality standards for the whole enterprise, and which offered the opportunity to produce direct for the market. Playing cards could also be printed in the slack season, the early months of the year, and held conveniently in stock for later sale. Two further features of the market were also attractive: the UK market had been divided 80–20 per cent between only two firms, Charles Goodall & Co and De La Rue, and became a monopoly with the takeover of Goodall by the latter in 1922; and it was also insulated to a significant degree from foreign competition by the Excise duty wrapper, which had to be attached to each pack sold, and accounted for a third of the average retail price of 9d.

Waddingtons sought entry to this market through technical superiority in lithography. To this end, Victor and his son Norman had already visited Zornhafer, Bavaria, soon after the war, to purchase the best quality lithographic stones, and had secured many years' supply. They had also managed to recruit in Charlie Brough the most expert craftsman in the field, and, as the card-printing enterprise was launched, under the direction of Norman Watson, further key employees were brought in: C.H. 'Clarrie' Hirst, from Petty's, as sales manager, G. Stuart Vivian as senior salesman and Mr Rossiter, paper mill manager from Goodalls, as adviser. Norman Watson's researches into the new business were meticulous, checking tooling, paper, lacquer, temperature, and humidity, for the equally critical finishing processes. The launch into the development of the new product in July 1921 therefore took place on the base of a strong core business, though its specific trigger may have been the invitation to quote for the printing of Oxo playing cards, reinforced by a clear project team, and with a sharp willingness to recruit critical personnel from outside.[24]

The venture was rewarded by fairly rapid success, winning large contracts for cards from the Great Western Railway (250,000 packs in 1924) and the LNER, whose advertising effectively sponsored the product for sale through the stationery trade, and exploring the export markets of Denmark and the USA.[25] Barribal's artwork for the cards reinforced the company's gains. A potentially damaging copyright dispute with the Goodall division of De La Rue was won, perhaps fortuitously, by exhibition in court of critical differences in the ace of spades in the same year. The action had been provoked by the successful inroads being made by Clarrie Hirst's sales team, circumventing De la Rue's defence of share offers to wholesalers, by dealing direct with clubs and then retailers.

Norman Watson's ambitions for the division extended further, however, and development work began on reel-fed printing of cards. Victor and Norman

Plate 6.6 *Beaver*, 1923, Waddingtons' first game, and illustrative of early card production.

approached the machine-makers in Bristol behind the screen of a shell company, the Lamonby Manufacturing Co, and experiments began with a two-by-two reel-fed machine in an old building in Keighley. The development costs, and the nature of the first products of this continuous process—the cards were produced cross-grained, and were only suitable for magicians—led to an attempt to abandon the project by the board, and Victor Watson's counter-offer of resignation and purchase in March 1923. Success was eventually achieved with a three-card width reel—the original concept, and in 1926/7 the playing card operation as a whole moved to a factory in Keighley, a new investment in excess of £10,000. Somewhat surprisingly, in view of the competition of this upstart firm and the subsequent litigation, Sidney Lameurt, Chairman of De La Rue, revealed to Victor Watson the attempt by an employee of Crabtrees, the punch manufacturers in Shipley, to sell the secrets of this new process for £500. This sharply pointed the commercial value of the innovation, and of Lameurt's business ethics.[26]

There existed a further challenge to the firm in the 1920s in labour relations. Victor Watson modelled some of the paternalist culture of the firm from the early 1920s explicitly upon successful companies he admired:

I had often looked with envy upon the efforts made by large firms in order that

157

better conditions for employees should prevail. I had looked with longing eyes upon such firms as Messrs. Reckitts, Messrs Lever Bros. and Messrs. Bryant & May. I say looked with envy, not that I wanted to take away the advantages from their employees, but to do something on similar lines for John Waddington Limited.

The motivation was clearly mixed, and reflected in part his own keen interest in sports and recreations, a belief in the team spirit as a positive factor in company performance, and a keen desire to ensure that office and shop floor co-operated fully. Accordingly he secured investment of £1000 in sports grounds at the Wakefield Road factory in the early 1920s, financed the sending of the entire workforce to the British Empire Exhibition in 1924, and encouraged social and cultural associations. Within a highly skilled workforce in which a culture of quality was being consciously developed, such welfare measures, if effective in retaining employees, were probably positive contributors to performance, although a specific link with productivity would be hard to demonstrate. More significantly, it meant that the events of the mid-1920s, with the four-week Typographical Association strike against wage cuts in July to August 1922, and the General Strike of 1926, were likely to place the harmonious ethos extolled by the company under severe stress.

The first seems not to have had the longer-term adverse effects on industrial relations that characterized so many other parts of the trade. Victor Watson accepted and admired his trade union opponents in what was 'a genuine, honest, straightforward battle between employer and employee', involving blackleg labour, smuggled into the works to sustain the output of the dated printing business, and the firm neither lost jobs nor became non- or anti-union in the aftermath. The timing of the dispute, perhaps coupled with the TA's isolation from the other print unions, and emphatic defeat, may also have reinforced the firm's commitment to measures of industrial harmony.[27]

But the General Strike was perceived as a quite different dispute, almost as an affront to the 'team spirit' and harmony the firm had so assiduously cultivated. The shocked and surprised rather than recriminatory tone of Victor Watson's retrospective account of 1929 is particularly revealing:

...On a certain Monday night I had for the first time realised that a General Strike throughout the whole country was imminent, because I never for a moment imagined that Britishers would allow the Bolshies to have their own way to such a degree, and I delivered a speech in the canteen, when I did my best to prevent my greatest friends (the employees) making a huge mistake. I pleaded with them, I pointed out the advantages of being members of the greatest empire that ever existed, and so forth, but all my efforts were unavailing.

The decision was made to battle on patriotically and cost a great deal, £4 for every £1 of business sent out according to Victor Watson's estimate. The Wakefield Road factory was besieged, and the non-striking workers and the management slept in the factory, on beds brought in, and for many of the predominantly young workforce, concentrated in the playing card department, the atmosphere of the nine-day strike was one of a holiday camp.[28] The outcome, as elsewhere in the business was more serious, despite Victor Watson's respect for trades unionism, and employment attitudes hardened somewhat, and short-time working and lay-offs became more common. The impact was lasting.

Despite these challenges and problems, and the impact of the continuing coal strike on electrical power supplies, Waddingtons went ahead with the Keighley plant, which was in production at 10,000 packs per week by June 1927, and was expected to reach 30,000 by that autumn. Diversification had been achieved by the late 1920s, with a radical improvement in the quality of customers—a contract for the programmes for all the Moss Empires struck in 1925 lasted to 1963—the introduction of new technology, and the advance in technique. Waddingtons were clearly established among the ranks of Master Printers.

IV

The 1930s saw critical innovations, within a context of generalized expansion. The quality colour work continued and grew, and benefited from the growth of commercial advertising and branded products, which characterized the decade. As part of the same development in consumer goods, printed packaging and cardboard carton manufacture was established, and became a central part of the business. Colour printing and cardboard work were linked in jigsaw puzzle manufacture, and joined with the playing cards in the formation of the games division. Expensive research and development work established the *Satona* waxed carton manufacture, the ultimate progenitor of the largest segment of the modern business. These developments were the outcome of some far-sighted perhaps intuitive decisions, the exploitation and cultivation of an excellent network of contacts, and exceptionally nimble footwork. Increasingly, Norman Watson, Victor's son, became the central entrepreneurial figure in the firm.

By 1930, De La Rue had clearly accepted that the playing card market was to be a duopoly, and were approaching an accommodation, within a diminishing market. In September that year they made the first approach to suggest limiting competition, to stabilize falling profit levels. Waddingtons bolstered earnings in this area for a while, with the 'Wills scheme' of 1931, for distributing miniature playing cards inside cigarette packets, part of the generalized free gift, card, and coupon competition between the tobacco companies that charac-

Plate 6.7   A Selection of Waddingtons' Advertising Playing Cards.

terized the early 1930s. Although Waddington's also did well from the contract with Imperial Tobacco in March 1932, they had, by the autumn, entered into agreements with De La Rue over prices and discounts, and with them and Alf Cooke & Co on the pricing of advertising playing cards. The Martin Scheme, led by Imperial [Wills], ended coupon competition and its boost to the printing trade from 31 December 1933.[29]

From 1933, the company again sought to diversify, and the first main outcome was in cardboard printed cartons. Waddingtons had an established reputation for the reproduction and printing of display cards, based on the skills of Vauvelle and Cameron, and this led Lever Brothers to seek 'display outers' for *Lux* and *Lifebuoy*, bearing the portraits of film stars from the firm. This was problematic, card proving much more difficult to work than paper, and standard letterpress methods of production, using carton-cutting formes, producing work of insufficient quality.[30] Solutions were provided first by the tool-design skills of a new foreman, Jim Allen—another example of strategic recruitment being used to acquire human capital—and subsequently by the import of dedicated machinery from the USA, including, in due course, rapid-gluing equipment. Later in the 1930s, the securing of a large contract for cartons for electric light bulbs from F. & A. Parkinson helped to increase scale, and thus to improve the economy of purchase of folding boxboard, from abroad and home suppliers.

In this context, the development of the cardboard jigsaw puzzle, was a logical extension of the key skills and processes possessed by the firm. Victor and Norman Watson met with Mr Gondar of Louis Marx, the American toy and poster firm, at the Queens Hotel, probably in 1933, to discuss possible purchases of poster designs. Rejecting these as unsuited to their market, they enquired whether he had other proposals, and this led to the suggestion of Waddingtons printing the Lumar brand jigsaws in the UK, for sale by Woolworths. This was agreed, and after the purchase of the requisite machinery from the US, production began, with the standard edition of each of six designs being 50,000, for 150-piece, $14\frac{1}{2}'' \times 9\frac{1}{2}''$ puzzles, selling to Woolworths at 3s. 9d. per dozen, and retailing at 6d, a new venture worth upwards of £4000 a year to Waddingtons. After a year of successful operations, relationships with the Woolworth buyer deteriorated, and Waddingtons resolved to market their current order directly, under their own name, and marshalled the sales force to the task. The orders obtained sold out the edition, and some weeks passed before Mr Bott, the Woolworth buyer, started asking questions.[31] Waddingtons had again piggybacked their way into a lucrative new product market.

Two elements of the future games division were thus in place, and in 1934 the critical stages of the third took place. Waddingtons marketed a new card-based game, David Whitelaw's *Lexicon*, in 1932, at the modest price of 1s. 9d. but with poor sales, but its relaunch in the autumn, in the characteristic and distinctive book package at 2s. 6d, was accompanied by an intensive advertising campaign, and was a major success. More significant still was the deal struck with Parker Brothers to market the game in the USA; this led the following year to the reciprocal offer of their new product, developed by Charles Darrow from Mrs Phillip's 1924 *The Landlord's Game*, the ultimate brand for both companies, *Monopoly*.[32] Late in 1934, Norman Watson tested the game against himself, became captivated, and persuaded his father to conclude the deal on the Monday morning. It was clinched through a transatlantic telephone call, the first ever received by Parkers. From its launch in 1935, it proved an instant and consistent success story. The first 2000 sets produced by Waddingtons in 1936 sold out immediately.[33] That year, Parkers agreed to Waddingtons taking rights in continental Europe, South Africa, and Australia, all at a 15 per cent royalty, and, as made clear by Robert Barton, President of Parkers from the

The NEW CARD GAME

Skill · Laughter · Interest

LINEN GRAINED.

Lexicon is an entirely new Card Game ; fascinating and instructive. It is suitable for all classes of people and all ages.

Attractively boxed in Single and Twin Cases.

Complete with Rules

FOR PRICES SEE PAGE 50.

Plate 6.8 *Lexicon*, 1932, the very successful playing-card based game.

late 1930s, good relationships between the firms made this flexible contact one of immense mutual benefit.[34]

By the later 1930s, then, the Waddington business had established a broader games division; introduced ambitious board printing and carton making to establish the carton and packaging division; and continued to develop high-quality colour printing, for both commercial posters and, increasingly, for the labelling of branded goods. By 1934, a large contract for Heinz labels had been won, and Waddington's were asked not to supply their rivals, a clear testimony to their superior quality in the field of 'bright' printing. Later in the 1930s, this was shown to be no empty request, when Sir Frederick Eley, Waddingtons' insouciant Chairman, became Chairman of Crosse & Blackwell, and prejudiced their poster and much of their label business.[35] Though the Floral Street plant had been sold in 1931, their Stoke Newington works expanded as national advertising demand helped replace the theatrical business.

162

Plate 6.9   Early Waddingtons Games.

Plate 6.10   The Wakefield Road Works in the 1930s.

V

The final critical innovation of the 1930s bridged the Second World War, and ultimately generated the products which now account for 41 per cent of total business. The board-printing business had sensitized the company to developments in Scandinavia, its principal source of supply, and it was from Denmark that they derived the new product, *Satona*, via the first licensees, Thyne of Edinburgh. Even more than with the expensive experiments in the 1920s that produced the reel-fed playing card process, *Satona* revealed the enormous costs

Plate 6.11   Paperwork, Wakefield Road, 1937.

and uncertain returns of innovation, and how the personal vision and commitment of the Watsons was needed to bring it to fruition, against the reservations of the rest of the board.

Satona was a product patented by the Hartman brothers, for the proofing of printed paper with paraffin wax, and was seen as the answer to the retailing of milk, the replacement for bottles. It was established in the UK in 1933, through a joint venture between the Hartmans and two members of the Edinburgh Thyne family carton firm, but seems to have met with limited technical and commercial success. Victor Watson saw the product as one of great potential when he saw it first early in 1936, and resolved to acquire rights to manufacture when they were offered in May 1936, but faced strong opposition from the board. That may have been well founded: the technical problems of producing a leakproof container of the requisite quality compounded market resistance to the non-glass packaging, had made difficulties for the Scottish *Satona*, and perhaps motivated them to seek licensees for the rest of the UK. To many in the trade, it may have appeared that Victor Watson was determined to acquire a waxed pup, and it was the Watsons, assisted by Rupert Hicks and Edgar Lupton, rather than Waddingtons that were the initial investors in the ailing Satona Ltd. The company followed the Watsons' lead some months later.

The early results appeared to confirm the negative assessments of the board. The milk market continued to resist the new packaging, even without the negative impact of major short-term increases in the price of paper in 1937, although orders for *Satona* packaging and machinery did build up to the eve of war. Machinery was installed at Wakefield Road, and through the licensing agreement, machines manufactured at Lyngby (Denmark) were supplied to

Mortlocks in London. Contracts were also gained for the supply of one-third pint cartons for school milk with Oldham Co-operative Society, and for exports to South Africa, and Canada, but commercial success was more promise than attainment in 1939. The principal market successes lay after the war in the unexpected direction of soft drinks, with the beginnings of the long-term contract with Schweppes. After the war, raw material costs made *Satona* prohibitively expensive for milk use.[36] There were, however, indirect benefits: Waddingtons' technical skills in carton-forming were tested and improved by the challenge of producing cartons for liquids, and *Satona* thus provided a further 'gold standard' of technical quality for the firm as a whole.

War restricted the supply of raw materials, and precluded that of further *Satona* machinery, but did create new market possibilities, as conventional packaging became still more restricted in supply, and the beginning of 1944 saw the formal creation of the Research Department, under Norman Gaunt. This decision created the basis first for the post-war development of waxed paper packaging, and the introduction of new features to the general printing work, principally the use, from the early 1950s, of 'fluorescent' inks through silk-screen processes. Gaunt's development work underpinned the successes of *Satona*, wholly owned by Waddingtons from 1944, but proved critical in the next technological shift, from around 1957, into vacuum-formed plastic containers. Taking a long view, the significance of the move with *Satona* into liquid packaging, though commercially valuable in its own right, lay more in being the progenitor of the plastics business.

Schweppes had long provided the core market for *Satona*, but by the mid-1950s were keen to secure packaging that provided longer shelf-life for their juice products. Under Norman Gaunt, Waddingtons' research department had already been experimenting with plastics, and found in machinery produced by Hydro-Chemie of Switzerland the technical answer to production. Another UK company, Mono Containers Ltd had, unfortunately, already secured rights to the process, but were vulnerable, having recently infringed one of Waddingtons' *Satona* patents. The outcome was a Waddington-Mono joint venture, Plastic Packaging Ltd in 1957, using the Hydro-Chemie technology. This lasted sufficiently long to establish the plastic container as publicly acceptable, but the forced alliance was uncomfortable, and within a year Waddingtons were left in command of the field. A new plant, on the opposite side of Wakefield Road, was purchased for the extrusion of the plastic sheeting. Once more, the aggressive business practice of Waddingtons had combined with their R&D to secure a wholly new product market.

These plastic containers did not immediately conquer the market place. As late as 1960, the prospects for paper containers were felt to be excellent, and the trade expected the market to double if and when the public accepted this

Plate 6.12 The *Satona* waxed-board carton, and its replacement, the *Plastona* plastic carton.

as the mode for the distribution of milk. Waddingtons secured the exclusive UK rights to the American Pure-Pak machine, the device through which the Ex-Cell-O Corporation had secured the US milk packaging market. This gave the company an immensely strong negotiating position with Metal Box and with the International Paper Co (US), both of whom were keen to secure rights to Waddington-controlled processes, and in April 1961 two new companies were the outcome: Waddington International Company Ltd, jointly-owned with IPC, manufacturing and selling milk containers; and Liquid Packaging Ltd, which owned the patents and rights to *Satona* and to *Pure-Pak*, and leased them to Waddington International and to Metal Box.

The whole episode may have been, as Douglas Brearley suggested, an outstandingly successful strategic withdrawal. The UK milk market never accepted the paper package to the anticipated extent, and Schweppes did shift from *Satona* to vacuum-formed plastic containers. Faced with huge capital costs for further development of waxed-paper milk packaging, Waddingtons disposed of their waxed-paper interests in February 1965 for a considerable sum. They appeared thus to have managed both sides of the demanding innovation process with aplomb: they had secured and perfected a new technology while selling the old for an unwarranted premium.

VI

Satona was the most striking of the developments on either side of the Second World War to make significant contributions to the success of the company in the 1950s and 1960s, but there were many others. The War provided a number of new opportunities, and validated the company's reputation for the highest quality colour printing, while frustrating some advances. The mix of new product lines, usually closely related to existing core business, improvements upon existing products or their adaptation to new markets, and judicious acquisitions and disposals were the key to Waddingtons' success in these years, and can be briefly surveyed before considering the final phase of the history, the difficult years of the 1970s and early 1980s.

The effective founder of the modern company, Victor Watson, had died in 1943, to be succeeded by joint Managing Directors, his son Norman, already a major creative force in the firm, and George Spink, whose financial expertise had been critical during the 1930s, but who had been with the firm since 1907.[37] Both had been brought on in the Waddington 'Auxiliary Board', established around 1929, and which focused on production issues.[38] In this respect, the succession planning of the firm was advanced, and meant that the transfer of direction in 1943 was largely unproblematic.

Plate 6.13   Norman Watson in his office at Wakefield Road, summer 1960.

167

The War created different patterns of demand, and, in common with many other companies, Waddingtons adapted to war work. Given the high degree of dependence across the business as a whole upon consumer-oriented printing, they had little choice in the matter. The top quality colour work was employed in part in the production of escape and evasion maps on silk, 'Bemberg silk' (rayon), or mulberry paper for MI9, perhaps to be secreted inside a playing card, thus marshalling two of the company's leading sectors to the war effort. Instructions were passed on by word of mouth through Norman Watson.[39] Other escape aids, such as compasses and currency, were secreted in special *Monopoly* sets.[40] Cartridge casings were produced for ICI Metals, and *Satona* adapted to other products and raw materials. Despite labour and raw material problems, playing card manufacture was continued on Churchill's orders, to sustain morale. Additional capacity was secured through the acquisition of Henry Jenkinson Ltd, Kirkstall (Leeds), late in 1944, to cope with the overspill of work from Wakefield Road.

The blitz also created for Waddingtons a strategic alliance with De La Rue which was to last to 1964. De La Rue lost their main plant through bombing in December 1940, and this triggered the contingent agreement made between the two firms before the War, for mutual aid in the event of war damage. It brought Waddingtons security printing, as hosts to the displaced De La Rue banknote business, and directly as lithographic initial printers of the banknote sheets. Waddingtons also produced playing cards for DLR, their production line having been destroyed in the same raid. Some of the production was relocated to Gateshead in 1943, as part of wartime dispersal policy, and management unified under the local DLR man, Claxton Prudhoe. During the 1950s, much of the work was taken to the Gateshead plant, but, as both businesses developed, work on foreign banknotes for DLR increasingly interrupted printing schedules for Waddingtons' own work, and the alliance ended in 1964 because it had been outgrown by both parties.

Waddingtons' research also extended to further development of the carton business, and produced in 1949 a new concept in the packaging of light bulbs, the shock proof container, a significant design advance on the corrugated sleeve of the pre-war contract. It was promoted with panache, and sixty-five lamps in the new packaging were thrown out of a light aircraft above Yeadon airport with Victor Watson and a colleague running round to collect them. As validation of the 'shock-proof' claims, only two were damaged, one by hitting the aircraft door on expulsion. Despite experimental work to reduce them, the costs of the new pack proved prohibitive for the trade, but a new application was identified and developed through Eric Watson, Norman's younger brother. The package proved ideal for development for the sale of Cadbury's Easter eggs, which, with the post-rationing boom in confectionery, it helped make

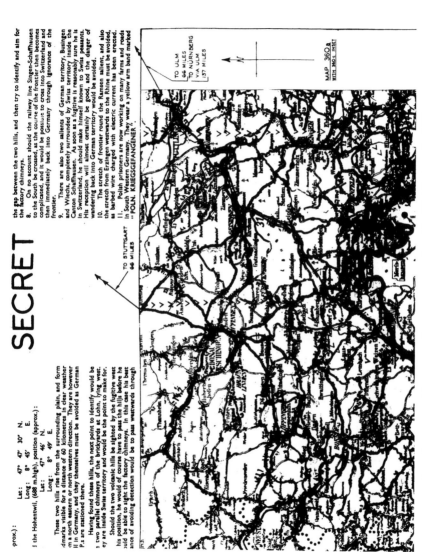

SECRET

(prox.):

Lat: 47° 47' 30" N.
Long: 8° 45' E.

f the Hohentwil, (688 m.high), position (approx.):

Lat: 47° 46' N.
Long: 8° 49' E.

These two hills rise from the surrounding plain, and form
dmarks visible for a distance of 60 kilometres in clear weather
m a north eastern or north western direction. They are however
ll in Germany, and they themselves must be avoided as German
Ps are stationed there.

Having found these hills, the next point to identify would be
: two parallel chimneys of the brickyards at Lohn, lying west.
ey are inside Swiss territory and would be the point to make for.

Should the two volcanic hills be sighted by the fugitive west
his position, he would of course have to pass the hills before he
uld be able to sight the factory chimneys. In this case his best
ance of avoiding detection would be to pass westwards through

the gap between the two hills, and then try to identify and aim for
the factory chimneys.
8.   On no account should the railway line Singen-Schaffhausen
to the South be crossed, as the course of the frontier then becomes
complicated, and it would be possible to cross into Switzerland and
then immediately back into Germany through ignorance of the
frontier.
9.   There are also two salients of German territory, Busingen
and Wiechs, completely surrounded by Swiss territory inside the
Canton Schaffhausen. As soon as a fugitive is reasonably sure he is
in Switzerland, he should make himself known to Swiss peasants.
His reception will almost certainly be good, and the danger of
wandering back into German territory would be avoided.
10.   The stretch of frontier round the Ramsen salient, and also
the stretch from Erzingen westwards to the Rhine must be avoided,
as barbed wire charged with electric current has been erected.
11.   Polish prisoners are now working on many farms and roads
in South Western Germany. They wear a yellow arm band marked
'' POLN. KRIEGSGEFANGENER ''.

TO STUTTGART
66 MILES

TO ULM
66 MILES
TO NURNBERG
VIA ULM
157 MILES

N

MAP 360a
WITH 360 INSET

Plate 6.14   Section of an Escape Map—one of a vast range produced by Waddingtons for MI9.

169

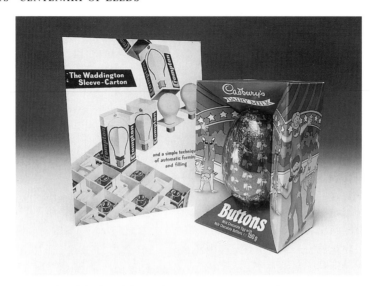

Plate 6.15   From the original Waddington lamp carton to the packaging of the modern Easter egg.

feasible, and developed packaging links with the chocolate trade which stretched back to Rowntrees in the early 1930s. It became and remains an important element of the business, in which chocolate is a valuable product for a printer, where packaging accounts for a large proportion of retail price at the luxury end of the market.[41]

Export markets were a recurrent theme of corporate development in the 1950s and 1960s, both by direct sale and through acquisitions and alliances. Picasso had been induced to supply a playing card design in 1949, but the principal French venture was the joint acquisition, with DLR, in 1962 of Ets J-M Simon, producers of the brand-leader in France, *La Ducale*. This was conceived as the first stage of a multinational consortium, The International Card Co, but the impact of double taxation made this a short-lived project, and Waddingtons disposed of their interests in 1967, followed shortly by De La Rue.[42] Other overseas ventures were also short-lived: the majority share-holding in Collet-Sproule, the Toronto-based box manufacturers, purchased in 1957, with the intention of exporting *Satona* and other carton production, and developing the alliance with Parker Brothers, produced losses of nearly £400,000, and was sold in December 1961. The new plant at Scarborough (Ontario) which proved essential to achieving scale economies in cartons was undercapitalized from the beginning, and exchange controls precluded its support from the mother company. Both ventures suggested weaknesses in the intuitive approach to strategy in the firm, and the problems of both might

170

have been avoided with deeper preparation, issues that were to become recurrent themes in the company's history.

An earlier strategic decision appeared better founded, the entry into the greetings card market. While longer-lived, this was not able to establish an enduring position in the business. Rust Craft of Canada had used Waddingtons to print greetings cards during a domestic industrial dispute, and Norman Watson had inserted a letter of overture into each case despatched, and this led in 1953 to negotiations which set up a joint venture, based upon the acquisition of the Leeds-based Cardigan Press, from 1954. A subsequent takeover of the parent company in Canada, led by Lew Birkman and Raymond Lewenthal, took the company into US ownership, and Waddington's were squeezed out of the venture by 1959. This led them to merger with Valentines of Dundee, perhaps Europe's leading postcard and greeting card manufacturer, with its own American design links, with Norcross Inc. in May 1960: the remainder of the Valentines stock was acquired during 1963 and 1964. The financial press had been hostile to the merger, and may have been correct, although excellent profits were made in some years. The greetings card market was becoming international, and was not sustainable in the long term on a UK base, and Waddingtons' cash needs after the *Videomaster* affair led them to sell the company in 1981.

Development of the games portfolio continued throughout this period, ultimately at the cost of complexity and lack of focus. In 1960, the Waddingtons' 'Big Five' games were certainly established market leaders—*Monopoly*, *Totopoly*, *Cluedo*, *Careers*, and *Buccaneer*—and were governed by a clear philosophy, of making adult games for children to play.[43] Acquisitions were made during the 1960s, principally of Tower Press (jigsaws) in 1966, which brought another London plant into the firm; *Art Master*, of Chelsea, in 1973; and *Subbuteo*, of Tunbridge Wells in 1969. The last brought Waddingtons a product still buoyant from the stimulus of the 1966 World Cup, and which continued to perform well.[44] Even before its acquisition, however, rapid growth in the games division had caused financial problems, and in the late 1960s, reorganization gradually brought the division's production and distribution under one roof, at the new Gateshead plant, installed at Castle Gate, and formal divisional autonomy, established from April 1975.[45]

Two other innovations took place during the period, both of which established continuing and profitable products. From 1958, Waddingtons began the development of their business forms, which formed a successful element of the company to 1993, and in 1961 began the negotiations which led to the formation of another joint venture, Eureka Waddington. From 1962, this company, owned 55 per cent by Waddingtons, and 45 per cent by the Eureka Speciality Printing Company of Scranton, Pennsylvania, began operation in the business

Plate 6.16   Postage Stamp printing at John Waddington of Kirkstall Ltd.

forms plant, producing *Green Shield*, the first and most successful of the UK trading stamps enterprises. Though their direct involvement did not last beyond 1967, when Litton Industries, who had acquired the US parent, transferred the operation to their factory in Huddersfield, Waddington's had probably enjoyed the boom years of the business. They had also laid the basis for more extensive stamp and related printing technology, and from 1970 they became established in the design and printing of postage stamps, securing their first orders from the GPO in 1980.

Despite some setbacks and false starts, the later 1960s saw the company with a broader base, and cash-rich from the disposals of 1963–5, which included that of the Stoke Newington factory to Sapphire Press.[46] The fundamental strength of the business, with its strong positions in several markets, attracted

a takeover approach in February 1967 from Mardon International, a complementary printing business jointly owned by Imperial Tobacco and British
America Tobacco. Norman Watson's health was failing—he was to die in
1969—and he was inclined to sell, but his son and successor, Victor, and other
directors retained a vigorous spirit of independence, and the overtures were
rejected. Mardon returned formally to make three successive bids between
May and July, raising the offer from 33s. 6d., to 39s., and to 45s. for 'A' shares,
and ultimately placing a value of £5.7 million on the company. They were
fought off with a tenacious campaign, stressing improving profit levels, and
making the determination of the company to resist very clear. Their capacity
to do so was strongly reinforced by the fact that over 49 per cent of the 'A'
shares were held by the board and their families (41.54%), employees (3.45%),
and 'friends' (4.10%). Surprisingly, the entire bid was left to Mardon, and
neither parent company became involved, and although the market expected
a fourth approach from BAT, it never came. The ultimate market assessment
of the failure was that Mardon had been too inexperienced to carry through
a hostile bid, and that it was a mistake 'to send a boy to do a man's job'.[47]
The increasingly profitable company had retained its independence.

VII

The 1970s and 1980s showed the many strengths and weaknesses of the firm,
its structure and management, and its heavy dependence upon consumer goods
industries. Thus the early part of the 1970s saw continuing strength in performance, were followed by a serious drift downwards, compounded by a number
of nearly catastrophic new ventures, and were followed in 1983 and 1984 by
two spectacular takeover battles with Robert Maxwell, before a reorganized
and leaner company began again to prosper in the later 1980s.

Growth certainly continued through the earlier 1970s, although, with the
benefit of hindsight, the 'Barber boom' may have helped to mask some of the
incipient weaknesses in the structure and management of the firm.
Thermoformed and printed plastic containers had been perfected by 1970, and
led to the contract with Van Den Berghs in 1971 for their premium product
Flora; other packaging grew; and a further new game, *Campaign*, had been
launched successfully in June 1972 on the battlefield of Waterloo. Despite
disruption by the electricity and Post Office strikes of 1970/71, consumers'
expenditure surged, and Waddington products benefited, and continued to
advance beyond the first steps to control inflation, from late 1973. By 1975,
the firm had a clear marketing strategy—'patents, trademarks, brand leader-

ship, and marketing penetration'—was engaged in a policy of decentralized, divisionalized management, and saw the historic peak of employment, at 3525.

Profits had already dipped, under the anti-inflationary measures, and consumers' expenditure began to fall from the later part of 1975, after five years of growth. The Waddington *Plastona* division was particularly hard hit by the impact of the world-wide rise in oil prices, and the company found itself squeezed badly between price ceilings and rapidly rising cost floors. Even the market-leading new product, the printed plastic-formed margarine tub, already suffering from the rise in raw material costs, had to sustain further reverses after doubling its sales between 1970 and 1975, as Britain's EEC entry exposed the product to intense competition from hugely-subsidized butter.[48] Foreign dumping of cheap playing cards on the UK market made matters worse for the group, and during the years 1975–8, the weaknesses of the company's position became increasingly exposed, with many of the games showing their age in the tougher and changing market conditions.

Part of the response to well-founded anxieties about the company's prospects, was a characteristically Waddington bold stroke, designed to reposition the games division at the leading edge of electronic leisure product market. The early Magnatron-based games had devastating effects on the board games market, and most games companies sought to enter production as an essential defence of their position. Waddingtons purchased *Videomaster* from the receivers for £700,000 with effect from March 1978, and within a year had become aware of the strategic error they had made in entering an unfamiliar business too far from their core activities; in dealing with an already bankrupt firm and its technically essential but managerially unfit executives; and in dependence upon extended and wholly unreliable networks of component supplies, from the Philippines. Unable to produce sufficient for an effective launch onto the Christmas market in 1978, managerial weaknesses led to poor quality in the subsequent year, and a second seasonal peak was effectively missed, and by December 1979 it was assumed that the company would have to be closed down, with losses of £2.8 million to be borne by the 1980/81 accounts. Waddingtons had lost around £6m over four years, roughly their stock market valuation, and hence the need to sell Valentines. That they survived and bore subsequent lesser trials, is a tribute to the managerial skills: in the US, games companies, including Parkers, succumbed under similar electronic disasters.[49] The disaster was compounded by other environmental effects on the games market, with VAT increases and the ITV strike of 1979 adding to the reverses, and a new game, *Bombshell*, promisingly based on the BBC *Dad's Army* programmes, launched but withdrawn and written off in the face of adverse tabloid publicity, at a loss of £200,000.

The years 1979–81 generated cumulative losses in excess of £5m, and the period to May 1983 saw a continuing fall in Waddingtons' share price, spectacularly shown when deflated by the general movements in the *Financial Times* index (Fig 6.1). Inflation and high taxation were tackled by price freezes, greatly damaging Waddingtons' capacity to generate sufficient income to retain working capital: the company needed profit margin of 1 per cent to finance inflation of 2 per cent.[50] Victor Watson initiated radical action to conserve cash and improve profits through increased efficiency, and several of the divisions were merged, and employment levels scrutinized before the beginning of 1983, placing the company in a good position for the recovery of that year. Between 1979 and 1983, partly because of disposals, including that of Valentines, total employment fell from over 3300 to 2062. Cost-cutting measures in excess of £3m were taken in the keen awareness that the company was vulnerable to predators, but may in fact have triggered the first bid, from neighbours Norton and Wright [hereafter Norton Opax], as redundancies signalled the extent of the firm's troubles.[51]

Figure 6.1   Waddingtons' Share Price, 1976–87, deflated by the *Financial Times* Index.

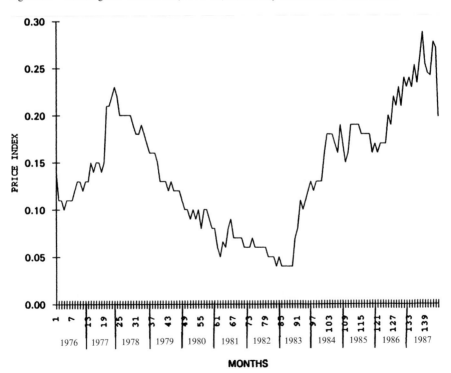

Plate 6.17   Victor H. Watson II, Chairman of Waddingtons to July 1993.

This bid was announced on 17 May 1983, and formally issued on 28 May, with a closing date of 20 June. Although it was felt by Waddingtons and their advisers, Kleinwort Benson, that it was both opportunistic and too low to succeed, it did direct attention sharply to some of Waddingtons' weaknesses, principally that attributable profits had not covered dividends paid over the previous four years, and that the Chairman's optimism about recovery, expressed from 1979, had not stopped the position of the shareholders from deteriorating, year by year. They also argued, without real conviction, that there were benefits for both sides in a merger that produced diversification. The reverse was in fact the case, but could not be used to deter the bid: a major contract with Van Den Berghs was about to be signed, and they had made it clear that this would go elsewhere if the bid succeeded, and both Heinz and Schweppes were among the other major customers who expressed concern, and suspended discussions for the duration of the bid. Although extended to 4 and then 18 July, the Norton bid was already being beaten unaided, when, at 7.30 on the morning of 17 June, an unlikely 'white knight' entered the fray, Robert Maxwell. In Victor Watson's words, this began part two of the summer, subtitled 'Enter the Bouncing Czech'.

The bid was described by Victor Watson as 'very persuasive', and valued the company at £12.8 million, twenty per cent above the Norton bid. Waddingtons remained independently minded, and concluded that 'Mr Maxwell wants to cash in on our recovery'. Although the bid was announced on 17 June, the formal offer documents did not appear until 9 July, with a closing date of 2 August, giving Waddington's further time to spike his guns with the disclosure of improved financial performance based upon actual results, the strategy already in play against Norton Opax. A reference to the

176

Monopolies Commission was tried in late June, and parliamentary questions asked about the risk of further unemployment on 18 July: David Perry, the managing director who had recently joined Waddingtons from the British Printing Corporation (by now Maxwell's BPCC), was able to confirm that these fears were well founded. However, as pointed out in the press, this was perhaps the first of Maxwell's predatory raids against a live company, rather than one being rescued from receiver or liquidator 'from the imminent knacker's yard', and Waddingtons were probably helped in these initial stages by being underestimated.[52]

Maxwell raised the cash offer to 250p from 184.8p per ordinary share on 1 August, and this expired before the share offer, of 11 BPCC ordinary shares for each 5 of Waddingtons. The battle became significantly hotter, as fund managers strongly preferred cash, given the doubts already existing about the real value of BPCC shares. Maxwell had already purchased the Norton Opax holding to take him to nearly 15 per cent, the critical first threshold in the takeover panel regulations, when Victor Watson engaged in a new defensive strategy, designed to retain the loyalty of the leading shareholders. He and fellow directors, assisted by their merchant bankers, started a series of personal visits to the principal shareholders, designed to persuade them of recovery and to stay with the existing management. In this they were adopting a new tactic in a takeover battle, but fund managers tended to prefer existing management, provided that the long-term prospects for the company were sound, and were satisfied that earlier problems had been remedied. It therefore proved very effective.

By 17 August, this tactic had delivered 46.2 per cent into Watson's hands, although Maxwell's claim of 45.85 per cent on 24 August indicated that a major holding had transferred its allegiance (it turned out to be 'a defecting friend', Watmough's, Bradford printers). BPCC's share value was hit by Waddingtons promotion of 'bad news' about his proposed property development in Wapping, and a last minute meeting with Norwich Union saved the day. Maxwell's offer lapsed on 7 September. Two days later an envelope was returned to Waddingtons: it contained the up-to-date share register sought by Maxwell on ten-day notice on 25 August, which would have given him the information with which to target shareholders, and might have brought him success. It had been understamped, and BPCC had refused to pay 11p excess postage.

Many lessons had been learned from this summer, and new defences were erected on the basis of the enormously enhanced share value, despite Maxwell's demands for a seat on the board. In February 1984, Vickers Business Forms were acquired for £3.3 million, and additional shares issued, principally to the institutions, to dilute the Pergamon/BPCC holding to 25.8 per cent, from the 29.9 per cent it retained from the bid. The further acquisition of the House of Questa, a rival printer of postage stamps, in late June 1984 provided the basis for a rights issue, which Maxwell did not hold, selling them on to Lonrho, and in July Waddingtons offered through Kleinwort Bensons to 'place' his shares. This, and subsequent offers were refused, and a final bid from Pergamon was launched on 25 October. On this occasion, neither Waddingtons nor the press were so inhibited about discrediting Pergamon, and its mysterious ultimate owners, in Liechtenstein, and KB released vital figures through the press to demonstrate the huge cash flows out of the Maxwell companies during 1984, and the corresponding shakiness of any shares offered. Maxwell may have intended his second bid to allow him to dispose of his shareholding at enhanced value, but it clearly damaged his standing, and enhanced that of Waddingtons, who had attracted much larger shareholdings by institutional fundholders by the time Maxwell abandoned his 'bid', on 12 December.

These episodes, the first of which came desperately close to success, had left Waddingtons much stronger. It had reinforced the benefits of reorganization, albeit at high human and financial cost: over £500,000 had been spent in the two battles. Thereafter, with better focus and quality in senior management, the company resumed the strategies which had established its earlier success. Rationalization of plant, judicious acquisitions and disposals, the strong marketing of new products, such as *Plastona* microwave frozen food trays from 1984, and a clear focus on the core businesses of printing, packaging, and publishing games marked the later 1980s, and sustained both the share price and the development of the business.

The retirement of the third generation of the Watson family from the Chairmanship, in July 1993, left a strong company, built by a strong sense of direction, the careful cultivation of helpful friends, and the use of strategic alliances, often over long periods. The good relationships with De La Rue, for example, forged in the 1920s from outwardly unpromising circumstances, lasted for almost fifty years, to considerable mutual benefit. To this was added a strong sense of vision, which made the company consistently innovatory, both in technology and in its early commitment to a strong marketing approach. Learning, perhaps, from past experience, Waddingtons' current US operations—Comet Products Inc, California Cutlery Corp, the Carthage Cup Company, and Hopple Plastics Inc—are closely related to the UK core businesses, particularly the plastics division and Jaycare Ltd, pharmaceutical and related packing based at North Shields, and generate around a fifth of operating profits.[53] For almost a century, this pattern of enterprise has made it one of the leading firms of Leeds.

Notes

[1] I am indebted for research assistance on this chapter to Ms Jane Durham, and for much information and advice to Mr Victor H Watson, Mr Christopher J. L. Bowes, and Mr Douglas Brearley.

[2] The latest accounts, for 1993, p. 28, list 2692 employees, and sales of £221,556,000.

[3] *Kelly's Directory of Leeds 1897*, 1897, pp. 267 and 707. Subsequent discussion is based upon further analysis of the series of *Kelly's Directory*, to the early 1920s; to that of *Robinson's Leeds Directory*, Leeds, 1897-; *White's Clothing District Directory*, Sheffield, 1894-; and the *Leeds and District Trades Directory for 1909*, Edinburgh, 1910.

[4] Father of Cicely.

[5] As above, and V. H. Watson, *Waddington Team Magazine*, 19 March 1927, pp. 3–4.

[6] *Robinson's Leeds Directory 1901–2*, pp. 726, 932.

[7] Douglas Brearley, 'A History of Waddingtons', part 1, 'The early days continued' in the house magazine.

[8] The material from 1897 is preserved at the Grand Theatre, Leeds—I am indebted to Mr C. J. L. Bowes for this information. For the Theatre Museum material, I am indebted for this information to Mr Andrew Kirk, Museum Assistant, Theatre Museum, National Museum of the Performing Arts.

[9] *The Waddington Team Magazine*, 25 April 1927, p. 3.

[10] Igor Ansoff, *Corporate Strategy*, revised Penguin edition, 1987, pp. 257–9.

[11] Leeds had long been established as a major printing centre, and by 1901 had 165 firms listed in its directories, with employment in excess of 6700 in the sector. It was predominantly letterpress, as one would expect: *Kelly's Directory for 1902*, lists 117 'Printers, Letterpress', including both Waddingtons, and only 48 'Lithographic Printers and Lithographers'.

[12] V. H. Watson in *The Waddington Team Magazine*, 19 March 1927, pp. 3–4.

[13] Board minutes, 6 March 1913.

[14] 6th Annual Report to the Board, 1919. The earlier parts of the paragraph are based upon accounts by V. H. Watson in the *Waddington Team Magazine*; Douglas Brearley's 'History of Waddingtons'; and a slightly different account published by James Thompson, *Leeds Born and Bred*, Clapham, 1982, pp. 12–13.

[15] The magazine must have been another, so far as one can tell in the world of ephemeral publications: *Toby* was published between 1921 and 1925, and cannot fit with Douglas Brearley's account. Financial details derived from report to the board, 1919.

[16] Account of V. H. Watson, *Waddington Team Magazine*, 3; Russell details from directories.

[17] Hugh Barty-King, *Her Majesty's Stationery Office: the story of the first 200 years, 1786–1986*, 1986, p. 56.

[18] Manager's report to the board, for years ending 31 March 1917 and 1919, the unmistakable language of VHW.

[19] The details on the takeover of Waddingtons Ltd are provided by V. H. Watson in *The Waddington Team Magazine*, 7 and 8. No financial details appear to survive.

[20] Brearley, *art cit*, I, continued; V. H. Watson, report *c* 1921 on reorganization of Waddington plant.

[21] The relationship between Sir Frederick and the Watsons, was not comfortable, and both Victor Watson and his son and successor, Norman, clearly felt that Eley took from the company without putting very much—internal memoir dated 3 May 1948, by N. V. Watson, reflecting upon the relative contributions of Eley, Stephens, and Lupton to the development of the firm.

[22] V. H. Watson, memorandum to the board, 1921, making the case for investment in a new unified works.

[23] Recollection of Mr Cyril Holland, 20 June 1955.

[24] The first cards were shown to the Board, 20 February 1922: they were cut out, not punched, and according to Douglas Brearley, Waddingtons' first card game, *Beaver*, of 1922 or 1923, was far from satisfactory, large stocks remaining when he joined the firm in 1924. Information from C. J. L. Bowes.

[25] Based largely upon 'How Waddingtons got into the playing card business' [by V. H. Watson II] and board minutes, 15 July 1924.

[26] *Ibid.* The chronology is not wholly clear, though the culprit was: Bernard Smith, a schoolfriend of VHW, and son of a University of Leeds professor. He was treated charitably, and retained his post at Crabtrees.

[27] On the strike in general, see A. E. Musson, *The Typographical Association: origins and history up to 1949*, 1954, pp. 399–401; V. H. Watson, *Waddington Team Magazine*, 11, p. 5.

[28] There survives a remarkable account from inside the factory by Ruby Hawker, personal secretary to Victor Watson, and subsequently Norman Watson's wife, the mother of Victor Watson II, which is reproduced in the appendix.

[29] Brearley, 'History'; B. W. E. Alford, *W. D. & H. O. Wills and the development of the UK Tobacco Industry 1786–1965*, 1973, pp. 338–55. Imperial tobacco seem to have commissioned promotional material at both group and divisional level, hence the appearance of both Wills and Imperial in the text.

[30] Skilled craftsmen in the letterpress division were not a problem, after JW took over Stembridge & Co, and high-quality letterpress operation, in 1929. J. A. Stembridge, the proprietor, had been President of the Master Printers' Federation in 1926, had been the foreman on that side of the business at John Waddington in 1908, when Victor Watson had been his opposite number in litho. Stembridge joined the board, and his staff of seventy were taken on by Waddington.

[31] Recollections of Norman V. Watson, recounted to Victor H. Watson, and transcribed 17 January 1967. The dating by NVW was '1928 or 1929', which conflicts with other records, and with Brearley's account, which provides a more convincing chronology. Louis Marx did have a UK subsidiary in Birmingham, but, like so many US toy firms, seem to have preferred to develop the product through European partners. The critical skills acquired in the Stembridge merger, in the person of Sid Benson, provided the technical solution to the problem in jigsaw production, that of cutting but holding the puzzle together until boxing.

[32] Darrow's 'development' cannot disguise the essential origins of the game as Elizabeth Phillips's tax propaganda game. What is also curious is the willingness of Parker Brothers to agree sale by licence in the UK: as indicated by Wojahn's study of Parkers, and Waddingtons' earlier dealings with Louis Marx, US games companies seem consistently to have followed this policy, the outcome of which was the consistent 'failure' of their European subsidiaries. This held true into the 1980s.

[33] Board minutes record the arrangements being made with Parkers in 17 December 1935, and the sell-out on 28 April 1936. Information from Mr C. J. L. Bowes.

[34] Correspondence between R. B. M. Barton and Victor Watson.

[35] Board minutes, 16 October, 1934 [Heinz], and recollections by N. V. Watson on Eley, dated May 1948.

[36] Sales were boosted by the rationing of confectionery, and J. Arthur Rank commented that he made more from the sale of orange drinks than he did from that of cinema seats. I am grateful to Mr Victor H. Watson for this point.

[37] Spink was General Manager in Leeds, but had clearly long been used as a trouble-shooter, and had been sent into Stoke Newington soon after its acquisition in 1919, where the workforce had nicknamed him 'The Silent Menace'.

[38] Established on the merger with the Stembridge letterpress printers, see note 30.

[39] Some examples survive with the company, but HM Government documentation of their side of the work is poor. There are references, none explicitly discussing Waddingtons, in M. R. D. Foot and J. M. Langley, *MI9: The British secret service that fostered escape and evasion 1939–1945 and its American counterpart*, 1979, p. 55, which might appear to describe Norman Watson, anonymously, as a 'jobbing printer'. On 'Bemberg silk', personal communication from Victor H. Watson.

[40] Again, I am grateful for this information to Mr C. J. L. Bowes. Christopher Clayton-Hutton of MI9 had noted Waddingtons ability to print well on silk from their Royal Command Performance programmes, pre-war.

[41] Some suggestions of this can be found in *Industrial Challenge: the experience of Cadburys of Bournville in the post-war years*, 1964, pp. 20–1.

[42] All playing-card manufacture became part of the Waddington Playing Card Company, when DLR sold out all their interests in the trade.

[43] Chairman's statement, 1960.

[44] Subbuteo was conceived and developed by Peter Adolph in 1947. A keen ornithologist, he took the name from the Latin name of the hobby hawk, *falco subbuteo*. An attempt to restart production of a game identical in all but name, after the sale to Waddingtons, had to be suppressed. The history of Waddingtons increasingly suggested that they were themselves magpies.

[45] Unexpectedly high costs had also been incurred in the development of *Future Scientist* kits. Rationalization of the division was not completed until the early 1980s. The board took the decision to establish Waddingtons House of Games Ltd on 16 August 1974 at the same time as it set up another separate unit for its business forms division, which has been recently (23 June 1993) sold.

[46] This was revealed to be a front for Edward Martell's anti-union campaigning, and embarrassed Waddingtons, who accepted the redundancy costs of their former employees, and placed future print orders elsewhere.

[47] Norman Watson died at the age of 65, 18 October 1969, having been in the company for fifty years. The exact details of the Mardon side of the bid are unknown, as is their specific motivation. This account is based upon a memoir of the bid by Victor H. Watson, a specific file on takeover bids, board minutes, and Victor Watson's annual address to the Leeds Chamber, of 1985 [?], presented in the context of Robert Maxwell's current second bid, but looking back to his first experience of defending the company. Mardon had long been the principal printers for Wills (information from Professor B. W. E. Alford).

[48] Information on the margarine industry from Paul Clark, 'The Marketing of Margarine', paper presented to the Business History meeting, 1983, kindly supplied by my colleague, Katrina Honeyman.

[49] Wojahn, *Playing by Different Rules*, pp. 75–91, 200f.

[50] Information from Mr Victor H. Watson.

[51] This and the subsequent paragraphs on the bids of 1983 and 1984 are based upon Waddingtons' 'Bid File', articles and speeches by Victor Watson, detailed internal chronologies of events, and, on 1984, articles from the *Financial Times* and the *Guardian*.

[52] *Guardian*, 14 December 1984, in a survey of the two Maxwell bids, and the general state of Pergamon.

[53] *Annual Report and Accounts 1993*.

APPENDIX

Ruby Hawker's letter to her mother from Wakefield Road on the General Strike, 26 May 1926

A remarkable letter which reveals the polarization of attitudes taking place among those affected by the General Strike, and here transcribed in full, with original spelling and punctuation.

Dear Mother,

I am afraid you will think I have been rather negligent, but all the time the strike was on I handn't a minute to sit down and write to anybody. We had a terrible time here, we kept about 30 girls in the place for ten days and a few men and about 25 apprentices. Mr Watson had beds from Longleys fixed up in the canteen for the men, and in the board room for the girls and Miss Childs, Mrs Talbot (a lady forewoman), Ivy, Jessie and myself slept in the room where we do gilt edging, and we five had to cook meals for about 70 people. We had to get up at 6.30 to cook bacon and eggs for the multitude, then the ordinary cook came in about 9 o'clock and she looked after the dinner but we had to stay in the canteen all the evening and help to entertain and then get the supper ready and wash everything up afterwards, so you can see how busy we were. All our people went out on strike except these few and on the first day of the strike we had about a thousand people howling like a lot of lunatics. All the same, although it was hard work, we had some fun out of it all, we have a piano in the canteen and they danced most evenings and we had two ping pong sets and a gramaphone [*sic*] so I think they all enjoyed themselves, a lot of them didn't want to go home anyway when it was over, I'll bet they had never had such good meals in their lives or slept under better conditions, some of them of course (particularly the girls) are filthy and no matter what you do they would never be any better. I would rather have had twice as many boys to look after as those girls, the boys were far better behaved and would do as they were told and were much tidier and everything, but the girls were most unruly and we never had one girl come into the kitchen to volunteer to help with the washing up, but we had at least four boys to help wash up every night and they quite enjoyed it too. The girls in the works have called the office girls everything, snobs and goodness knows what but it was the office girls who looked after them, and it just shows you what people like that would really be like if the positions were reversed, the world wouldn't be worth living in, if the working class, ignorant people had lots of money and better positions, they would be the biggest snobs out. I have learnt more about politics and been deeper into the actual things during this strike than ever before and I know this much, I wouldn't like to live in a world where they were all Socialists. Some people can't rule people without bullying them. The way these girls in the works treated us, just as if we were dirt and were there to wait on them hand and foot without even a 'thank you'. I never heard one girl say 'thank you' or 'please', and one of the girls about 16 or 17 she was one night said to me 'Get me a knife Ruby'. While girls of my own age in the office call me Miss Hawker, this cheeky little imp was so familiar and never said 'please' at all, so I took no notice until she asked again and then I said 'Oh were you speaking to me' and gave her a gentle hint in manners, and another boy, about 20, a big fat greasy looking individual came in one morning in the kitchen (the kitchen by the way has 'PRIVATE' written on the door but he scorned to look at that) he said '*I want* some dip'. We were absolutely disgusted with a lot of them, there were just a few nice ones that you could pick out here and there.

Mr Watson of course was heartbroken when all his workpeople left him and it has made him very very bitter, and you can quite understand his feelings when you think how he has worked and slaved to give these men work to do and his motto has always been 'No slack time' and whenever our men have had nothing much to do, they have *never* been sent home, and some of them have been here for years and just simply walked out of the place. The firm has lost £5000 owing to the strike to say nothing of the loss of trade, and I can't possibly see how a general strike could help the miners, the trade of this country will be put back again, and in business mother you realise that it is trade that keeps a country going, we want as much trade as we can get don't we to employ people. They don't seem to see that the more trade we get the more people will be employed, and as somebody said here 'How can ruining a printer help a miner?', and the miners don't care about everybody coming on strike to help them! Why lots of the girls and apprentices here, their fathers were miners so why in the world did they let their children go on working? Another thing, did you know that about four or five miners had applied to the railway office in Leeds for jobs and were set on? If it wasn't so tragic for some people it would be humourous wouldn't it?

Of course I know that lots of firms are not like Waddingtons, they don't all treat the workpeople like we do, and in Norman's department it was practically a non-Union department but a lot of his girls went out just because they were frightened. It might interest you to know that Brotherton's daughter (he is Labour M.P. for South Leeds)[1] worked in Norman's department and she got them all to strike, and mind you, these girls are paid the Union rates of wages although they are not in a Union. The reason that this department is now strictly non-Union is because a lot of the girls work on what we call the 'bonus system' which means to say that if they do so much more work than is usually allotted to them, they are paid bonus accordingly. This of course makes them work harder which is what we want and incidentally it is better for themselves, they are glad of it, and Mr. Watson has told them that the more bonus they earn the better he will be pleased. That girl Brotherton was a perfect devil, she was out here every day trying to get the girls out and causing mischief all round.

I know you are a great believer in Unions, I am not, I never quite understood it before but I quite agree that they have done a lot of good and they are necessary but they shouldn't rule the country should they? and I don't think they were right in bringing everybody out on strike.

[1]John Brotherton, MP for Gateshead, 1922–3, a native of Leeds who had entered a flax-spinning mill at the age of ten, and a Leeds City Councillor, 1927–30, 1932–41.

Well, anyway, it is all over now but I do wish you hadn't put me in that Federation, it has been money wasted all these years and here I go on paying 6d a week and I expect I shall eventually get a tenth of it back, if that, and if Mr. Watson knew I expect I'd be sacked on the spot, to say nothing of losing my future husband. Raymond says he thinks I ought to tell Norman, but after I have helped them all this strike it will look so rotten won't it? and besides if I resign where do I get my insurance card from and wouldn't they find out? I've been thinking of going to see Mrs. Arnott about it but I'd like to hear what you say first.

I have been to Pateley Bridge this holiday with the Watson family and Mr. & Mrs. Jack Spencer (Fanny Gregg) and the two children. It was just what I wanted, we stayed at a big house just on the outskirts of Pateley Bridge and the view was absolutely gorgeous, it is right at the top of a hill, and you look right down into the valley and right across the other side, it is very hilly but most beautiful. Really speaking, I prefer the north country to the south and it suits me much better, it is certainly more bracing. When I am down in Beckford I like the country and all that but I can't seem to get my lungs properly full of the air and it makes me feel awfully lazy. They were awfully nice people at the house, a widow and two daughters looked after us and her name was 'Mrs. Waddington' wasn't that funny? Tizzie went with us too and I was glad about that because she doesn't get anywhere much. You would love the country round there if you could stand the hills, and I'm sure it would brace you both up.

We haven't heard from Len for a long time, and I don't know whether he has been down to see you or not, I hope so.

Well mother after all this I think you will have your head full won't you, and you will think your daughter has turned into a rank Tory, but don't you believe it, I can quite see all your labour views and all the rest of it but I don't see how you can see all points when you have not actually experience now can you? You only see one side, you don't see the point of view of all these top men, and you wouldn't believe how human and sympathetic they were, I am in constant touch with lots of these men in Leeds (through Mr. Watson of course) and I find myself unconsciously taking their part and turning things over in my mind about right and wrong, they are not the money-grabbers that some people dub them, they don't make the huge profits that people believe, and some of them are far worse off financially than their own workpeople because they have to live up to their positions more. I'm glad I've got to be a private business man's secretary, you have no idea how interesting it is and how strange it is to look on both sides of a question. I do think Raymond made a mistake in coming out on strike, he has lost his opportunity there absolutely. If he had stayed in, it wouldn't have passed unnoticed and I'll bet that would have been just the step towards the promotion that he is always wanting, I don't think he'll ever get any further *now*, they will treat him just the same as all the men and not recognise him at all, I think he was a perfect fool, his opportunity was staring at him and he missed it, and although the men are making a fuss of him for coming out with him [*sic*], they will soon be criticising him as usual and what can *they* do for his future, or what do they care? I was a bit surprised when he came out because if he had offered his services, they would have seen that he wasn't victimised, I'm convinced of that. Of course I have never said anything to him, he resents any advice you are willing to give, he thinks it is downgrading to accept advice from his sister I expect, I don't see why it should be, but he does resent it, he resents it if you find fault with him in any way, he hasn't the sense to see that if you weren't fond of him you wouldn't bother to tell him at all.

I really must close now and get down to work. You never feel like work after a holiday do you? By the way, are you coming up this summer or do you want me to come down at Bank Holiday? Norman of course wants me to go to Blackpool with them at Bank Holiday but I haven't committed myself yet, I consult you first.

With very much love to Dad and yourself.

Your loving daughter

Ruby

185

CHAPTER 7

Montague Burton Ltd: The creators of well-dressed men[1]

Katrina Honeyman

A T ITS PEAK in the 1930s, Montague Burton Ltd. was the largest single employer in Leeds and among the top ten in the country. The firm's founder, Montague Burton, had emerged from Lithuanian origins and a small men's outfitting business in Chesterfield and Sheffield, to become a major maker and seller of men's bespoke suits based in Leeds. It was his vision and determination that successfully combined mass production and made-to-measure. His massive factory at Hudson Road produced individually fitted suits at a price a working man could afford. Burton's success was extraordinary. Until the 1950s, when demand for suits began to decline, his 650 shops and his several factories worked to capacity. Clients, whose measurements were taken in the shop and then dispatched to the factory, received a made-to-measure suit within a week. Since 1960, the business established by Montague Burton has been transformed. His personal and proprietorial management style, which failed to create a successor, has been replaced by a succession of short-lived and ruthless management teams. The manufacturing side of the business has disappeared, and retailing now dominates the activities of the Burton Group. The company has survived thirty turbulent years through a painful process of adaptation to a new social and economic climate.

This chapter traces the development of the firm of Montague Burton Ltd. with emphasis on its special contribution to the organization of the clothing industry and to the clothing habits of two generations of British men. The success of the firm will be analyzed in terms of product and marketing innovation and of Montague Burton's peculiar financial and managerial strategies.

I

Leeds became the centre of the modern tailoring trade in the second half of the nineteenth century.[2] The local specialism of men's and boys' wear, which has endured to the present, permitted greater scale economies than was possible in the more volatile and fashion-dictated women's wear. It was in the more profitable area of male tailoring that Montague Burton constructed his empire. Men's tailoring was traditionally craft based and more highly regarded than the sections of the industry producing women's wear, underwear, or working clothes. The widespread adoption of the sewing machine from the mid-nineteenth century, however, threatened the skilled men's trade as a novel ready-made sector emerged on the basis of low paid, unskilled factory labour.[3]

The opening of John Barran's clothing factory in Leeds in 1850 signified the foundation of the ready-made trade and the onset of the rapid growth of the industry in Leeds. Large numbers of manufacturers were attracted to the town during the second half of the nineteenth century and they congregated in a small district in the centre of Leeds. Localization apparently offered great advantages for the diffusion of technical and other expertise. This was important in the early stages of the industry's development and particularly because many important innovations originated in the town. John Barran himself developed the band knife, which cut many layers of cloth at a time; and a mechanism for controlling the heat of irons. Herman Friend, a colleague of Barran, is credited with devising the 'divisional system', which rather resembled Adam Smith's earlier ideas on the division of labour, and which extended the possibilities of large-scale production.[4]

Until late in the nineteenth century, Barran and other specialist manufacturers produced for independent retail outlets nation-wide. From the 1880s several of the major tailoring firms in Leeds, including Blackburn and Hepworth, opened their own chain of shops and thus introduced the concept of multiple tailoring.[5] This in itself was a significant departure in the history of the Leeds clothing industry, but within a decade, further transformations were to take place. In fact the 1890s can be identified as a watershed both in the industry and in the City's development. There had been a sharp increase in the number of clothing firms and workers from the 1870s. By 1890, the Leeds industry employed 15,000 people and produced some five million garments annually. Most of these items were cheap ready-made suits for lower middle class customers. In the 1890s, however, expansion of supply was so great that there were indications of imminent market saturation.[6] It was this problem that the firm of Montague Burton sought to address.

Montague Burton arrived in England at the turn of the century, fleeing the persecution endemic in his native Lithuania. Leeds was not his first port of call, but from his early years as a men's outfitter in Chesterfield and Sheffield, he purchased wholesale from Leeds' manufacturers. Burton's ambition was to become a manufacturer of suits; and his early years in England were devoted to building up his capital and his contacts. Burton began manufacturing on

Plate 7.1 The Band Knife, first devised by John Barran in the 1850s, in operation at the Hudson Road Mills, 1942.

his own account in both Sheffield and Leeds around 1908, and by 1914, Leeds had become the focus of his activities. One of Burton's aims was to improve the quality of the clothing that was accessible to all social groups. Although Burton is associated with improvements to both the product and the working conditions of the clothing industry, the trend towards quality enhancement had begun in Leeds and elsewhere before his arrival. Superior and more varied materials were introduced together with new methods of retailing, which included a form of wholesale bespoke. Indeed factory made-to-measure was identified at the turn of the century as the most likely saviour of the men's tailoring trade.[7] Several firms in the 1890s had established the practice of measuring clients in their shops and then making up 'bespoke' garments in either their own or another's factory. In this way it was possible to retail a made-to-measure suit for as little as thirty shillings. This threshold, which significantly extended the market, was recognized by Burton in one of his early enterprises, 'Walker's Thirty Shilling Tailors', opened in Sheffield in 1906.[8] That Montague Burton was a creative and imaginative merchant is beyond doubt. That he was a true innovator is less clear.

During the inter-war period, as the relationship between manufacturer and retailer drew closer, competition within men's tailoring, particularly the bespoke section, became more intense. Turnover of firms was most marked in multiple clothing, which Montague Burton attributed to 'style monotony': 'no industry can prosper with stationary fashions', believed Burton, 'people would spend on clothing double the amount they do at present if their garments were dated as their motor cars are'.[9] Developments in the post-war years reveal the accuracy of this assessment, yet the history of Burton's suggests that the firm was singularly ill-prepared to respond to the opportunities that fashion-led marketing presented. Indeed it is 'style monotony' that epitomizes Burton's own approach; an approach which for several decades served the firm well.

Montague Burton became a limited company in 1917. The phenomenal growth and success of the firm at least until after the Second World War has been attributed to the founder's identification and exploitation of a unique market opportunity. Yet Burton was acutely aware of the competition wrought by the multiple tailors and other wholesale bespoke firms. Competition was particularly fierce during the inter-war period, with severe downward pressure on prices. Most of Burton's immediate competitors—Hepworth, Henry Price and John Collier—charged a standard fifty shillings for a made-to-measure suit. At the time, this price was roughly equivalent to one week's wages.

Plate 7.2   The end of the day: an empty machine room at Burton's factory in the inter-war years which indicates the vast scale of the operation.

189

Hepworth's targeted customers were somewhat downmarket than Burton's, and their prices ranged as low as 37s. 6d. Burton's on the other hand, had the 'man of taste'—who wished to emulate his betters—in mind, so his base price was 55s. with 'superior styles' available at extra cost.[10]

While Burton was certainly not unnerved by his competitors, he nevertheless took them seriously, and engaged in many advertising campaigns. Intensive publicity in national newspapers characterized the strategy of both Burton and his competitors through much of the 1920s. Burton also introduced the mail-shot during the inter-war period, sending his catalogue to every man on the electoral register of each town that contained a Burton shop.[11] He also used 'sandwich' men, underemployed shop porters whose task was to spend part of their day parading the High Street in the vicinity of Burton stores. The most imaginative scheme, however, was the payment of a retainer and the provision of free suits to a temporarily impecunious Colonel Freddie Cripps (Stafford's brother) between 1948 and 1952 to impress the members of his several exclusive clubs with the quality, style, and good value of Burton's suits.[12] Although it is impossible to measure the direct impact of Burton's advertising strategy, the firm surmounted the competition of the inter-war years, and became the largest clothing manufacturer in Europe in the 1940s.

After the Second World War, the competitive environment was quite differ-ent. The expansion of fashionable casual wear for men, most recently reflected in 'lifestyle' dressing, undermined established divisions in the market. Thus although 'wholesale bespoke' implied a degree of individuality, especially in sizing and style and in material choice, the product was essentially static and homogeneous. In the event, the manufacturing sector of Burton proved in-sufficiently flexible to respond to the volatile demand of the now fashion-oriented clothing industry. While most of Burton's direct competitors moved more decisively into ready-made suits and casual attire, Burton's was slow to confront the new competitive conditions. It retained its traditional framework of activities and for much of the 1950s and 1960s struggled to remain profitable. Its reluctance to diversify served only to delay the inevitable shift from whole-sale bespoke and eventually brought the end of manufacturing.

II

Even in the highly competitive context of the early twentieth century, it was possible to enter the clothing trade either as a manufacturer or as a retailer on the basis of a modest initial capital outlay. Indeed, the high labour content, the simple and inexpensive technology, and the potential for small-scale pro-duction, permitted the survival of the small enterprise until very recently. The

£100 provided by an uncle was ample for Montague Burton to establish a small business. Although his first outfitter's shop was not opened until 1905, he had apparently become acquainted with the trade through peddling second hand clothes from the time of his arrival in England. His first retail outlets, in Chesterfield and Mansfield, operated on the principle of narrow margins and high turnover, which characterized Burton's strategy to the end. He purchased quantities of suits, shirts and overalls from such manufacturers as Zimmerman Brothers of Leeds with whom the earliest record of such transactions exists, and retailed cheap on the basis of a thirty per cent mark up.[13]

Burton's long term objective was to widen the access to good quality men's suits. His retailing enterprise provided the means of raising sufficient capital to establish a wholesale bespoke business. This he achieved by retaining the profits from the shops and by developing a solid relationship with Parr's Bank in Chesterfield. The first step towards his ultimate goal was marked by the opening of his 'Walker's Thirty Shilling Tailors' in 1906. Customers' measurements and orders were taken in the shop and made up in Leeds tailoring workshops. The significant move into manufacturing came in 1909, when he acquired the Progress Mill in Leeds, adding Elmwood Mill, also in Leeds, the following year. Both of these factories produced ready-made as well as made-to-measure suits, but with growing emphasis on the latter. Although Leeds became Burton's manufacturing base, Sheffield served as the firm's Headquarters as well as his home. His marriage to Sophia Amelia Marks, daughter of a prominent member of the Sheffield Jewish Community and Freemason, coincided with the onset of an expansionary period in the business. By the outbreak of the First World War, the firm had acquired an additional eleven shops and a shirt factory. The shops were apparently taken on lease and/or low rental, for there is no evidence of assets in the form of freehold purchases before the end of the First World War. In this way, fixed capital was minimized, while circulating capital was engendered by a combination of bank overdraft and retained profits.[14]

During the hostilities, the expansion of the Burton enterprise accelerated, though Montague's concept of wholesale bespoke, where manufacturing and retailing were perceived not simply as interacting functions but rather as part of the same process, had not yet been realized in its pure form. By 1919, Burton had forty shops, with turnover approaching £300,000 (net profit £10,000) and had greatly extended his factory capacity in Leeds, partly to satisfy the retailing requirements of the business, but also to fulfil government orders for uniforms. Indeed, the mass market for uniforms inspired critical refinements in the standardization of production and gains from economies of scale. Between 1914 and 1917, the number of manufacturing employees, outworkers as well as workers in the five factories, rose from 56 to 400.[15] The years between the two World Wars marked a critical period in the growth of Montague Burton Limited. Its expansion displayed several unusual features. Firstly, it was tightly controlled by its founder who retained the bulk of the shares even after flotation in 1929. Secondly, the rapid growth of fixed capital assets, especially shops, required dextrous manoeuvring. Burton's financial advisers developed a range of strategies that allowed the Burton family to retain control of the firm. These will be examined below.

Despite the impressive growth of the firm in the inter-war period, there are indications that financially Montague Burton sailed rather too close to the wind. Until the early 1920s, the business operated on the basis of a very small proportion of fixed capital. In the years immediately following the First World War, massive demand for demob suiting indicated an opportunity for further expansion which Burton readily grasped. Between 1918 and 1920, Burton's turnover trebled to £689,832. During the same years, however, with profits reaching just over £27,000 and assets (mostly shop fixtures) slightly less than £22,000, Burton's overdraft at the bank stood at more than £83,000. Much of this debt was used to meet immediate commitments of wages and other production costs. Fixed capital requirements were largely financed by mortgages.[16]

It was in these circumstances that Parr's Bank, with whom Burton had enjoyed a harmonious relationship for almost twenty years, pulled the plug. Burton failed to meet a repayment deadline and, after several apparently unheeded warnings, was refused further financial support. The bank was particularly concerned that the expansion of Burton's business as indicated in

Figure 7.1   Montague Burton Ltd: early growth performance.

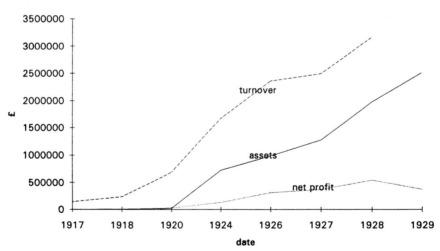

Source: Montague Burton Ltd, balance sheets, 1917–29, Burton Archives, Box 119, Leeds District Archives.

turnover growth was not accompanied by an equivalent growth of assets.[17] This is not surprising, however, as working capital requirements would absorb the bulk of profits and loans at this relatively early stage of the firm's existence. Only later, when a steady expansion had been achieved, would a greater proportion of these sources of finance be used for fixed capital purposes. Burton was only temporarily incommoded by the actions of his bank and several years later, having secured the services of another institution, the firm seemed to be based on more solid foundations. By 1924, turnover had risen to £1,674,828, an increase of 2.5 times the 1920 level, and net profit to £131,477, a five fold increase from 1920.[18] (Fig 7.1). In 1924, when the manufacturing capacity of the firm was sufficient to fulfil its retailing requirements, Burton's wholesale bespoke concept was realized. For the next fifteen years, sustained expansion was achieved. By 1929, prior to flotation, turnover approached £4 million, the chain of shops numbered 200, and the partially expanded factory premises at Hudson Road (purchased in 1920) employed 6,000 people. Assets totalled £2.5 million. It was at this point that Montague Burton was urged to raise capital for expansion through the sale of shares.[19] Although growth in

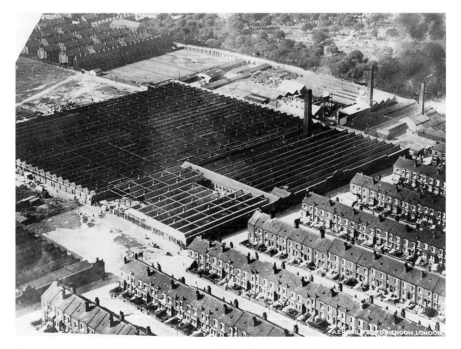

Plate 7.3   Aerial view of the Hudson Road Mills. The factory at Hudson Road was bought in 1920 from the clothing firm of Albrecht and Albrecht. Additional buildings were constructed during the 1920s, and its maximum size was reached in the mid-1930s when 10,000 people were employed there.

the 1930s was absolutely greater, its financing was more straightforward than in the 1920s.

Part of the expansion after 1924 was financed by bank loans supported by freehold property. Most other investment, however, was raised in the normal manner through retaining the company's profits. Because Montague and his wife were the only shareholders until 1929, this caused no difficulty. A constant increase in the bank overdraft, which exceeded £1 million in 1929, also provided much needed capital.[20] Useful too, was the extended credit offered by suppliers. More complicated was Burton's system of purchasing properties, which permitted rapid expansion. A type of lease-back arrangement was adopted whereby property acquired by Burton was typically sold on to an insurance company, which in turn leased it back to Burton for a fixed, long term period. A term of 999 years was common at this stage, though later 99 years became more usual.[21] Before mid 1927, freehold or long leasehold properties were acquired for the business by Montague Burton in his own name through a loan advanced by the company that also met outgoings on the property. Burton then charged rent to the company which was credited to his loan account. Having raised the purchase price from the company, Burton then immediately sought a mortgage from a bank or insurance company, and paid such proceeds into his bank deposit account.[22] From 1927, the system became more complex. Two new companies were incorporated: Henry Holding Limited (wholly owned by Burton or his nominees), and Key Estates Limited (mostly owned by Henry Holding Ltd). Properties for the company were acquired by Key Estates, on the basis of finance lent by the company to Henry Holding and then advanced from Henry Holding to Key Estates, which also received rent from the company.[23]

The choice of financial structure was influenced by tax avoidance motives. It enabled the firm to acquire essential fixed assets while minimizing tax liabilities. Indeed, such were the suspicions of the Inland Revenue that they instigated court proceedings on the grounds that prior to 1929, the company had failed to distribute a 'reasonable part of its income' to its members (the Burton family) which enabled them to avoid surtax.[24] The company was also criticized by the Inland Revenue for failure to raise finance through shares or debentures, which would have been appropriate given the volume of business, and for operating on a negligible amount of permanent capital. In the event, the judgement was in Burton's favour, but the real problem of raising capital remained. The company could not resist going public indefinitely. In 1929, some 10 per cent of the company's holdings was floated onto the stock market. Thereafter, Burton's raised capital through share issues or debentures but continued to retain the great majority of shares within the family and to implement tax avoidance schemes.[25] Although the flotation of the company did little to change the overall structure of ownership, it permitted a more sustained and secure growth of output and sales during the 1930s. Profit levels rose rapidly to a peak of more than £500,000 in 1935, and although they fell during the war, they picked up in the context of post-war demand for demob suits. Much of the firm's expansion was financed by retained profits. This was as true in the 1960s as in the 1930s.[26] (Fig 7.2). By 1940, fixed capital in the form of freehold or leasehold properties was valued at £7.5 million, and the important phase of the company's expansion was complete. A point of saturation had been reached on the retailing side of the business. Until the absorption of shop chains in the 1970s and 1980s, no more shops were acquired. The only major change was monetary as revaluation of assets took place in 1961. Some expansion of factory premises occurred in both the 1930s and in the post-war restocking boom.[27]

By the late 1930s, therefore, Montague Burton's wholesale bespoke business had reached its peak. Its position, before and after the Second World War seemed unassailable, but the epoch of rapid and solidly based growth was at an end. In the early 1950s profits fell, but from the late 1950s until the mid 1970s, growth of turnover and profit was respectable. By this time, however, the trading foundations of the business were weak, and for several years in the 1970s, the Group's profits became excessively dependent on the property division. Despite attempts at diversification, weaknesses in the manufacturing division were not rectified and in the late 1970s, divestment and rationalization

Figure 7.2   Burton's profits 1932–62: final and retained.

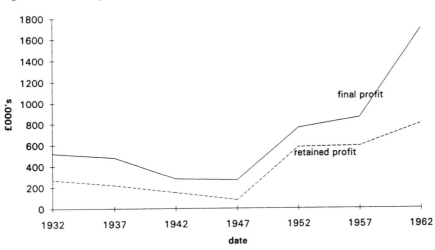

Source: Montague Burton Ltd, accounts, 1932–62, Burton Archives, Box 185, Leeds District Archives.

became the key to improved performance.[28] Following the closure of loss-making activities and the strengthening of the retailing sections, the company moved into the black. By late 1979, the Group as a whole and all retailing divisions became profitable (Fig 7.3), reducing overall dependence on the Property division. The early 1980s saw a continued emphasis on retailing. Manufacturing was further rationalized and by 1983 had become profitable on the basis of the high technology garment manufacturing service 'Farndale' located at Guisborough. By 1984, fashion retailing recorded a profit of £36.7 million.[29] The rebirth of Burton's had begun.

III

Montague Burton's fortune was based on a homogeneous product. His dream was to clothe the entire male population in good quality, well-fitting suits. His concept of wholesale bespoke, which was to mass-produce upmarket suits at a sufficiently low price to generate a mass market, ensured the attainment of the dream. Montague Burton perceived equality of dress to reflect a more spiritual social equality in which he strongly believed. In addition, he anticipated an enduring market as each male generation came to be fitted at Burton's just like their forebears. His vision was at least partly realized. During the 1930s, 1940s, and in the early part of the 1950s suits became common attire

Figure 7.3   Burton's profits 1962–87: final and retained.

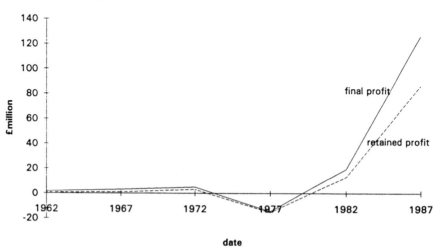

Source: Montague Burton Ltd and Burton Group plc, accounts, 1962–87, Burton Archives, Box 185, Leeds District Archives.

amongst working men at leisure. In fact for almost thirty years, the demand for Burton's suits seemed unquenchable. In these circumstances, the firm's specialization on this single item was entirely appropriate. As Ralph Halpern was to observe from the very different vantage point of the 1980s, retailing formulae had at one time changed slowly[30] and in such a slow moving market for men's fashions, the company had not been penalized. In Montague Burton's case, it was several decades before a fundamental change in direction was required.

Before the 1950s, the only significant catalyst for change in Burton's product was not fashion but war. Early in the First World War, Burton's became an official war contractor, and the expansion of manufacturing capacity was driven by government demand for uniforms. By 1917, in addition to his bespoke trade, Burton had fulfilled £150,000 worth of uniform orders, with a further £60,000 worth outstanding.[31] Immediately after the war, both retailing and production were boosted by demand for demob suits and by the release of pent-up demand for bespoke suits. In the Second World War, Burton became even more committed to the national effort. On the outbreak of hostilities, Burton's factories immediately switched production to greatcoats and battle-dress. In total, Burton's made some 13.6 million garments, or 25 per cent of all uniforms produced for the three services.[32] It is for this reason that Hudson Road Mills became an early Luftwaffe target.[33] As in 1918, the return to peace in 1945 marked a post-war expansionary phase. Burton's factories continued to operate at full capacity immediately after the war, despite raw material constraints, as government contracts for demob suits provided a vital stimulus. These suits made economical use of material and were devoid of trimmings, yet they retained the quality characteristic of a Burton's suit.

The death of Montague Burton in 1952 created an opportunity for the firm to reduce its traditional commitment to wholesale bespoke and to respond to changing markets. The firm was injected with new blood. The Jacobson brothers, whose successful 'Jackson the Tailor' chain of shops was based, like Burton's, on wholesale bespoke, were brought in to rejuvenate the firm. Despite their undoubted ability, their presence served only to confirm wholesale bespoke at the heart of the business. The Jacobson's tackled the pressing financial problems, but failed to implement any long term strategy in response to changes in consumer taste. The Burton stores were rationalized and the number of Jackson's shops increased.[34] Some change in the product structure was achieved through the acquisition of complementary businesses and shops; and the firm responded in a small way to the growing fashion market by treating the outlandish demands of teddy boys with indulgence.[35] Burton's, however, satis-fied only a small proportion of the new youth market. It was predominantly a middle-aged firm meeting the requirements of a middle-aged market.

Plate 7.4   Gender divisions at work: the machine room at Burton's. The vast majority of machinists at Burton's as at most other clothing firms, were women. During the 1930s and 1940s, more than half of the female labour force of Leeds was employed in the clothing industry.

Throughout the 1950s and for much of the 1960s, despite enormous changes in fashion and in the men's wear market in general, which suggested a shift to ready-mades and casual wear, the core of Burton's business remained in conservative, made-to-measure suits.[36] Market share declined noticeably. Nevertheless the company was reluctant to relinquish its traditional lines of activity. Neither the purchase in 1963 of the French made-to-measure tailoring specialists, *Alba*, nor the move into mail order, did much to alter the product structure.[37] The attitude of top management was critical in determining strategy; and it was not until the Chairmanship of Ladislas Rice from 1969 that changes took place within the men's tailoring sector. The proportion of ready-mades increased; the firm reduced its dependence on men's suits and diversified both into other men's wear and into other clothes retailing. The closure of two small factories in 1970 marked the beginning of a long process of manufacturing divestment through which Burton's was to become almost wholly devoted to retailing. During the 1970s, Burton's acquired a range of retail outlets, some unconnected to clothing.[38] (Fig 7.4). Many of these were unsuccessful, and in the difficult trading conditions of the mid 1970s, men's and women's

198

Figure 7.4   Montague Burton Ltd and Burton Group plc, diversification in retailing.

1946 Acquisition of Peter Robinson
1953 Purchase of Jackson the Tailor
1960 Acquisition of Brown's of Chester
1963 Acquisition of Alba, Paris
1964 Introduction of Mail Order (Burton-by-Post)
1969 Opening of first 'Top Shop' branches
1970-1 Acquisition of: St.Remy(French clothing retailers)
                         Trumps(employment agency)
                         Evans Outsize(later renamed Evans Collection)
                         Ryman Conran

        Internal Development: 'Orange Hand' (Boys' Wear)
                               'Break Out' (Jackson's, for young men)

        Unsuccessful bid for Wallis
        Closure of Mail Order

1972 Trumps sold to Alfred Marks
1973 Acquisition of Green's Leisure Centres
        Expansion of 'Top Shop'
1975 Closure of 'Orange Hand'
        Development of 'Top Man'
1979 Acquisition of Dorothy Perkins
1983 Internal development : 'Top Notch'
1984 Internal development : 'Principles' and 'Principles for Men'
        Acquisition of 93 Harry Fenton shops
1985-6 Acquisition of Debenhams

Source: Montague Burton Ltd and Burton Group plc, Annual Reports, 1946–86, Burton Archives, Leeds District Archives.

fashion retailing (especially Top Shop and Evans) provided the only profitable segment of the Burton business.[39]

The turnaround associated with the later 1970s was accompanied by the closure of ninety Burton and Jackson shops and four further factories.[40] The Hudson Road site was reduced to a cloth cutting and warehousing centre.[41] The men's wear component of the business underwent a change of image and became more clearly segmented. By 1980, after a tortuous decade, Burton's had finally disposed of its wholesale bespoke culture as well as the involvement of the Burton family.[42] The company had become committed to the fashion retailing of men's and women's clothing. By the mid-1980s manufacturing capacity was further reduced and the activities of the business were evenly divided between Men's wear (Burton, Principles for Men, Champion Sport, Top Man and Collier) and Women's wear (Top Shop, Principles for Women,

Evans Collection and Dorothy Perkins). The young, sophisticated and casual segments of the market were thus targeted with some success.[43]

From the mid-1980s to the present, the fashion activity of the business had remained fundamentally unchanged. There has been, however, a shift into products for the home. The take-over of Debenhams in 1985, was originally conceived as a joint venture with Conran's Mothercare/Habitat Group, but before the deal was struck Conran bought BHS and formed the Storehouse Group.[44] Undaunted, Burton proceeded with the purchase, which has proved to be a relative success. Burton's retailing strategy for the 1990s will focus on the older customer (people in their 30s and 40s and above) and on enduring personal style rather than fashion.[45] The founder would no doubt have approved of this direction.

IV

The clothing industry was not a classic site of mass production. From the late nineteenth century to the present, the manufacture of clothing took place within a range of organizational forms. On the face of it, the coexistence of such diverse forms of production as outwork, homeworking, 'sweating' and large- and small-scale factory, is surprising. It is widely believed that developments in the organization of industry proceeded in a unidirectional manner and specifically that the modern factory superseded more traditional forms of production. Recent research, however, suggests that capitalist development, rather than destroying apparently outdated organizational forms, in fact incorporated them within its structure. The clothing industry exemplifies this alternative view.[46]

The mid-nineteenth-century invention of the sewing machine, itself a highly advanced piece of technology that embodied the latest developments in interchangeability, extended rather than reduced the variety of organizational forms. The sewing machine was compatible with pre-modern forms of production. Its diffusion also encouraged the expansion of factory production and permitted the introduction of such regressive methods as 'sweating', which made intensive use of low paid labour in squalid conditions.[47] From the late nineteenth century the clothing industry developed through a symbiotic relationship between the factory sector, which used advanced techniques and an extensive division of labour, and a 'secondary' sector where labour was used intensively. The non-factory sector was particularly important in sustaining the expansion of an unstable industry with unpredictable markets. Before the First World War, many clothing factories would have failed to survive the seasonality and

Plate 7.5   Men only: the cutting room at Burton's. Cutting was perceived as a skilled task and was confined to men who jealously guarded their position as the élite of the clothing trade. It was only during the two World Wars that women were employed in the cutting room.

intermittent vagaries of the industry without the support provided by the flexible, usually female, sweated labour and outworkers.[48]

It was within this complex and unstable structure that Montague Burton created an outstanding position for himself, eventually heading the largest clothing factory in the world. He was not the first manufacturer of clothing to retail his own product. Burton's contribution was more subtle. His vision was of a wholly integrated process that allowed for the effective control and planning of output. It was this vision that transformed the whole of the clothing industry. In the early days, Burton subcontracted work to satisfy his customers' requirements at his 'Walker's Thirty Shilling Tailors'; and until the early 1920s, the needs of his shops outpaced his manufacturing capacity. A balance between manufacturing and retailing was achieved during much of the inter-war period, when production became concentrated at the Hudson Road site, but periodically Burton sent garments out to other factories in Leeds. Manufacturing capacity was extended outside Leeds from the mid-1930s, partly because of constraints of labour supply and partly because of government

201

inducements to relocate to the depressed textile regions. Accordingly factories were acquired in Walkden, Bolton, and Worsley in Lancashire in the late 1930s and in the late 1940s factories in Goole and Doncaster were opened with government assistance.[49]

During the difficult years of the 1950s and 1960s when the demand for made-to-measure suits was falling, Burton's factories were modernized and production streamlined.[50] Some shift towards ready-mades did little to reduce the clear excess of capacity in the factories. The new management team of the late 1960s was reluctant to featherbed the manufacturing side of the business, and in any case believed it to be incompatible with the new retailing focus. Attempts to improve the efficiency and profitability of manufacturing proved inadequate. Rationalization became inevitable. This meant factory closures, and these continued through the 1970s as the manufacturing sector recorded increasing losses, which reached over £3 million in 1978. In the early 1980s only the Goole and Guisborough factories remained. At Guisborough bespoke production was retained, but was completely updated. It became the first factory in the world to introduce computerized marking for made-to-measure suits; and was responsible for the profitability of the manufacturing division achieved in 1983.[51]

Plate 7.6 Burtonville clothing works, East Lancs Road, Worsley. This factory was one of several opened with government assistance in the late 1930's and eased Burton's labour supply constraints.

Burton's early factories operated on a small scale and until the end of the First World War production expanded through the purchase of additional small units. The Hudson Road Mills were acquired in 1921 with a view to concentrating production on a single site. After a period of construction, the desired manufacturing capacity was reached by the early 1930s. At its peak, the Hudson Road factory employed 10,000 workers in three great halls. Most of the workforce was local. 'Everyone in the area worked at Burton's—fathers, mothers, sisters, brothers—whole families'.[52] Ultimately, however, labour was sought from further afield. 'Like a huge octopus, Burton's spread out its tentacles and pulled in its workforce from as far as Castleford, Swillington, Garforth, Rothwell'.[53] A form of mass production characterized parts of the manufacturing process, while other sectors remained labour intensive. After inspection, the cloth was dispatched to the cutting room where each garment was cut out separately from individual specifications. At this stage, few economies of scale could be achieved. The pieces for each suit were passed on to the making up departments where the division of labour became quite complex. Suit-making was sectionalized with separate rooms for trousers, coats (jackets) and vests (waistcoats). Within each section, tasks were subdivided: 'machining in all its stages is done on systematic lines, down to the pressing and finishing stages after which regular and orderly collection of the completed garments are made and transported to the dispatch room'. Coats, vests and trousers reached the dispatch room separately and were then 'efficiently sorted by a sound system and placed in compartments, each one of which represents a branch and bears its number'. Items for each branch were then packed and transported to its destination by lorry or rail.[54]

All machinery used in the factory was, according to Burton, the latest model. Many types of sewing machine were adapted to every phase of tailoring. In practice, the technology of clothing production underwent little radical change during Montague Burton's lifetime, and some widely diffused technical improvements, such as the Hofmann Press, were insignificant in terms of productivity gains. In the decades after the introduction of the sewing machine, improvements were confined to such 'work aids' as needle positioners; to raising stitching speeds; and to the diffusion of dedicated machines for such special tasks as buttonholing. Throughout the period from the late nineteenth century clothing production has been dominated by the sewing machine, 95 per cent of which remains the straightforward, single operator-controlled type; and the pressing equipment.[55] Much of the recent progress in micro-electronic application has followed the course of previous technical innovation to develop special purpose equipment for high volume, repetitive operations.[56]

Once the winning manufacturing formula had been established at Hudson Road, little change was made to the technology and organization of production. In 1952, the basic structure was as in 1930. The subdivision of tasks had

Plate 7.7 One of the Bedfords operated by Montague Burton Ltd from its headquarters in Hudson Road. Burton's transport arm was later replaced by 'High Street Transport' which served other clothing firms as well as Burton's.

become more complex, however, and the making of jackets entailed between 50 and 70 operations; waistcoats 39 and trousers 55. The factory contained 32 conveyer belt production units, each of which comprised a team of workers, sitting at machines arranged on each side of a moving belt.[57] The subsequent modernization programme focused on methods of production and progress control, supervisory control and quality control, and involved a rearrangement of the layout.[58]

Hudson Road Mills remained the largest clothing factory in the world for at least thirty years. Thousands of workers were crowded together in great halls protected by an archetypal paternalist employer. Burton was proud to have introduced formal welfare provision. His appointment of a Welfare Officer in the early 1920's predated by several years that of Marks and Spencer who are often portrayed as innovators in this field. Meals were provided at the Hudson Road factory from its early days. Indeed the works canteen, which could accommodate and feed the entire workforce at a single sitting has become legendary. The seasonality of the clothing trade meant that some months were a great deal busier than others but Montague Burton made strenuous efforts to provide regular employment for his workforce and, apparently, never laid workers off during the slack periods.[59]

Plate 7.8   Work and play: Hudson Road Mills and its Bowling Green on the occasion of its fiftieth anniversary. Montague Burton provided a range of sporting and other recreational facilities.

Montague Burton achieved a commendable record on industrial relations. He believed strongly in collective bargaining, and made a contribution to the improvement of pay and conditions in an industry characterized by irregular and poorly paid work. Strikes occurred infrequently at Burton's, although the story that work stopped only once, in 1936, is an exaggeration. Burton's workforce may well have enjoyed better conditions of work than others in the trade, but there were episodic grievances. Correspondence between management and the National Union of Tailors and Garment Workers in 1945 illustrates one such episode, which greatly disappointed the firm's management and highlights Montague Burton's ideas on industrial relations that emphasized formal channels of communication.[60] Despite episodes of unrest, Burton can be identified as one of the few industrial leaders with a commitment to negotiation and arbitration in cases of disagreement.

V

A key feature of Burton's success, both before and since Montague's time, has been its policy towards property. Property has provided a secure foundation for the sometimes volatile clothing industry and an instrument for raising

Figure 7.5   The expansion of the Burton retailing empire.

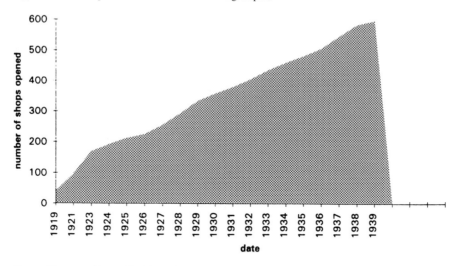

Source: Montague Burton Ltd, branch records, Burton Archives, Box 119, Leeds District Archives.

funds for expansion. Prior to 1920, Montague Burton avoided accumulating property assets, preferring to lease or rent. By 1924, a complete reversal of this policy was evident, and during the inter-war years, a massive property portfolio was acquired (Fig 7.5). Acquisitions ceased in 1939, and between 1931 and 1961 the value of Burton's property grew from a little over £6million to less than £9million. A revaluation of the company's properties in 1961 raised the level to £41million. Since then, Burton's properties have been regularly revalued both to enhance borrowing power and for use as a basis for market rents to be charged to the retail divisions (Fig 7.6). In 1972, Montague Burton Property Investments Ltd was created as a separate division within the group. This formalized the position of property acquisition, management and disposal within the company. The tangible assets of the Burton Group (including more than 2,000 shops) are currently valued at more than £1 billion. Within that figure the assets of the Burton Retailing Division (the original Montague Burton Ltd) lie between £250 and £300 million.[61] The Group's dependence on property is double-edged. It could be argued that such valuable, if depreciating assets from a secure basis from which to confront the current difficult trading situation. Equally, such a dependence in the present slump in the property market, underlines the Group's inherent vulnerability.

Since the early days, Burton's have displayed an imaginative and innovative approach to the vital property part of the business. Within Burton's concept of wholesale bespoke, his shops were perceived not as mere receptacles from which to offload the products of his factories, but rather as an integral feature

206

Figure 7.6   Burton's property values 1960–91.

Source: Montague Burton Ltd and Burton Group plc, financial accounts, Burton Archives, Box 119, Leeds District Archives.

of his grand design of egalitarian clothing. As retail outlets, Burton's shops were striking in several respects, which, in distinguishing them from the competition partly accounts for the company's long term success. Montague Burton seemed to possess a keen locational sense. Even his first outfitting stores in Chesterfield and Mansfield were centrally placed to catch the passing trade, and thereafter he devoted huge amounts of time and energy gaining knowledge of potential city centre sites. Montague's preference was to purchase and then demolish a redundant corner pub, and on the site create a standard Burton store in granite, bronze and other fine materials. Although they may not have justified the description of 'outstandingly handsome'[62] the shops were readily identified as Burton's.

The prescribed uniform appearance and organization of the interior of Burton's shops suggested a scientific approach to selling. The external architectural distinctiveness, which was simple yet striking in spacing and proportion, was matched by an interior decor designed to resemble a contemporary Gentlemen's Club. This was confirmed not simply by the overwhelming maleness of the atmosphere, but also because the place barely resembled a shop. The interior was not cluttered with goods for sale. Instead there was simply a counter, some lengths of cloth and books of styles and patterns. The uniformity of the shops was matched by a uniform routine for the shopworkers. Regulations governing the activities of the salesmen were detailed in the 'Managers Guide' and focused on codes of dress and behaviour. These rules,

Plate 7.9   Burton's shop front in the 1930's: Leeds city centre. It was typical of the stores that Burton acquired during years between the wars when a corner position was preferred.

which emphasized staff smartness and a courteous approach to all customers except those unfortunate individuals over-endowed in waist or chest measurements, were masterminded by Montague and enforced by an elaborate inspectorate, in order to create a pervading ethos of good taste. The invisibility of women in Burton's shops, until the era of sex discrimination legislation, confirmed the clothing trade as a man's world. Women became employed as cashiers, and as such they recorded measurements and dealt with payments and accounts. They were kept well out of sight, however, behind a hatch, to spare the embarrassment of the clientele.[63]

The influence of Montague Burton on the external and organizational style of the shops was ubiquitous. It is also clear that, despite engaging an estate manager, the choice of properties to be purchased or rented and the transactions involved, were conducted by Burton himself using a *nom de plume*. His capacity for travel, his photographic memory and above all his extensive connections, provided him with an unusual knowledge of towns and cities and suburban shopping centres. His awareness of property values in diverse locations was such that he struck some neat deals. He very often bought when the market was at a low ebb. Much of Burton's expansion in the 1930s was undertaken at a time when retailing, industry and property were generally

depressed. Burton's anonymity was essential in completing property transactions particularly once his predilection for corner positions and other key
sites became known. He thus often operated through a nominee, typically the
estate agents Healey Baker. When the transaction was particularly sensitive,
however, he used James Walker the jeweller (owned by his friend Sydney
Saunders) as a front.[64]

There is no doubt that Montague Burton appreciated the investment value
of property. From an early date he would purchase sites which were never
used by the company for its normal activities. In many such cases, the properties
were sold sometime later at a substantial profit. His foresight was particularly
impressive during the Second World War, when he purchased a number of
shops at a time when few other retailers were interested in buying. By 1945,
the company owned 120 unoccupied sites. On all of these a killing was made
on the subsequent resale.[65] Many of the buildings owned by Burton, but only
partially occupied by shop premises, had considerable rental potential that was
readily exploited by Burton. Spare capacity fulfilled objectives other than
financial gain, and a scrutiny of the Burton shops of inter-war vintage, com-
monly reveals the existence of Billiard Halls and/or Dancing Schools above or
below the store. It is said that young men in an unfamiliar town, seeking a
diversionary game of Billiards, would make for the Burton's landmark.[66] This
was cleverly designed by Burton to fulfil the dual purpose of catching the
passing trade of young men at leisure, and encouraging them towards modes
of behaviour appropriate to their style of dress. In particular, Burton hoped
that the absence of alcohol in these settings, which were quite unlike modern
snooker emporia, would assist in reducing the level of youth drunkenness.

VI

Until 1952, the management style of Burton's was dictated by the founder.
From the moment of his firm's inception, Montague Burton had assumed
responsibility for all aspects of its operation. The rapid growth of Montague
Burton Ltd. during the inter-war years was largely attributable to the vision,
determination and industry of the founder. Despite the greater scale and
complexity of the organization from the 1920s, full control remained with
Montague Burton. The objectives of the firm and such overall strategy as
existed, were known only to him. He had a deep reluctance to delegate.
Montague Burton's style of benevolent dictatorship may well have served the
company well in the short term, but over-dependence on the founder ultimately
caused severe problems for the company.[67]

Montague Burton Ltd was, above all, a family firm. It was led by the founder until his death in 1952, with a supportive Board of Directors. From the 1920s until 1952, the composition of the Board changed little. For most of that period it consisted of Montague's three sons; his step-brother Bernard Burton; Emmanuel Hurwitz, formerly a business associate; A. W. Wansbrough, whose original appointment with the company before the First World War was as Inspector of Shops; and C. E. Benson. Benson, a Director of the City Merchant Bankers, Kleinwort Benson, was co-opted in 1931 at the time of a large issue of preference shares.[68] While Montague Burton clearly believed in his own ability to steer his company, he was not afraid to acknowledge his shortcomings. He thus appointed trusted key personnel to remedy such weaknesses. His particular expertise in marketing was not matched by a competence in manufacturing. Thus he acquired the services of Emmanuel Hurwitz and made him responsible for the manufacturing side of the business. Hurwitz's small clothing business had supplied Burton's outfitters' shops in the early twentieth century,[69] and having thus gained Montague Burton's respect was appointed to the Board in 1910, where he remained until 1952. Bernard Burton was given responsibility for purchasing materials-shop fixtures and fittings as well as cloth. Benson provided a much-valued City connection. Other, rather vague, areas of responsibility were allocated to Montague Burton's three sons as they matured, but they were given little autonomy or decision-making powers. Raymond was allotted an administrative function and was influential in the shift in the company's activities to include women's wear. Stanley's role in the firm was determined by his early interest in manufacturing and especially in technology. This particularly pleased his father whose talents did not embrace these areas.[70] Arnold had overall responsibility for property. These able and highly educated sons made contributions of great worth to the company both during and after Montague. Their father's strategy of tight control, however, impeded a successful succession to take place. The sons were ill-equipped to sustain the company after his death.

In principle, a hierarchical structure of middle management existed, but was denied effective decision-making powers. Heads of Departments and other executives merely followed instructions. There was no formal network of interaction. The executives consulted and communicated with the Chairman but not among themselves. Ultimately this resulted in an absence of team spirit, and prevented the emergence of new talent and innovation. A better use of managerial talent and a reorganization of the management structure would not only have improved current operating conditions and future performance but would also enhance the position of the company in the eyes of the lending institutions. Shortly after Montague Burton's sudden death in 1952, the founder's failure to provide for succession was revealed. Initially, C.E. Benson assumed the Chairmanship of the company. Within weeks it was recognized

Plate 7.10   The conveyor belt in operation at Hudson Road in the 1960s. A decade later most of Burton's manufacturing plants were closed.

by the Board that the survival of the firm depended upon an urgent strengthening of its managerial talent. The strategy was to acquire a compatible firm with a strong management team. Jackson's the Tailor, a north-east company run by Lionel and Sidney Jacobson, was thus identified. Shortly after the take-over in 1953, Lionel became Chairman of Burton's.[71]

The new management team generated some change at the margin of the firm's activities, yet its vision, like Montague Burton's, was founded in whole-sale bespoke. By the mid 1960s the days of made-to-measure were over, and as the business began to suffer, pressure for more extensive change developed. In 1967 the search began for a more visionary management team. The strategy, as before, rested on the acquisition of a company with proven management strength. A deal negotiated with UDS (including John Collier) was referred to the Monopolies Commission which, unconvinced by Burton's argument that satisfactory top management was unavailable elsewhere, rejected the merger.[72] The Burton Board responded to this by head-hunting. The outcome of this creative strategy was the appointment, in 1969, of Ladislas Rice as Chief Executive and Joint Chairman (with Raymond Burton). Rice, whose previous

211

managerial experience was in the metal and engineering industries was the first Chief Executive of any of the major UK clothing multiples to come from outside the industry. He approached his task with a freshness of vision, untainted by the world of wholesale bespoke. Rice's appointment marked the end of the old regime, the retirement of the Jacobsons and the renaming of the business to The Burton Group.[73]

A new management hierarchy was established under Rice. His corporate team, with the exception of the Finance Director, was appointed from outside Burton's. In 1970, Rice moved the Head Office from its traditional Leeds base to London where Company strategy was developed. This represented a significant change in the culture of the business which had previously failed to appreciate the value of strategic planning. The shift in the focus of the Company's activities from manufacturing to retailing required new approaches and managerial capability. The appointment of Ivan Richard from Marks and Spencer as Buying Director was designed to enlarge Burton's product range. The shift in Burton's remaining manufacturing capacity from made-to-measure to ready-mades, was expedited by Martin Frankel (from Daks Simpson), Managing Director of the Manufacturing Division. Further action was taken to develop the management capacity within the group (by 1970, 50 new senior executives had been recruited and a management training centre established), and to extend strategic planning initiatives, through a system of management by objectives and annual divisional plans.[74]

The Rice era was characterized by necessary experimentation within what had become unquestionably a conservative company. The need for further diversification was recognized by the Board, but in retrospect, the activities of the company under Rice's Chairmanship seem uncoordinated. During the 1970s, the Burton Group acquired a range of companies which integrated poorly into its existing structure and many of which were subsequently sold. By the mid-seventies, the company's performance was causing concern among City institutions. In 1974, profits were 'an unmitigated disaster'; and the old two-tier share structure, which retained control within the family, was perceived as a serious deficiency.[75] Members of the Burton family were seen as a constraint on the Group's development. Their commitment to employee security and welfare retarded rationalization and deterred factory closures. In 1975, a leaked report prepared for the Company's shareholders by the stockbroking firm, Scrimgeour, revealed significant weaknesses in management strategies and suggested the replacement of Rice and other senior management by a more dynamic team experienced in retailing. In the event, Rice retained his position but his influence was diluted by the addition of two new Directors: Power and Spencer. The following year, Spencer became Chief Executive while Rice was retained as Chairman; and Ralph Halpern joined the Board.[76]

In 1979, non-voting shareholders became enfranchised, family control of the business was lost; Spencer was elevated to Chairman and Joint Managing Director (with Halpern), while Rice was demoted to Deputy Chairman. Spencer's apogee was short-lived. He stepped down in 1981 when exposed in scandalous business circumstances by Halpern, who in turn became Chairman and Chief Executive.[77] Halpern had joined Burton's in 1961 as manager of Peter Robinson and progressed rapidly through the hierarchy. His particular strength in retailing was revealed in the striking success of 'Top Shop', and from 1981 in his capacity as Chairman he developed the retailing culture of the Burton Group. He challenged the traditional approach to strategic planning and established a new open system of business planning with clear channels of communication, high rewards and incentives and the continual involvement of outsiders to prevent complacency. Thanks to Halpern, the early 1980s witnessed the rebirth of Burton's as a company committed to 'multi-strategy market positioning' in response to the new, fast pace of retailing.[78] Halpern's extraordinary energy and dynamism was responsible for the healthy performance of the Burton group in the 1980s. It also became the subject of intense press scrutiny, and in 1990 he was replaced by Laurance Cooklin whose tenure was to last only eighteen months. Both men received generous golden handshakes. In April 1992, a new Chairman was appointed and a new era began.

Forty years after the death of Montague Burton, the company he founded is the largest men's wear retailer in the UK. In the intervening decades, the company appeared several times on the verge of collapse, and has changed beyond recognition. But for the sound property base established by Montague Burton in the inter-war years, failure would have been inevitable. Because of it, and some creative management decisions, the company is set for some time yet, perhaps even a further 100 years.

Notes

[1] Many thanks to Jane Durham for able research assistance, to Jeremy Burton for documentary evidence and enthusiastic support; and to Raymond Burton for his valuable information. I am grateful to my colleagues at the Centre for Business History at the University of Leeds, to Andrew Godley of the University of Reading and to Peter Scott of Pembroke College, Oxford for helpful comments on an earlier draft of this chapter.

[2] Jenny Morris, 'The characteristics of Sweating: The late nineteenth century London and Leeds tailoring trade', in Angela V. John, *Unequal Opportunities: Women's employment in England 1800–1918*, 1986, p. 113.

[3] Deidre F. Busfield, 'Sex and skill in the West Riding: Women's employment in Yorkshire, 1850–1914', Unpublished PhD thesis, University of York, 1986, pp. 257–60.

[4] Joan Thomas, *A History of the Leeds clothing industry*. 1955, pp. 5–7.

[5] *Ibid*, pp. 47–8.

[6] *Ibid*, pp. 48–51.

[7] *Men's Wear*, 19 April 1902.

[8] Described in *Men's Wear*, 6 February 1932, p. 37.

[9] *Ibid*, p. 38.

[10] Oral record. Interview with William Blackburn, conducted and transcribed by Paul Smith, 1976.

[11] E. M. Sigsworth, *Montague Burton: The tailor of taste*, 1990, p. 50.

[12] A. Orchard-Lisle, 'Recollection on Sir Montague Burton', unpublished ms, October 1963, p. 15.

[13] Zimmerman Brothers Account book, kindly loaned to the author by Mr Dick Zimmerman of Leeds 17, son of the firm's founder. See also Sigsworth, *Montague Burton*, p. 16.

[14] Sigsworth, *Montague Burton*, pp. 22–4.

[15] *Ibid*, p. 29.

[16] Montague Burton Ltd. balance sheets, 1917–29, Burton Archives, Box 119, West Yorkshire Archive Service, Leeds District Archives, Sheepscar, Leeds 7.

[17] Correspondence between Mr Howson, Manager of the Chesterfield branch of the London County Westminster and Parr's Bank and Montague Burton, between 19 October 1920 and 14 November 1920. Burton Archives, Box 31.

[18] Montague Burton Ltd., balance sheets, 1917–29, Burton Archives, Box 119.

[19] Information from interview with Raymond Burton (son of Montague), London, June 1992.

[20] Montague Burton Ltd., balance sheets, 1917–29, Burton Archives, Box 119. As Sigsworth points out this represented a smaller proportion of total liabilities than had been the case with the 1920 overdraft when the firm was expanding into the Hudson Road Mills. Sigsworth, *Montague Burton*, p. 74.

[21] Information from interview with Raymond Burton, London, June 1992. For a full analysis of Burton's property activities, see Peter Scott, 'Financial institutions and the British property investment market 1850–1980', unpublished D.Phil. thesis, University of Oxford, 1992.

[22] Court of Appeal: Montague Burton Ltd. v Commissioners of the Inland Revenue, 4 July 1934, p. 2, Burton Archives, Box 29.

[23] *Ibid*.

[24] *Ibid*.

[25] During the 1930's there were two separate issues of preference shares of £1m and £2m respectively. Information from interview with Raymond Burton, June 1992.

[26] Montague Burton Ltd., Annual Report for 1961 stated that 'the expansion of this group since 1946 has been financed from its own internal resources.

[27] The expansion of the 1930s took place in the depressed textile regions of Lancashire with government support. In the post-war years new factories were opened in Doncaster, Goole and Guisborough. Government help was again forthcoming especially with the cost of new machinery.

[28] Gerry Johnson and Kevan Scholes, *Exploring Corporate Strategy*, 1989, pp. 545–552.

[29] Burton Group plc, Annual Report, 1984.

[30] Letter from Montague Burton (though using his original name of Meshe David Osinsky) to the Board of Trade, 2 October 1917, claiming exemption from an Act of the previous year which would have required him to publish documents under his original surname. He had not yet legally adopted the name Burton. Burton Archives, Box 31.

[31] Johnson and Scholes, *Corporate Strategy*, p. 556.

[32] R. Redmayne, *Ideals in Industry*, 2nd edition, Leeds 1951, pp. 156 and 158.

[33] *Ibid*, p. 154.

[34] Information from interview with Raymond Burton, London, June 1992.

[35] Ray Gosling interview with Arnold Burton (another son of Montague), broadcast on Radio 4, 10 July 1992.

[36] Some attempts were made to diversify the company's activities through, for example, the extension of Peter Robinson stores (the London shop was bought in 1947) into the provinces, and the purchase of Brown's of Chester. Chairman's Reports, 31 August 1956 and 31 August 1960.

[37] Chairman's Reports, 31 August 1963 and 31 August 1964.

[38] Chairman's Reports, 1970–76.

[39] Burton Group plc, Profit and loss account, 1974–5.

[40] Chairman's Reports, 31 August 1977 and 31 August 1978.

[41] Chairman's Report, 31 August 1980.

[42] Johnson and Scholes, *Corporate Strategy*, pp. 552–55.

[43] Burton Group plc, Annual Report, 1984.

[44] Johnson and Scholes, *Corporate Strategy*, p. 558.

[45] Burton Group plc, Annual Accounts, 1990.

[46] See, for example, Jordan Goodman and Katrina Honeyman, *Gainful Pursuits: The making of industrial Europe*, 1988, chapter 3; C. Sabel and J. Zeitlin, 'Historical alternatives to mass production: politics, markets and technology in nineteenth century industrialisation', *Past and Present*, 108, 1985, pp. 133–76. Specifically on the clothing industry is James Schmiechen, *Sweated industries and sweated labour*, 1984.

[47] Schmiechen, *Sweated industries*, passim.

[48] S. Fraser, 'Combined and uneven development in the men's clothing industry', *Business History Review*, 1983, p. 531.

[49] The Yorkshire factories were located in areas of traditional male employment where surplus female labour existed.

[50] Johnson and Scholes, *Corporate Strategy*, p. 534.

[51] *Ibid*, p. 555.

[52] Leslie Rosen, 'An outline history of the Jewish association with the clothing trade', lecture delivered to the Leeds branch of the Jewish Historical Society of England, 25 February 1985. Transcription in Burton Archives, Box 204.

[53] *Ibid*.

[54] This description of the early operation of the works at Hudson Road is presented fully in Anon, 'A modern garment factory: Montague Burton Ltd., Leeds', *Garment Manufacturer and Fabric Review*, August 1930.

[55] Clothing economic development council, 'New technology and the clothing industry', NEDO, 1971, p. 6.

[56] Jonathan Zeitlin, 'The clothing industry in transition: international trends and British response', *Textile History*, 19, 1988, p. 224.

[57] Fuller description contained in 'Factory of the month: Montague Burton Ltd., Leeds', *Works Management*, June 1952.

[58] Recommendation of Industrial Consultants, 1953, conveyed in Chairman's Report 31 August 1954.

[59] Oral evidence, including interviews with Raymond Burton and a number of former employees of the company.

[60] The industrial relations perspective of Montague Burton was contained in a letter from E. Hurwitz (Factory Manager) to A. Conley (then General secretary of the NUTGW), 11 May 1945, during a period of industrial unrest. Burton Archives, Box 62.

[61] Annual Report, 1991.

[62] Orchard-Lisle, 'Recollection', p. 6.

[63] The image of the interior operation of a Burton shop was vividly presented by Arnold Burton during his interview with Ray Gosling, broadcast on 10 July 1992.

[64] Orchard-Lisle, 'Recollection', p. 3.

[65] *Ibid*, p. 7.

[66] Arnold Burton in interview with Ray Gosling, 10 July 1992.

[67] These difficulties were anticipated by E. Beddington Behrens (who married Montague Burton's daughter Barbara) in a written survey of the company, produced in September 1931. His report was kindly loaned to the author by Jeremy Burton (son of Arnold). Behrens particularly identified Montague's failure to delegate and to plan for his succession as weaknesses, but he was also concerned about the unconventional financial arrangements.

[68] He took temporary control of the company following Montague's death. I am grateful to Raymond Burton for the information about C. E. Benson.

[69] Information from interview with Raymond Burton, June 1992.

[70] *Ibid.*

[71] *Ibid.*

[72] The Monopolies Commission, 'United Drapery Stores Ltd. and Montague Burton Ltd.: A Report on the Proposed Merger', CMND 3397. During the six hearings, it became clear that there was strong opposition from the wool textile industry and from the relevant trade unions. Ultimately, the commission was not satisfied that Burton's had made sufficiently sustained efforts to acquire management elsewhere, and were not convinced that it would be impossible to achieve satisfactory top management without the merger. It was also revealed that the market share of the merged company would reach about 40 per cent.

[73] Johnson and Scholes, *Corporate Strategy*, pp. 532–4.

[74] *Ibid*, p. 534.

[75] *Ibid*, p. 541.

[76] *Ibid*, pp. 541–4.

[77] *Observer*, 24 January 1981.

[78] Chairman's Report, 1984.

CHAPTER 8

Soapy Joe's: The History of Joseph Watson and Sons Ltd. 1893–1993[1]

Katrina Honeyman

THE Whitehall Road soap factory of Joseph Watson and Sons Ltd. was a Leeds landmark for over a century. From the 1880s until 1987, it produced a variety of soap-based items. In the early days it specialized in general purpose household soap, the most famous brand of which was *Matchless Cleanser*. Later, when the firm became incorporated into the Unilever Group of companies, its product lines became more diverse. After 1930, the success of Soapy Joe's depended on its flexibility in production and marketing.

Joseph Watson's shares were sold to William Lever in 1917, whereupon Soapy Joe's ceased to exist as an independent enterprise. Nevertheless it continued to operate as a semi-autonomous unit within the Lever Group of companies. Lever acquired several other major soap companies during the 1920s, so that by the end of the decade, he controlled most of the British soap industry. In 1930, upon the formation of Unilever, Joseph Watson and Sons Ltd became one of its Associated Companies, along with Crosfield and Gossage. As such it retained some individual identity, yet its manufacturing and marketing activities were to be centrally directed by Unilever's Home Soap Executive. In order to reduce the extensive overlapping interests of the component firms, Unilever established a trend towards specialization of product and function. This ethos created separate manufacturing and selling companies, and changed the range of operations at Joseph Watson and Son's Ltd. In 1936, Whitehall Road became a specialist manufacturing unit. A separate trading branch of Watson's was established in the same year in association with Gossage. In 1942 the selling side of Crosfield was added, to form Crosfield, Watson and Gossage.[2]

A critical chapter in Joseph Watson's history was opened at the end of the Second World War. The process of consolidation of Unilever's soap interests reduced the number of competing firms and removed soap production from the Whitehall Road plant. For the first time in its existence, Soapy Joe's produced no soap. In the early 1950s it began to concentrate on toiletries, and thereafter produced a range of shampoos, toothpastes and shaving creams.[3] In 1962 the firm of Joseph Watson and Son's Ltd. became part of a larger enterprise. Unilever's sustained practice of rationalization and coordination led to the merger of Watson's with two other companies within the Unilever Group, D. and W. Gibbs and Pepsodent Ltd. to form Gibbs Pepsodent Ltd. This enterprise was renamed Gibbs Proprietaries Ltd in 1965. It was subsequently transformed by the addition of Elida, an Austrian toiletries company with particular expertise in shampoo and toothpaste. This development, from which Elida Gibbs was born in 1971, reflected Unilever's commitment to expansion in the field of toiletries especially in the overseas market.[4] Throughout this period of growth and change, the manufacturing activities of Joseph Watson and its successor companies were maintained primarily at Whitehall Road. Some production was introduced at Seacroft from 1969 in a former shoe warehouse.[5] Since 1987, when the Whitehall Road site was closed, all production and independent development activities have been concentrated in a purpose built factory unit at Seacroft, which contains a Watson building in memory of the founder of Soapy Joe's.[6]

This chapter examines the expansion of Joseph Watson's in the context of its position as one of Unilever's Associated Companies. Its history provides an excellent opportunity to analyze the operation of a quasi-independent unit of one of Britain's most successful companies. Particular emphasis will be

"WATSON'S MATCHLESS CLEANSER" SOAP WORKS
(Showing the 1909 Extensions.)

Plate 8.1   The Whitehall Road soap factory of Joseph Watson and Sons Ltd which, until the 1930s was the largest works in the country exclusively devoted to the production of soap for the home market.

218

placed on the role of Joseph Watson in marketing and in product innovation and the way in which these activities were subsequently coordinated centrally by Unilever.

I

The competitive environment of soap manufacture was transformed during the nineteenth century alongside broader social and economic changes. Domestic soap consumption rose from just 24,000 tons in 1801 to 260,000 tons in 1891.[7] This growth reflected population expansion, urbanization, improved standards of personal hygiene and rising per capita incomes. Between 1861 and 1891 soap consumption per head doubled, as it became impossible to avoid the need to wash.[8] The grime produced by factories in the industrial towns emphasized the requirement of an efficient means of removing dirt from person and clothing. At the same time, the sharp expansion of washable cotton goods introduced to the masses such novel habits of personal hygiene as a more frequent change of clothing.

Joseph Watson of Leeds was one of the most successful and enduring of the soap manufacturers to become established within this dynamic context. As early as the 1840s the founder of the firm, Joseph Watson (I), had created a thriving business in skin and hide dealing from which soap making was a natural outcome.[9] From the outset, Watson's had engaged in a profitable sideline in fat and tallow lubricants for industry. From this it was a small step into the production of tallow candles and then into the making of solid bars of tallow soap.[10] It was Joseph's sons, Charles and George, however, who shaped the future of the company. It was they who persuaded their reluctant father to specialize in soap production. In the 1860s Watson's manufactured mainly soap and production became concentrated at the site on Whitehall Road.[11]

Watson's soap business was thus born of expediency. Other major soap manufacturers of the time took a more scientific route to success. The Merseyside firms of Gossage and Crosfield, through links with the chemical industry, influenced the scientific development of soap making. William Gossage, a chemist by training, turned his attention to soap making in the mid 1850s, and successfully produced an effective and cheap item from palm oil and silicate of soda. His competitor Joseph Crosfield began work as an apprentice chemist and druggist and subsequently developed techniques for the making of silicate of soda and for the recovery of glycerine.[12] The firms of both Crosfield and Gossage maintained their early reputation in the field of industrial chemistry well into the twentieth century.[13] It was William Lever, however, who became Joseph Watson's closest rival in the years before the First World War. Lever had become well acquainted with soap and its market while employed in his family's grocery business. From this experience he identified both the potential demand for wrapped soap and the ideal moment to enter manufacturing. In 1885, when raw material prices were depressed, he purchased an ailing soap factory in Warrington. After a period of experimentation he produced a 'pure' oily soap. This was to be known as *Sunlight*, whose success is legendary.[14]

The growing market for soap in the nineteenth century stimulated developments in its production. As a result of this progress the concentration of soap manufacture became more pronounced. Traditional soap makers had processed home grown tallow, which imposed few locational constraints. From the mid nineteenth century, however, vegetable oils replaced tallow as an essential ingredient of soap, and manufacturers became reliant on supplies from the Far East and from tropical Africa. As a result, soap makers sensibly began to locate their works close to one of the major ports. Merseyside was a popular choice. By the 1880s, with Gossages at Widnes and Lever and Crosfield at Warrington, the soap industry became concentrated around the port of Liverpool. A further group of enduring manufacturers was located near Bristol, with a smaller number at Wapping in London.[15] The position of Joseph Watson, many miles from the nearest port, was an unusual one for a soap manufacturer. Its Leeds location reflected its early business dealings in skin and hide. The firm enjoyed a sustained demand for its products from the industrialists of the West Riding and from further afield.[16] Its development of a lucrative export market was eased by the position of its Whitehall Road factory on the banks of the River Aire, adjacent to the Leeds-Liverpool Canal and at the junction of two railway lines.[17]

Although the disposal of the hide and skin elements of Joseph Watson's business was delayed until 1911, it had become apparent in the 1880s that the future prosperity of the firm rested on the production of soap. Watson's soap output rose from 100 tons to 600 tons per week between 1885 and 1893. The business also produced candle wax, and sold its glycerine by-product to dynamite makers. The expansion of the firm was securely founded and its ability to surmount the considerable local and national competition was a tribute to the vision of the partners. The greatest impetus came from the dynamic Joseph Watson (II), later Lord Manton and also known as 'Soapy Joe'. By 1893, the firm of Joseph Watson was established as one of the giants of the soap industry in an increasingly competitive environment.[18]

In the last few years of the nineteenth century soap makers enjoyed buoyant demand for their products. By 1900, however, the period of unconstrained expansion had passed. Saturated markets and rising raw material prices created

Plate 8.2 Wrapping and packing *Matchless Cleanser* at Whitehall Road at the turn of the century. The men are placing long bars of soap into the cutting machines; the women wrap the individual cut bars and place them in boxes ready for dispatch.

difficulties for soap producers in the first decade of the twentieth century. Competition among the major manufacturers became intense and the market shares of individual producers were retained only by the implementation of creative marketing initiatives. William Lever's activities introduced novel principles of marketing mass-produced consumption goods. He generated brand awareness and stimulated demand through attractive packaging and imaginative advertising. Conscious of the significance of Lever's ideas, Joseph Watson (II) was quick to implement and adapt them. Because of their corresponding approaches and visions, the two men became both natural allies and intense rivals.[19]

Competition among the major soap producers was, in 1906, temporarily replaced by a spirit of co-operation. Lever, Watson, Crosfield and Gossage united to seek a solution to the raw material problems facing the industry. Supply had become erratic and prices were soaring. Lever proposed a combination of the four firms to allow economies in the purchase of raw materials and in advertising costs. Lever envisaged a combination of the firms through the mutual exchange of shares. In principle, each firm would retain autonomy, but in practice the proposal amounted to a take-over of the participating firms by its most powerful member. Thus Lever would have been given effective control of the soap trade. In the event, however, Lever's project was insufficiently supported. It was finally killed by an anti-Trust campaign orchestrated by the national press.[20]

Despite the highly publicized failure of this attempt at amalgamation, Lever's determination to take control of the soap trade was undiminished. In the immediate aftermath of the 1906 debacle, several of the major producers co-operated more informally over some aspects of raw material supply and in the pooling of technical knowledge. Lever, however, had other plans and began to purchase some of the smaller soap companies. Before the outbreak of the First World War, Lever renewed his approaches to Watson as well as to Crosfield and Gossage. In 1912, Lever and Watson acquired a 'mutual interest in each other's business'. In 1917, Joseph Watson succumbed to Lever's pressure for a take-over, and sold all his shares in the company to his erstwhile rival. During the 1920s, Lever also acquired Crosfield and Gossage, which gave him control of 60 per cent of the British soap industry.[21] Watson's life with Lever is considered in the next section.

II

The firm of Joseph Watson and each of the other businesses taken over by Lever during this period were to be known as Associated Companies. Each retained its name and some independence. Lever insisted that he would not enforce unwelcome policy on any of the Associated Companies, yet the evidence suggests that he oversaw the operations of them all. He exercised general control over manufacturing, selling and advertising policy. He vetted proposals for major capital expenditure and new products. He examined accounts. Nowadays these functions are performed by the Unilever Board. Because Lever had acquired a number of structurally similar firms, he was forced to rationalize their activities. The process of rationalization was long and difficult. Some degree of competition was considered necessary for maximum efficiency and optimum profit for the whole enterprise, but the co-ordination of centralized control and competition among the Associated Companies posed an enduring problem.[22]

Until 1929, the extent of rationalization was limited. On the soap side of Lever's activities, 49 manufacturing companies coexisted with 48 sales organizations.[23] Production at the firm of Joseph Watson and Sons Ltd, and most other companies within the group, was largely unchanged. On the formation of Unilever in 1930, however, priority was given to the elimination of excess capacity and duplication within the group. Centralization of activities became more pronounced. Raw materials were secured for individual firms by the central Unilever (Raw Materials) Ltd. The manufacturing and selling activities of individual firms were supervised by Unilever's Special Committee. The rationalization strategy, which determined, among other things, the size and structure of Joseph Watson's product, was fixed by the Home Soap Executive of Unilever.

During the 1930s, the Executive identified unacceptable levels of overlap among the major soap producing firms and implemented change. The closure of several small firms within the Group and the manufacturing section of Gossage's, significantly reduced the number of competing products. The production of household soap was concentrated at Watson's Whitehall Road factory. In the later 1930s Watson's also became the centre for the development of soapless shampoo and shampoo powders. Interdependence among the Associated Companies became an important feature of the rationalization process and one that required careful planning. An agreement in 1933 formalizing this interdependence, affirmed the practice of production interchange, which further reduced the number of brands. The rationalization of marketing followed. In 1945 a General Agreement confirmed the practice of reciprocal selling and distribution of the products of all companies.[24]

The records of the firm of Joseph Watson illustrate the high degree of reciprocity and of specialization among the Associated Companies. During the 1930s, for example, Watson specialized in producing hard soap for Unilever. At the same time its production of soap flakes declined as Crosfield became the specialist in that area. During the Second World War, soap rationing and other features of the war effort required Watson and other Associated Companies to make major changes to their product structure. As total soap production fell to 25 per cent of the 1905 level, Watson, following the instructions of the Executive, extended its range of shampoo and toothpaste products. In the early 1940s it produced *SR* and *Solidox* for D. and W. Gibbs. In the shampoo line, it took over *Trixie* in 1944 and *Gloria* in 1948 from sister companies. Watson continued to produce some soap throughout the war, adding *Lifebuoy* and *Bodyguard* to its own long established product range.[25]

Changes to the organization of Unilever's soap production continued after the war. In the immediate post-war years, production ceased at several constituent firms including Watson's. Thereafter all Unilever's soap output came from Port Sunlight.[26] In the early 1950s a new division of Unilever was established which specialized in toiletries, later to be known as Personal Products. Joseph Watson was identified as the core production unit for this division, and all Unilever production within this category was transferred to Whitehall Road. Under the terms of the reciprocal agreements of 1933 and 1945, Watson's was required to produce a range of items for a number of companies within the Unilever Group.[27] Among many other products, it manufactured *Pears* shampoo; toothpaste for Gibbs and for Pepsodent; and a variety of products for overseas markets which were channelled through Unilever Export. This practice continued until the early 1960s; and details of Watson's *Sales to Allied Companies and Third Parties* in 1961, reveal an extraordinary range of products made to the specification of several sister firms. Gibbs and Pepsodent absorbed the bulk of these products, and the amalgamation of Watson with these two companies in 1962, cemented what had already become a close working relationship.[28]

The degree of autonomy enjoyed by Watson as part of the Unilever Group is difficult to assess. In spite of independent accounting, the activities of Watson's and the other 600 firms within the Unilever 'family', were circumscribed by the Central executive Committees. Watson's output from the 1930s was largely determined by the requirements of the group as a whole, and its ability to respond to dynamic demands was critical to its success. Its capacity to shift from its traditional emphasis on soap to the more varied demand for toiletries during the Second World War and beyond ensured its position at the centre of Unilever's new Toiletries Division in the early 1950s. Without this dynamism, Watson's may well have suffered the same fate as the other soap producers which were closed down in the late 1940s. In its new role, Watson's raw material requirements continued to be handled by Unilever through its trading company, *UAC*.[29] The marketing of Watson's products was arranged by a separate trading organization and largely determined by the Unilever centre. The firm's research and development programme was at least partly centrally conducted.

Following its amalgamation with Gibbs and Pepsodent in 1962, the activities of the company were structured by the co-ordinated strategy of the central Unilever organization. Since the establishment of Elida Gibbs in 1971, the operations of the firm are controlled by the Personal Products Co-ordination Group. This develops strategy in conjunction with the Boards of each of the toiletries-producing firms within Unilever. This Group, of which Elida Gibbs is a prominent member, establishes planning procedures and contributes to strategic thinking. Thus, the position of each of the Associated Companies and its interaction with the centre, can be understood in terms of a strategic planning model.[30] Within this context, the *corporate mission* established at the centre, guides developments across the business units. The control process provides some scope for individual firm initiative. Performance targets are set in broad strategic terms. Annual financial targets are considered less important than longer term strategic objectives. The mechanisms for control allow some flexibility and at the same time ensure that the activities of all member companies are complementary and well integrated.[31]

Within the Unilever Toiletries operation, Elida Gibbs makes independent decisions about relatively modest capital expenditure, about advertising styles and strategies and about product diversification. It implements its own product and packaging development programme. Its links with the centre, however, and with other companies within the Group are pervasive and unavoidable. A product developed by Elida Gibbs, for example, might be placed with another company within the Group for manufacturing. Equally, financial assistance for a major capital project might be forthcoming from the central unit. Operational control from the centre, however, is minimal unless the performance and profitability of the firm gives cause for concern.[32]

III

The soap industry developed on the basis of continual innovation in product and process. The discovery that soap making constituted a chemical process marked a turning point in the history of the soap industry and of the organization of the manufacturing firms within it. Traditionally, soap making was perceived as a mechanical activity, where animal fat and alkali were combined during a lengthy process of boiling to produce a solid block. Imported olive oil was occasionally substituted for the harder fat to produce a more malleable item. The scientific foundations of soap production became established late in the eighteenth century by Leblanc's pioneering work on the chemical composition of soda and by the discovery, in the nineteenth century, of the fundamental principles of the saponification process. A valuable by-product of this chemical process was glycerine which enhanced the profitability of the soap industry. The progress in the theoretical understanding of soap production was maintained through sustained research and development, which in turn brought long term changes to the scale and organization of its manufacture and to the range of products.[33]

Changes in the nature of soap and in the uses to which soap were put were particularly pronounced during the inter-war years. For centuries a single product sufficed for the cleansing of person, clothing and household. Marketing and technical developments from the late nineteenth century onwards, however, created diverse products with specialized functions. Laundry soap dominated the market during the early twentieth century and by the 1930s became available in a variety of forms. Bars, powders and flakes each served a specific purpose. A special soap for dish-washing was also created during this time. In the late 1930s toilet soap was the fastest growing area of sales. Developments in theoretical chemistry also encouraged the creation of such novel soap-based products as dry soaps and saponaceous cosmetics which included vanishing

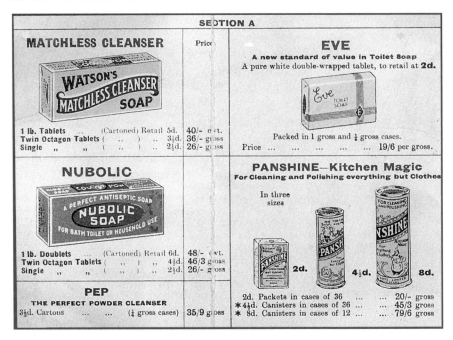

Plate 8.3   A range of Watson's best-selling products in the first forty years of the twentieth century.

creams and face powders and wet and dry shampoos. The dental creams and pastes of the 1920s contained a large proportion of soap, but later incorporated a greater silicate content.[34] After the Second World War, the focus of product development was on shampoo and other such soap-based toiletries as toothpaste and deodorants. The potential of this group especially in the overseas market was recognized by Unilever, which supported its growth through substantial research and development effort in the 1950s and 1960s.

In the early days of Joseph Watson and Sons, the production of soap owed little to chemical knowledge. Subsequently, however, the firm was to be instrumental in developing the scientific basis of the soap industry. The firm's raw material records indicate changes both in its product structure and in manufacturing techniques. It was known from the eighteenth century that soap could be made from a number of alternative oils each one generating a product of different appearance, texture and lathering quality. By the 1920s, properties of individual oils and their significance in soap manufacture had become more widely known. It was established that both coconut oil and palm kernel oil produced extremely hard and rather abrasive soaps with excellent cleansing properties. Coconut oil was particularly suitable for shaving and toilet soap. Palm kernel oil made the best household and dry soap. It was unusual for a soap to contain less than two or even three different oils.[35] The best toilet soap at this time was produced with a mixture of tallow and coconut oil.[36] By the 1930s, Soapy Joe's was consuming large quantities of palm kernel oil (PKO), as well as increasing amounts of cottonseed and soyabean oil, which were the essential ingredients for the new soap powders and flakes. As Table 8.1 shows, Watson's proportionate consumption of the various oils fluctuated year by year, partly because of product diversification but also in response to changes in the world market for fats and oils.

From the early days, Watson's soap manufacture embraced scientific principles. During the 1880s, the firm acquired the services of Dr Julius Lewkowitsch, a highly qualified chemist, who was placed in charge of a special glycerine refining works. Subsequently, the firm's commitment to research and development both before and during its time as part of the Unilever Group was an essential feature of its success. In the years before the Second World War progress in theoretical chemistry stimulated substantial product innovation. Process innovation, however, was limited. Thus, soap was produced in the same way in 1945 as it had been at the end of the nineteenth century. It was still boiled in pans, though these had become much larger. The manufacturing process remained batch though progress in continuous production after the Second World War was pronounced. In the post-war period great emphasis was placed on the pooling of research findings among the Associated Companies of Unilever. Watson's thus enjoyed the advantages of membership of a large group. Unilever established a number of independent research laboratories in addition to the development units attached to operating com-

Table 8.1 Joseph Watson and Sons Ltd., Consumption of Raw Materials (tons)

	Tallow	Palm Oil	PKO	Caustic Soda	Soda Ash	Salt
1931	3302	514	2425	1900	2634	2340
1932	2827	828	2327	1842	2540	2359
1933	1723	1952	2242	1879	2947	2835
1934	1004	2000	1902	1513	2298	2793
1942	1803	5484	1973	2434	4488	
1943	560	5337	2395	2272	4298	
1944	314	5242	2645	2510	3499	
1945	162	5757	1812	2259	3715	3552
1946	31	3189	2528	1530	1021	2572
1947	2	3953	2111	1565	408	2239
1948	126	4927	2165	1577	454	314
1950	3652	4573	1818	2018	186	2235
1951	2107	4494	71	1601	157	2114
1952	2416	896	9	782	94	1354

Source: Joseph Watson and Sons Ltd, Materials Stock Book, Unilever Historical Archives.

panies. By 1965, eleven major research establishments and many laboratories, together employing £10m worth of research staff, supplied the necessary innovation for the Unilever Companies to succeed within an increasingly competitive environment. Although such concentrated endeavour resulted in some duplication of results, it did maximize the chances of a successful discovery.[37]

The post-war transition in Watson's product base from soap to toiletries was integral to Unilever's long term strategy. The peculiar nature of toilet preparations and the market in which they competed, required intensive research and development effort. The short life span typical of many toiletry products suggested a greater emphasis on product innovation than was the case for other products within the soap group. In the 1960s research expenditure on toiletries was twice that of any other area of the Unilever soap group.[38] Commercial and technical considerations rank equally high. The success of Watson and more recently Elida Gibbs is testimony to the effective and enduring effort in marketing and technique.

IV

One hundred years ago the title 'Soapy Joe's' accurately described the product of the firm. Soap dominated Watson's production until the outbreak of the Second World War. Since then the structure of its product has changed several times. Currently, in 1993, the Elida Gibbs factory at Seacroft manufactures a greater variety of brands and products than any other Unilever plant.[39] Most of the items now made were unknown a century ago, and reflect progress in theoretical chemistry, industrial research and development, and innovations in marketing and advertising.

From the outset, Joseph Watson's soap making business made healthy profits. The substantial growth of the 1870s and 1880s was replaced by staggering expansion between 1893 and 1918. Soapy Joe's had transformed itself from just one of several Leeds soap boilers with a sideline in skin and hide dealing, to one of the nation's giant soap manufacturers. By 1917, the daily soap output of the firm exceeded its annual production of the 1880s.[40] In 1882, vat capacity was 160 tons. By the 1890s, it had reached 460 tons. In 1902, when a new mill equipped with electricity was added, the soap making capacity of the works approached three times its level of ten years earlier. The recovery and sale of glycerine, a by-product of the soap-making process, was vital to the overall profitability of the soap industry. Watson's engaged fully in this activity, and its own glycerine refining plant, established in 1886, supported a highly lucrative subsidiary interest.[41]

In 1897, Watson became incorporated as a public company with an authorized capital of £1.4m.[42] For the next twenty years the profits of the firm averaged £65,000 per annum.[43] The inter-war years marked a significant period of growth, as Fig 8.1 indicates. Profits stood at £265,000 in 1918 and £518,000 a year later. A noticeable dip in 1920 was replaced by unusually high profits in 1921. Through most of the 1920s annual profit levels lay between £200,000 and £300,000 and a peak of £350,000 was reached in 1930. The financial performance of the firm was most impressive during the worst years of the depression. As British economic activity picked up after 1932, Watson's profits slumped, reaching a trough of £93,000 in 1938.[44] This tendency to perform counter-cyclically was not unusual among soap manufacturers, and partly reflected the lower raw material prices during years of depression.

Watson's achieved a commendable profit performance during the Second World War as a result of extensive product diversification. Thereafter pressure on the firm's finances allowed profits to fall to just £35,000 in 1951–2.[45] For a short time during the later 1950s, the firm moved more convincingly into the black, and annual average profits exceeded £100,000 for the first time in over ten years. In the early 1960s profits dipped again to levels more typical of 1900 than of the heyday of the inter-war period. Thereafter the company underwent several changes of persona and a new lease of life. Organizational changes allowed steady increases in production and profit. By 1987, pre-tax profits had reached more than £9m. In 1991, sales turnover stood at £162m.[46]

Production trends follow closely those of profits. Watson's output multiplied in the pre-war years and by 1918, had reached over 30,000 tons. The

Figure 8.1 Joseph Watson and Sons Ltd, net profit 1918–62

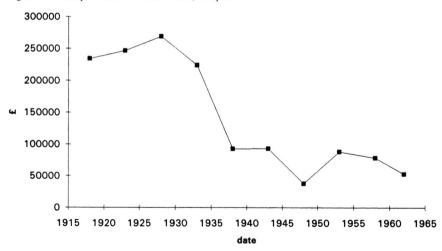

Source: Joseph Watson and Sons Ltd, annual profit figures, Unilever Historical Archives.

hard soaps—*Matchless Cleanser*, *Nubolic* and *Sparkla*—dominated production. During the later 1920s production levels and sales of hard soap fell following the withdrawal of the prize wrapper scheme which had supported previous expansion. Output was maintained during the years of depression, but from 1932 through the remainder of the 1930s, production of hard soap fell.[47] The growth areas of powders, including dry shampoo and flakes, accounted for only a small proportion of the total. Production of glycerine and caustic soda remained constant throughout. In spite of the wartime contraction of the soap market, Watson's production of hard soap was well-sustained. Buoyancy in output of powders was also achieved, but expansion was concentrated in the new shampoo and toothpaste products. During the 1950s, Watson's consolidated its role as manufacturer and packer for a group of Unilever selling companies, and, while it continued to produce growing quantities of toothpaste and shampoo,[48] it extended its range to include toilet water, shaving creams and hair preparations for export. Value of production which stood at around £8m during the 1960s, slumped during the recession of the 1970s, but recovered during the 1980s to reach unprecedented levels. In 1986 turnover stood at £102m and trading profit at £7m. By 1988 turnover had reached £142m and trading profit £11m.[49]

The records of Watson's output reveal a remarkable continuity of product between 1890 and 1940. A single brand of household soap *Matchless Cleanser* dominated the figures. This item together with *Nubolic* and *Sparkla* formed the basis of the firm's wealth. The Whitehall Road factory was known for many decades as Watson's 'Matchless Cleanser' soap works, and 80 per cent of the firm's profits in the 1920s and 1930s was attributable to this remarkable product.[50] *Matchless Cleanser* was advertised as an 'ideal soap', made from the 'choicest and purest' materials. It was sold as a good general purpose washing medium, but also had medicinal uses. It was recommended for the removal of ringworm from children's heads, for example. The development of *Nubolic* accompanied a growing awareness of the importance of personal and domestic hygiene. It combined the cleansing and detergent qualities of *Matchless Cleanser* with powerful disinfectant and antiseptic properties. It was marketed both as an excellent toilet soap and as an unrivalled floor scrubbing compound. *Sparkla*, the third brand in the 'famous three', performed scouring and polishing functions. It apparently 'cleaned and brightened everything' except clothes, and was advertised in the early years of the twentieth century as a 'state of the art' cleanser.[51]

Important changes in product began to appear during the 1930s, as shown in Table 8.2. These reflected developments in technique and in consumer preference. Watson's trading accounts reveal the growth of toilet and shaving soaps as well as dry soaps, flakes and powders. The variety suggested by this list in fact masks the underlying similarities in manufacturing inputs and processes.

Table 8.2   Joseph Watson and Sons Ltd., Output (Tons)

Date	Hard soap	Toilet soap	Soap flakes	Soap powder	Shampoo	Toothpaste	Glycerine
1918	30354						
1919	27925						
1921	15949						
1922	17446						
1924	18410						
1926	16035						
1927	12157						
1928	15538						
1929	14680	133	468	574			958
1930	15277	139	439	557			1044
1931	15784	127	295	589			1090
1932	15476	92	279	601			1021
1934	13613	42	280	661			881
1935	13522	33	319	927	56		918
1936	12379	112	303	1016	36		804
1937	13285	51	327	1502	62		904
1938	13273	54	428	1916	65		994
1939	12461	19	1119	1629	77		902
1940	13715		589	1859	53		869
1941	19151		660	3464	24	141	1335
1942	17218		82	2924	74	301	1243
1943	15946			3163	131	334	1153
1944	18371			3325	120	325	1134
1945	17942			2515	150	346	1099
1946	13656				194	504	
1947	14168				192	836	
1948	14660				143	1493	
1950	18150				78	1295	
1952	6073				44	2208	

Source: Joseph Watson and Sons Ltd., Sales reports, Unilever Historical Archives.

The products were differentiated only by the proportion and quality of the raw materials used. The most significant innovation of this era was the soapless shampoo *Eve* which marked the onset of Watson's transition from a manufacturer of soap to one with a major interest in hair care products.[52]

The next stage of Watson's product diversification occurred during the Second World War when soap manufacture was restricted through rationing. The future of Soapy Joe's was secured by the flexibility of production it achieved at this time. The firm's contribution to the war effort concentrated on the production of hand grenades, rifle grenades, anti-tank grenades, bomb tail units, and valve bodies for the J bomb, all of which made use of the glycerine by-product of the soap making process.[53] The firm also produced toothpaste during the war, which signalled the developing relationship with Gibbs. It also expanded further into shampoo production. This pattern of

Plate 8.4 A *Matchless Cleanser* Prize Wrapper. The highly successful prize scheme captured the public imagination and substantially boosted the sales of Watson's products. The scheme, which was adopted by other soap producers, lasted for fifty years in various forms.

diversification was perceived as a short term expedient, but the expected revival of soap production at Whitehall Road never materialized. A little soap was manufactured there after the war, but by the early 1950s the emphasis was on the production of toiletries which had been diverted from other Unilever companies. In 1952, soap production at Whitehall Road ceased completely.

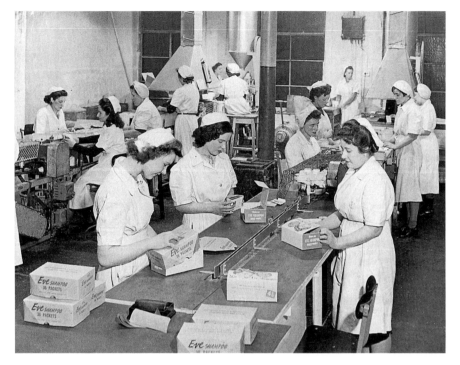

Plate 8.5   The packaging of *Eve* shampoo at Whitehall Road during the late 1940s. Shampoo was to become one of the major products at Watson's and its successor companies. The enduring *Sunsilk* and the more recent *Timotei* are justifiably the most famous.

The factory was stripped of its soap making equipment in anticipation of its role as Unilever's Personal Products division.[54]

The production of Unilever toiletries at Whitehall Road began openly from 1953, although its most successful item, *Mentasol*, a chlorophyll toothpaste, had been developed there covertly for some time.[55] By the mid 1950s, the Whitehall Road works produced 119 distinct items, in 437 packages, which were marketed by ten Unilever selling companies including Pears, Gibbs, Crosfields, and Atkinsons. Several years later, Watson's had become the largest single toiletries manufacturing unit in the UK and the largest toothpaste unit in Europe.[56] For a short time after amalgamation with Gibbs and Pepsodent in 1962, expansion was concentrated on the production of toothpaste. Later in the 1960s, however, the introduction of a new range of skin and hair products reflected the company's desire to reduce its dependence on a single sector. The aim of the company, as stated in the 1968 Annual Report, was that within four years, the structure of its output would be 35 per cent dental, 35 per cent hair care, and 30 per cent skin care and pharmaceuticals.

Accordingly, a growing market was secured for home perms, especially *PinUp*, *End Curl*, and *Twink*, for shampoos in sachets and for hair dyes and tints. Improvements in shaving stick design boosted sales of *Erasmic*. During the mid 1960s aerosol technology was applied to shaving foam, hair sprays such as *Sunsilk* and *Clynol*, and deodorants. In 1971 the output structure of the company, now Elida Gibbs, was subtly changed to enhance the position of deodorants.[57]

Since the early 1970s, the company's unquestioned strength in each of its three core areas of toothpaste, deodorants and hair care is revealed in its sustained position among the market leaders.[58] This has been achieved by building on traditional strengths and increasing the range of brands within its existing portfolio. Current policy for survival, however, combines 'innovative approaches in manufacturing systems' with the search for new and exciting products which are essential to the maintenance of market share.[59] Not all novel products contribute to the financial well-being of the company, however, as the fateful 1970s excursion into sunglasses exemplifies.[60] In 1987, following the acquisition of the skin care specialists Chesebrough-Ponds Ltd., Elida Gibbs supplied 20 per cent of the British market for shampoo and conditioner, and almost 30 per cent of the hair spray market. It also met 20 per cent of demand for skin care products and accounted for 30 per cent of deodorant sales. Thus it maintained a strong position in every key area of the personal products market, outpacing Beecham, Colgate, Proctor and Gamble, and Gillette, its main rivals.[61] The company is justly renowned both for product innovation and for longevity of brands. *Sure* and *Vaseline* continue to generate demand several decades after their original appearance. In 1991, male fragrance and shower gels entered the Elida Gibbs sale figures for the first time, and this sector is likely to become the growth area of the 1990s.[62]

V

The soap business was a pioneer of modern advertising. Even now, the highly competitive industry into which Joseph Watson diversified over a century ago, stands at the forefront of creative selling. Various techniques to enhance market share were developed late in the nineteenth century to counter the downward pressure on the rate of growth of demand. The most popular forms of publicity in the early days included such pictorial advertisements as posters and hand-bills. Those for *Pears* soap and *Sunlight* are justifiably the most memorable. Watson pioneered mobile advertising. Travelling salesmen in decorated horse and carriage were employed to promote *Venus* soap, Watson's earliest product.[63] The most spectacular results, however, were achieved through nationwide competitions. The success of these drew the larger soap manufacturers apart from the rest of the field and accelerated the demise of the smaller businesses.

The publicity generated by the Prize Wrapper scheme, for which both Joseph Watson and William Lever claimed credit, greatly enhanced the profitability of the two companies.[64] The scheme, introduced in the 1880s, continued to the 1930s with only minor alterations. Prizes, which ranged from teaspoons to a house, were exchanged for appropriate quantities of soap wrappers. Such was the force with which the scheme took off, that Watson's soon required new premises and 250 additional staff to provide the necessary administration. At its peak, Watson's employed as many sales representatives as shop floor staff. Even the Post Office in Leeds city centre was forced to acquire additional staff and buildings during the forty years of the scheme's existence.[65] The cost of this form of publicity for Watson's was estimated to be £10 per ton of soap sold.[66]

Following the formation of Unilever, its Associated Companies accounted for the bulk of Watson's sales. These companies financed the direct costs of manufacture and contributed to indirect expenses. During the 1940s Watson's toothpaste sales of £500,000 per annum consisted of *SR* and *Solidox* for D. and W. Gibbs. Shampoo accounted for the remaining sales, 70 per cent of which was *Eve* for CWG.[67] Most of the remainder was *Gloria* for A. and F. Pears. As Watson became the focus of Unilever's toiletries' production during the 1950s, sales to Associated Companies rose steadily and were valued at £2.75m in 1958. Toothpaste produced for Gibbs and for Pepsodent accounted for 65 per cent of this figure. CWG and Unilever Export Ltd each took a further 10 per cent of sales.[68] In 1961 immediately prior to the merger of Watson, Gibbs and Pepsodent, the sales to the latter two companies were even more overwhelming.[69]

The formation of Gibbs Pepsodent in 1962 with an independent marketing function, coincided with a particularly volatile and competitive period in the marketing of toiletries, in a trade whose oligopolistic structure indicates the importance of product differentiation through branding. The company operated in tight markets and felt justified in spending massive amounts on publicity. In 1963, with the launch of its range of combined toiletries' products, Gibbs Pepsodent allocated 37 per cent of its £3m turnover to advertising.[70] The introduction of commercial television in 1965 presented irresistible, if expensive opportunities for participants in the competitive toiletries' business to enhance their market share. Gibbs Pepsodent was at the forefront of television advertising. The first advertisement to appear on British television was that for *SR Tingling Fresh*. The company retained its commitment to this form of publicity and since the mid 1960s television promotion has absorbed the bulk of its large advertising budget.[71]

Plate 8.6   Filling tubes of toothpaste at Whitehall Road in the 1940s. Most of Watson's toothpaste production at this time was for D. and W. Gibbs with whom they subsequently merged. As Elida Gibbs, the company now controls one-fifth of the British toothpaste market.

The incorporation of Elida and the formation of Elida Gibbs in 1971 strengthened the company's position in the hair product market. By 1972, *Sunsilk* alone accounted for 13 per cent of the £25m shampoo market.[72] The market for hair care products was and remains distinguished by low growth, high competitiveness and very low levels of brand loyalty. The sales of these products, therefore, are even more influenced by advertising than other toiletries.[73] Elida Gibbs' publicity in this area during the 1970s emphasized the distinctiveness of products and highlighted the original attributes of newly developed items. This approach succeeded in the cases of 2in1 and Protein shampoos; but the campaign to promote the anti-dandruff shampoos, which have enjoyed some popularity in recent years, failed spectacularly in the early 1970s.[74]

Elida Gibbs has also sustained high profile marketing of toothpaste, building on its successful promotion of *SR* in the 1960s. *Close-Up* was launched in

1972 using the concept of the 'Close-Up zone' to challenge Colgate's 'Ring of Confidence'.[75] Such was the success of this promotion that it was later alleged that sales of *Close-Up* had increased the size of the market and had not been achieved purely at the expense of other brands. The toothpaste campaign of the early 1970s was consolidated with the relaunch of *Signal* as *Signal 2* (with fluoride) and *SR* as *Arctic Fresh SR*.[76] By the late 1980s, £30m per annum was allocated to advertising, almost twice the amount spent on raw materials and well over double the entire wages and salaries' bill. The company believes that this extraordinary expenditure has been necessary to maintain Elida Gibbs share of the core markets. It currently holds 17 per cent of the £331m hair care market, 17 per cent of the £197m skin care market, 20 per cent of toothpaste (£119m) and 36 per cent of deodorants (£118m).[77]

VI

In 1893, Watson's was a large firm by contemporary standards. Of its 700 employees, one-third were sales representatives and 50 were clerks and managers.[78] Production workers made up the rest. Until the Second World War, total wages and salaries of managerial and sales staff stood consistently at twice the wage bill for all shop floor workers. The total number of employees remained fairly static until the end of the First World War. Thereafter employment fluctuated in line with production. Thus by 1927 the workforce had fallen to 570, of which 300 were productive workers. During the 1930s as employment particularly in the packing section grew, the number of productive workers rose to 450. The proportion of the workforce engaged in non-manufacturing activities was sharply reduced upon the separation of the selling and productive functions of Watson's in 1937. During the Second World War, expansion of the manufacturing section reflected both the firm's contribution to the war effort, and its diversification into toothpaste and shampoo. Between 1940 and 1943, the workforce doubled through the recruitment of additional female workers for munitions' production. The removal of Government contracts caused some redundancies before the end of the war, but the revival of soap and toothpaste production in the late 1940s expanded the workforce once more.

Production at Watson's ceased completely for six months in 1953, but employment remained stable. Four hundred women and 200 men were engaged in the preparation of the factory for its new role as toiletries' producer. The subsequent growth of output was reflected in the size of the workforce. At its peak in 1959, the Whitehall Road factory employed 1200 people, of whom 1000 were women. The total number of employees changed little during the

1960s and 1970s. Well over 1000 people, predominantly women are currently employed at the new factory at Seacroft.[79]

A pronounced gender division of labour has always characterized work at Soapy Joe's. Women's employment has embraced clerical, packing and sorting functions, all of which have become steadily more important over the years. Men's jobs which mainly entailed manufacturing and selling have accounted for a smaller proportion of the total since the 1930s. Women played a particularly significant role in the administration of the Prize Wrapper scheme. Women processed the daily mountain of coupons and organized the selection and dispatch of prizes. At its peak in 1908, 250 people, mostly women, were employed in the prize department.[80] As the Scheme was dismantled in the 1930s, women's work became concentrated in 'packing' activities. Packing incorporated a greater variety of functions than the description implies. Such tasks as the filling of toothpaste tubes, shampoo bottles and sachets, the placing of hot wax into tins for *Kurl-Out* for the West African market, and the boxing of these for dispatch, accounted for a large proportion of the productive work at Watson's.[81] This category of work was particularly susceptible to fluctuations in trade and as a result, women's employment at Watson's was less stable than men's.

The flexibility of women's work, which was not confined to this firm, was revealed in both frequent changes in working conditions, especially between shift systems and relay work, and in strikingly rapid turnover. Despite the growing proportion of women workers (5:1 by 1963) and their crucial role in the success of the company, women seem to have been undervalued. The annual reports of the company from the 1940s reveal exceptionally high rates of movement in and out of employment, with many women leaving and re-entering several times during any given year. In the late 1940s for instance, total time lost by women was more than twice that of men and stood at 20 per cent of actual hours worked. The bulk of this loss was through 'sickness' (twice the male level) and 'other causes' (seven times the male level), while time lost as the result of accidents was much less than that for men. Fifty per cent of the female workforce was married at this stage, and child care difficulties probably explain both the high level of lost time and the high rate of turnover.[82]

Turnover increased during the 1950s and 1960s. In 1955, for instance, 16 per cent of female workers resigned before completing one month of service. The comparable figure in 1970 was 26 per cent. In 1955, one-third and in 1970, two-thirds of women resigned in less than three months, while fifty per cent and eighty per cent respectively failed to survive more than six months. This poor employment record was not perceived as a constraint on the company's performance, nor was it seen as an indication of dissatisfaction among the female employees. The management interpreted the volatility in terms of the

Plate 8.7 Packaging *Mazo* in the early 1940s. The bulk of women workers at Watson's were engaged in packing, which included filling bottles and tubes, wrapping bars of soap and preparing cartons for dispatch.

peculiar local labour market conditions about which they could do little; and failed to secure a more committed female workforce through improved conditions of work.

The male experience of work at Watson's was quite different. Before the formation of a separate trading company in 1937, an extensive marketing and sales staff was employed. These, and the executive and managerial staff, were exclusively male. Manufacturing employment was likewise confined to men. Over time, the move to the greater automation of the production process has reduced the demand for men's work. There has been a steady decline in the proportion of men in the workforce since the Second World War.

In terms of remuneration, Watson's was relatively generous. Such relevant evidence as exists suggests that employees were often paid above the standard rates. In 1958, for instance, unskilled workers at Watson's received about fifteen per cent above the Leeds minimum rate for the job; while those in the skilled sector earned almost twenty per cent more than the minimum. Wage costs as a proportion of the company's turnover has ranged between eight and thirteen per cent throughout the period since 1918, with the higher levels in more recent years.[83] In addition to basic wages, the workers at Watsons and successor companies, have had access to various bonus schemes. Piece rates were quite common in the years before the Second World War, and in the 1950s, a job evaluation system, redolent of scientific management, was introduced whereby each worker was allocated a 'job rate' based on the mental and physical requirements of the task.[84] In the packing section, for instance, the standard set for each operation was expressed in 'Girl Hours per gross'. This was regarded as a measure of efficiency, though in fact it was based entirely on estimation and experience. The figure enabled production managers to estimate employee requirements and it formed the basis on which Watsons recovered costs from the selling companies for whom they manufactured and packaged products.[85]

The principles underlying this scheme and the incentive payments associated with it, gradually lost popularity among both workers and managers, and in the mid 1960s, following an extensive work study programme, it was replaced by the Standard Achievement Payment. This rewarded exceptional performance, and as such it was designed to enhance 'efficiency', that is, productivity and profitability. The investigations from which this scheme emerged established a 'Standard Performance' or a normal day rate of working. The workers in any department achieving more than ten per cent above the standard during the course of a week would be suitably rewarded.[86] The scheme was apparently accepted by the workforce and was a feature of the company's industrial relations strategy, yet ultimately it was divisive and produced dissent.

In general the company was satisfied with its industrial relations record and low incidence of strike activity. Joseph Watson was a typical paternalist employer; and many of the trappings of late nineteenth century paternalism have persisted within the firm to the present. Watson's took the welfare of its employees seriously and provided the usual range of facilities including in-house health treatment, convalescence homes and support for the chronically sick. The ubiquitous works outing was instigated in the 1880s, along with regular sporting activities. Christmas entertainments for the workforce and their families provided the social high point of the year.[87]

VII

This chapter has illustrated the vitality of Joseph Watson and Sons Ltd. and its successor companies in a dynamic and competitive market. In recent decades, the competition among producers of soap and toiletries has become increasingly intense. The integration of the European market has introduced new opportunities and new challenges for such producers. Elida Gibbs appears to be responding to the European challenge. It is sustaining its position as the largest manufacturer of mass market toiletry brands in the UK through a continuous process of self improvement. The company's commitment to 'Total quality' and its goal of 'manufacturing excellence' are recent indications of its quest to remain on top.[88] It is seeking to establish a more flexible business capable of responding rapidly to customer and consumer needs. By the end of 1993, Elida Gibbs should be placed to secure a long term future within the European market.[89]

Notes

[1] I am indebted to Peter Collins, formerly Technical Director of Elida Gibbs Ltd, for providing access to documentary material and his own wealth of knowledge, and for his unstinting support and advice. Thanks also to Graham Sykes for research assistance; to Jeanette Strickland, Archivist at Unilever Historical Archives for kindness in supplying information and illustrations; and to my colleagues at the Centre for Business History, University of Leeds, especially Stephen Caunce and Michael Collins, for valuable comments on a draft of this chapter.

[2] For more detail on the complex history of Unilever, consult Charles Wilson, *The History of Unilever: A Study in Economic Growth and Social Change* vol. 1 and 2, 1954.

[3] Charles Wilson, *The History of Unilever...*, vol. 3, 1962, p. 160.

[4] Information kindly supplied by Maureen Staniforth, Unilever House, London.

[5] Thanks to Peter Collins for this piece of information.

[6] Jane McBretney, *'Soapy Joe's': The story of a great factory 1861–1987*, 1987, p. 27.

[7] Wilson, *History of Unilever*, vol. 1, p. 9.

[8] An additional catalyst was the 1848 outbreak of cholera which changed the British attitude to washing and ended the soap tax which had been levied since the mid-seventeenth century.

[9] Alastair Laurence, *Woodside and its industries*, 1985, p. 28.

[10] ''A good thing to come out of Yorkshire'. The genesis of Matchless cleanser', *Progress*, 176, July 1927, p. 196.

[11] McBretney, *Soapy Joe's*, p. 5.

[12] Glycerine became a valuable by-product of the soap-making process and enabled some of the more marginal soap manufacturers to survive. Glycerine was available in two qualities: dynamite quality and the more refined 'chemically pure' glycerine. The market for both grew from the late nineteenth century and the two World Wars provided additional impetus for dynamite glycerine.

[13] Wilson, *History of Unilever*, vol. 1, pp. 11–13.

[14] The lathering qualities of this particular soap distinguished it from the earlier tallow soaps. *ibid*, p. 28.

[15] *ibid* pp. 9–20.

[16] P. Baring, 'Joseph Watson and Sons Ltd.', *Progress*, Autumn 1951, p. 43.

[17] McBretney, *Soapy Joe's*, p. 5.

[18] *ibid*, p. 7.

[19] Baring, 'Joseph Watson', p. 45.

[20] Unpublished ms on Soap Trust, Unilever Historical Archives.

[21] Wilson, *History of Unilever*, vol. 2, appendix 10.

[22] A. E. Musson, *Enterprise in Soap and Chemicals: Crosfields of Warrington 1815–1965*, 1965, p. 287.

[23] W. J. Reader, *Fifty Years of Unilever*, 1980, p. 24.

[24] Musson, *Crosfields*, p. 320–23.

[25] Joseph Watson and Sons Ltd, Sales Reports 1940–48, now at Unilever Historical Archives.

[26] Watson, however, did produce shaving soap, in stick form, from soap chips supplied by Port Sunlight and, until its closure, by Christopher Thomas Bros. of Bristol. Information from Geoffrey Chappell.

[27] Joseph Watson and Sons Ltd. and D. and W. Gibbs Sales Reports, 1945–65, now at Unilever Historical Archives.

[28] Information kindly supplied by Maureen Staniforth, Unilever House, London.

[29] United Africa Company. Reader, *Fifty Years*, p. 22 and 36.

[30] M. Goold and A. Campbell, *Strategies and Styles: The role of the centre in managing diversified corporations*, 1989, p. 42.

[31] Information kindly supplied by Peter Collins.

[32] I am indebted to Peter Collins for clarifying this point.

[33] Wilson, *History of Unilever*, vol. 1, pp. 10–20.

[34] The information in this paragraph comes from E. T. Webb, *Modern Soap and Glycerine Manufacture*, 1927, chs 1 and 2. I am grateful to Layth Alsaffar for identifying this reference and for other scientific information.

[35] Webb, *Modern Soap*, pp. 25–31.

[36] *ibid*, p. 25.

[37] Wilson, *History of Unilever*, vol. 3, p. 66.

[38] Wilson, *History of Unilever*, vol. 3, p. 67.

[39] *ibid*, p. 160.

[40] Joseph Watson and Sons Ltd, Production figures. Now stored at Unilever Historical Archives.

[41] McBretney, p. 6.

[42] Leeds Chamber of Commerce, 'Men who made Leeds: Joseph Watson'. nd.

[43] *ibid*.

[44] Joseph Watson and Sons Ltd., Profit figures. Now at Unilever Historical Archives.

[45] *ibid*.

[46] Elida Gibbs Ltd, Annual Reports, 1987–91, Unilever Historical Archives.

[47] Joseph Watson and Sons Ltd., Production figures, Unilever Historical Archives.

[48] Especially for D. and W. Gibbs, Pears and Pepsodent.

[49] Elida Gibbs Ltd, Annual Reports 1986–8. Unilever Historical Archives.

[50] Joseph Watson and Sons Ltd., Profit figures. Unilever Historical Archives.

[51] Joseph Watson and Sons Ltd., 'How d'you do?' book, 1907. This booklet contained cleaning and household hints, and was used as an advertising medium.

[52] Joseph Watson and Sons Ltd., Sales Report, 1934. Unilever Historical Archives.

[53] Joseph Watson and Sons Ltd., Technical Reports, 1941–43. Unilever Historical archives.

[54] Joseph Watson and Sons Ltd., Annual Report, 1952. Unilever Historical Archives.

[55] Secrecy was necessary because it was one of the real innovative toothpastes of its time. In the early days it was hugely successful. I am grateful to Geoffrey Chappell for this information.

[56] Gibbs Proprietaries Ltd. Annual Report, 1969. Unilever Historical Archives.

[57] Gibbs Proprietaries Ltd. and Elida Gibbs Ltd. Annual Reports, 1965–71. Unilever Historical Archives.

[58] Elida Gibbs Ltd, Annual Reports, 1971–91. Unilever Historical Archives.

[59] Elida Gibbs Ltd, Annual Report 1992. Unilever Historical Archives.

[60] McBretney, *Soapy Joe's*, p. 25; and information supplied by Peter Collins.

[61] Elida Gibbs Ltd, Annual Report 1987. Unilever historical Archives.

[62] Elida Gibbs Ltd, Annual Report 1991. Unilever historical Archives.

[63] Baring, 'Joseph Watson', p. 44.

[64] *ibid*, p. 45.

[65] McBretney, *Soapy Joe's*, pp. 8–9.

[66] Joseph Watson and Sons Ltd., Annual Reports, 1930–34. Unilever Historical Archives.

[67] Crosfield, Watson and Gossage was the selling arm of Joseph Watson and Sons Ltd.

[68] Joseph Watson and Sons Ltd., Sales Reports 1953–58. Unilever Historical Archives.

[69] Joseph Watson and Sons Ltd., Sales Report 1961. Unilever Historical Archives.

[70] According to Geoffrey Chappell, it was the first UK company ever to spend more than £1m in one year on advertising.

[71] This has stood consistently at 25–30 per cent of annual sales. Annual Reports 1963–91. Unilever Historical Archives.

[72] *Campaign*, 14 January 1972.

[73] *Campaign*, 21 January 1972.

[74] *Campaign*, 14 January 1972.

[75] *Campaign*, 17 April 1972.

[76] *Retail Chemist*, 27 April 1972.

[77] Elida Gibbs Ltd, Annual Reports, 1988–91. Unilever Historical Archives.

[78] McBretney, *Soapy Joe's*, p. 6.

[79] Annual Reports 1960–1980. Unilever Historical Archives.

[80] McBretney, *Soapy Joe's*, p. 9.

[81] Baring, 'Joseph Watson', p. 45.

[82] Gibbs Proprietaries Ltd. Report of Man (sic) Hours Worked, 1965. Unilever Historical Archives.

[83] Elida Gibbs Ltd, Annual Reports, 1987–91. Unilever Historical Archives.

[84] Baring, 'Joseph Watson', p. 48.

[85] Gibbs Proprietaries Ltd., Work Study Report, 1965. Unilever historical Archives.

[86] *ibid*.

[87] McBretney, *Soapy Joe's*, pp. 13 and 20–1.

[88] Elida Gibbs Ltd, Annual Report 1992. Unilever Historical Archives.

[89] This was the thrust of the message contained in *Link Line*, the Elida Gibbs newspaper for employees and pensioners, October, 1992. Kindly provided by Peter Collins.

CHAPTER 9

Chas. F. Thackray Ltd: suppliers to the surgeons

Penny Wainwright

W HEN Charles Frederick Thackray and Henry Scurrah Wainwright bought a Leeds retail pharmacy as a going concern in 1902, they could hardly have foreseen that their business would one day expand to employ more than 700 people, with markets all over the world. In less than a century, the corner shop was to grow into one of Britain's principal medical companies, manufacturing drugs and instruments, and pioneering the hip replacement operation which has changed the lives of hundreds of thousands of people.

The story begins with Charles Thackray's predecessor, Samuel Taylor, who came to Leeds from York as a young man in 1862. He took over a fruit and game dealer's premises in Great George Street to set up his own pharmacy. Leeds, suffering the effects of rapid expansion caused by the Industrial Revolution, might have seemed a surprising choice for a man from York, but against the background of smoke and grime was the spirit of enterprise and opportunity.

Samuel Taylor's pharmacy would have been familiar to Charles Thackray as a boy, as it was on the opposite corner to his father's butcher's shop at 43 Great George Street (then on the corner of Oxford Row), where Charles was born and where he lived until he was eleven. Charles's father acquired three additional premises in the 1890s and business was doing well enough to enable Thackray to send his son away to Giggleswick School.

At sixteen Charles began an apprenticeship in pharmacy at the Bradford firm of F. M. Rimmington & Son. He then went to work at the prestigious Squire & Son, Queen Victoria's official chemist's in the West End of London, and rounded off his education with a spell working on the Continent.

Thackray qualified in 1899. By this time, the profession of pharmacy had clearly emerged from traditional herbalism, a change that had begun with the creation of the Pharmaceutical Society in 1841 and the Pharmacy Act of 1852, which made provision for the Society to keep a register of chemists and druggists.[1]

In 1903 Charles married Helen Pearce, daughter of a leading Leeds jeweller. Their first son, Charles Noel, was born on Christmas Day two years later, followed by William Pearce (Tod) in 1907, then Douglas in 1909 and a daughter, Freda, two years after that. Charles and Helen Thackray had another daughter, but she was very frail and died when she was only ten. We can only guess at what effect the little girl's death had on Charles, but it might go some way to explaining the 'mental anxiety' from which he was later to suffer.

The Thackrays lived in Roundhay, moving to bigger houses as business prospered. A man in Charles Thackray's position would be expected to join a professional men's club. But the obvious choice, the Leeds Club, refused him membership on the grounds that he had committed the cardinal sin of being 'in trade'. Along with others barred for the same reason, including Snowden Schofield, founder of the Leeds department store which was to bear his name, and a couple of others in the clothing business, he set up a club of his own, which they called the West Riding Club. It had its premises on the first floor of what is now the Norwich Union building in City Square.

Much of Thackray's time there was spent playing bridge which, along with golf, was his abiding passion. He was fond of singing, too, and the family often joined in singsongs round the grand piano at home.

Thackray's financial partner, Henry Scurrah Wainwright, was the same age as his friend Charles and, like him, was Leeds born and bred. On leaving Leeds Grammar School at the age of sixteen, he became articled to William Adgie, Junior, at Beevers and Adgie, a leading firm of chartered accountants in Albion Street (now part of KPMG Peat Marwick). He qualified in 1899, the same year as his friend Thackray, and became a partner in Beevers and Adgie in 1905.

Wainwright, like Thackray, married a local girl, Emily White. Her father

Plate 9.1 Charles Frederick Thackray, joint founder of the company and after whom the newly-established Thackray Medical Museum in Beckett Street is named.

245

was an importer and manufacturer of botanic medicines—a herbalist rather than a pharmacist. The family business was built largely on the success of Kompo, their patent medicine for colds. Scurrah and Emily had one son, Richard, born in 1918, who was later to become financial director of the Thackray business and Liberal MP for the Colne Valley in the Yorkshire Pennines.

Scurrah Wainwright was actively involved in Leeds life: he became President of the Leeds Society of Chartered Accountants, was a long-serving director of Jowett & Sowry Ltd Printers and the Hotel Metropole and was Honorary Secretary of the Leeds Tradesmen's Benevolent Association. But it was as Chairman of the National Assistance Board's Advisory Committee in 1938 that he was appointed Officer of the British Empire, having achieved the monumental task of interviewing every unemployed man under 30 years of age in the city in an effort to help them find jobs.

As young men, Charlie and Scurrah, as they were known to friends, lived within easy walking distance of each other's homes in New Leeds—then a pleasant residential area on the east side of Chapeltown Road. As Scurrah's diary for the year 1902 shows, he and Charles met at least twice a week with other friends to play cards, snooker and ping-pong in the winter and to go for walks and play tennis in nearby Potternewton Park in the summer months.

Plate 9.2 Henry Scurrah Wainwright, who with Charles F. Thackray bought a corner shop pharmacy in 1902 from which the Thackray Company grew.

246

I

It was natural that the two young men, both recently qualified in their chosen professions, should have ambitions to start their own business. They saw their opportunity when Samuel Taylor's pharmacy came up for sale.

To assess its potential, as Thackray and Wainwright must have done, let us look at how Great George Street had developed since Taylor had opened his shop. By 1869 the Gothic facade of the newly built Leeds General Infirmary dominated the north side of the street—as it does today—and many medically-related businesses had grown up in the vicinity,[2] including an oculist, a surgical instrument and artificial limb maker, a homeopathic dispensary, a drug company and a 'specialist in artificial teeth'. Number 70, on the apex formed by the junction with Portland Street, was a prime site.

Many doctors at the Infirmary had consulting rooms in Park Square and would pass the shop on their way between the two. In addition, there were half a dozen private nursing homes in the vicinity, all providing potential customers. The dispensing side of the business looked healthy, too. Taylor's prescription books between 1890 and 1901 record between six and a dozen prescriptions dispensed each day.

Scurrah Wainwright's diary entry for Friday, 25th April 1902 reads: 'CFT arranged price of Taylor business. £900 + 13 wks at £5.' Then on 19th May, Whit Monday: 'CFT commenced business @ 70 Great George St.'

Two days later, Wainwright records: 'Opened bank a/c for CFT. Gave him cq £100 deposit for Sam. Taylor; put £50 in his bank a/c. CFT signed contract agreeing to purchase ST's business (£900). Evg. Tennis on grass courts. 1st this year. At CFT's shop re. books. CFT stayed [at HSW's] all night.'

Several late evenings of bookkeeping are recorded in the ensuing weeks. One evening in August Scurrah notes: 'Saw S. [Emily, his fiancée, known as Sis], then worked late at CFT's shop, 7.30–9.30, then with Mr A. [Mr Adgie] until 11.30 pm'. The same month a partnership was officially agreed between the pair; the original pencil draft of the agreement states that Thackray was entitled to an extra £30 salary in lieu of living over the shop.

The business traded under the name of Chas. F. Thackray. Wainwright might have added his name but for the fact that chartered accountancy was a relatively new profession and if accountants were seen to be involved in commercial ventures, their professional impartiality could be jeopardised.

Although the shop was considered to be a high-class chemist's under Samuel Taylor's ownership, Thackray and Wainwright immediately spent just over £40 on painting and repairs (when the buying power of £1 was equivalent to £41 today) and a further £20 on an oak bookcase, display cabinet, linoleum and an electric bell. Two apprentices were taken on in the first year, too. In all probability they lived over the shop, as was customary, to judge from food, drink and coal orders recorded in the accounts.

The first five years' accounts show profits rising steadily, from just over £226 in 1903/4, to nearly £400 in 1907/8. They also show the first investment in equipment: £5 12s. spent on a Humanized Milk Plant Separator in 1903 and £81 for a sterilizer three years later. Other purchases included a bicycle costing £2 14s, a typewriter for £7 and more than £30 on catalogue-printing.

In 1908, for the first time, profits were split two-thirds to Charles Thackray and one-third to Scurrah Wainwright, as opposed to the equal division they had shared previously. No doubt the extra income would have been welcome to Charles, now a family man with a wife, two sons and domestic wages to pay.

Advances in aseptic surgery in the early years of this century led to a new demand for sterilized dressings and instruments. The sterilizer bought in 1906 meant that Thackray could now develop another side to the business, supplying sterilized dressings to the Leeds General Infirmary, the nearby Women's and Children's Hospital and neighbouring nursing homes.

Meanwhile, common preparations such as eye and ear drops, mouthwashes, nasal sprays and cough mixtures, dispensed at a cost of between 9d. and 2/6, and the occasional pair of gold spectacle frames at 8/6, were the mainstay of the dispensing side of the business. Customers represented a wide range of social class, from aristocracy (Lady Harewood's name is recorded in the ledger for 1910) to servants.[3]

Plate 9.3 Thackray's retail shop on the corner of Great George Street and Portland Street.

The first instruments Thackray sold were supplied by Selby of London in 1908. This side of the business grew so rapidly that two years later he set up an instrument repairs department in a converted stable at the back of the pharmacy. Compared to prescription fees, the income from instrument repairs was in a different league altogether.

A large number of the physicians who patronized the shop, and sent their patients there, became lifelong friends of Thackray's and their role in his success should not be underestimated. They helped the Thackray name to become known all over Yorkshire and they played an important part in the development of the surgical instruments side of the business.

The early years of the firm coincided with major advances in surgical techniques. Leeds, in particular, was a renowned centre of high-calibre surgeons, many of whom made their names at the Infirmary; best known of all was Berkeley (later Lord) Moynihan, who achieved worldwide recognition for his contribution to abdominal surgery. It was Moynihan who first suggested to Charles Thackray that he should make instruments; and the firm, with its experience in repairs at their premises just across the road, was well placed to do so.

In 1908 Thackray bought the firm's first powered transport—a Triumph motorcycle—and advertised for the first time in a national magazine. He also took on his first representative. By 1914, he had taken on two more, marking the beginning of a shift in emphasis from retailing towards wholesaling.

Although the firm enjoyed regular orders for drugs and equipment from Yorkshire hospitals, they had to break into long-established names in the field if they were to expand. Thackray's insistence on employing only qualified pharmacists as salesmen resulted in a salesforce well above the average—and went some way towards overcoming any prejudice surgeons might have in talking to a sales representative.

By the outbreak of the First World War, turnover was about six times that of the first financial year. Thackray's was employing 25 people, including eight instrument makers and three full-time representatives.

Salesmen visited customers over a wide area, supplying wholesale pharmaceuticals not only to hospitals and nursing homes but also to general practitioners serving rural areas. Where chemist shops were few and far between, doctors did much of their own dispensing and therefore carried stocks of common medicines with them.

The First World War brought with it an increased demand for dressings, many of which were sewn on to bandages by hand in those days. Thackray's, looking to boost their production and not afraid to pioneer new methods, bought a machine which made the 'Washington Haigh Field Dressing' cheaply and quickly. Acceptance by the War Office of Thackray's 'Aseptic' range as standard field dressings was important to the firm, both ensuring large contracts for drugs and sundries and, to a lesser extent, instruments. Ministry approval also provided a useful testimonial for potential customers.

The Infirmary continued to place regular orders with the firm and in 1916 the hospital ordered sterilizers to equip its new operating theatres in the King Edward Memorial Extension.[4] The total for ten items, including water, instrument and glove sterilizers, dishes, copper cylinders and a cylinder sterilizer, came to more than £500 (worth about £17,500 today). The following year another substantial order was placed for theatre furniture, totalling £487. Instrument repairs for the hospital continued to be undertaken by Thackray's at least until 1926, after which the Infirmary's accounts stopped being itemized.

By the end of the war in 1918, Thackray's employed fourteen instrument makers, out of a total workforce that had risen to 32. The surgical equipment supply side of the business prospered, largely owing to the increase in surgery in Leeds and Thackray's realization that there was a limit to the amount of wholesale drug business that could be obtained from doctors.

The sales area for instruments now became greatly extended. Consequently more representatives were taken on and organized into a sales team. Unlike most, Thackray's salesmen were not paid on commission, but given a share of the profits, a practice which encouraged them to win their contracts on the most favourable terms for the company.

Thackray's reputation in the trade for having a first-class sales network throughout the UK won them important distribution rights and they acquired agencies for various American products, then in advance of home-grown equipment in terms of design and gadgetry.

The US company Davis & Geck, who manufactured soluble sutures and surgeons' gloves, saw Thackray's as an ideal distributor for their products. The sutures were Thackray's first national distributorship. They were a superb product and were to be both profitable and good for the firm's reputation. In due course, films were made of classic surgery being done with Davis & Geck sutures, and representatives were each equipped with a Kodak home cine projector to use with hospital audiences.

Davis & Geck's parent company, Lederle, front-runners in the 1920s in the production of serums for measles, whooping cough and other infectious diseases, also asked Thackray's to act for them throughout the UK and provided, at their own expense, three or four more representatives for the purpose. Later, when sulphonamide drugs were introduced, Lederle again made Thackray's their UK distributor.

By the 1920s, the firm's changing emphasis from pharmaceuticals and dressings to surgical supply brought rapid expansion, and Thackray's outgrew its Great George Street premises. By 1926, employees had doubled in number since 1914.

250

Plate 9.4   The offices and showrooms of Chas. F. Thackray, formerly the Old Medical School, Park Street, Leeds.

Thackray was fortunate to find the extra space he was looking for just round the corner in Park Street where the Yorkshire Archaeological Society and the Thoresby Society (the Leeds historical society) occupied the Old Medical School. The Park Street building had been purpose built in 1865 for the Leeds School of Medicine.[5] In the intervening years, it had been sold to the Yorkshire College of Science, precursor of Leeds University, then to the two historical societies. So when Charles Thackray made an offer the Societies considered 'too good to refuse', it was appropriate that it was to have a medical use.

When Thackray's took over the building in 1926, a lot needed doing to it. After alterations and repairs totalling more than £3,000, administration and most of manufacturing could be transferred to the new premises. Number 70 Great George Street was retained as a retail pharmacy and for the manufacture and fitting of surgical appliances.

Early days at Park Street are remembered clearly by staff who worked there: 'I left school at fourteen and joined Thackray's in 1928. I used to pack parcels and take them on a handcart to the post office in Park Square. Often the wheels got stuck in the tramlines.

'Mr Thackray impressed me very much. He was a very likeable chap, always smartly dressed. There was no barrier with him. It was nothing to see him take his coat off to wash bottles—Winchesters, they were called, holding three or four pints—in the basement. I remember he had a massive office with a massive desk in it; a contrast to the petite person who sat behind it. He travelled in a chauffeur-driven limousine, an American car.'

Though approachable, Thackray demanded high standards. As a sixteen-year-old apprentice in 1932, another employee recalls:

'I was scraping enamel off a trolley to be re-enamelled—this was before the days of stainless steel—and Mr Thackray came to inspect the work. He asked for some paper to be spread on the floor and he went on his hands and knees so he could check the underside of the trolley...I finished my apprenticeship when I was twenty-three.'

A thorough training by any standards, but the firm's reputation was built on first-class workmanship. It is fair to say that Thackray's was rated as one of the best employers in the Leeds area, an essential element in the production of high-quality instruments. (Even during the Depression years of high unemployment, Thackray's was able to offer a 58¾ hour working week for engineers, compared to the average 51¾.[6]) It is equally fair to say that the staff were exceptionally loyal and formed a closely-knit team who were willing to put themselves out on their employer's behalf when necessary.

'At holiday time, Whitsuntide and Easter, the firm closed for the Monday and Tuesday. We worked with a skeleton staff and one director on the Tuesday to open the post and despatch any urgent orders.

'Once, we had an order for six sterilizing drums—they're about fifteen inches tall and a foot wide—at Harrogate. The director on duty had a sports car. It was raining and, with the drums piled in my lap, we couldn't shut the roof, so we were wet through by the time we arrived. But you didn't mind.'

Recruitment of staff by recommendation rather than by advertisement meant that there were many instances of people from the same family working for the firm. A lively calendar of social events meant that everyone knew each other, whichever department they belonged to. A Social Committee, started in the 1930s and funded by weekly subscriptions and raffles, organized dances, outings and whist drives. It arranged cricket and golf matches with local organizations and started a football team which played at Roundhay Park.

The Thackray football team competed in Sunday Combination League matches; success in a rather different league was achieved by Jim Milburn, the former 'iron man' of Leeds United and uncle of the famous brothers

252

Bobby and Jackie Charlton. He worked as a labourer at Thackray's from 1966 to 1982.

II

The 1920s had seen sales in the home market flourishing. Turnover in wholesale pharmaceuticals was brisk and increased instrument sales led to the opening of a London depot in Regent Street. Now Thackray turned his attention overseas.

Much of surgery round the world at this time was British because Empire countries sent trainees and postgraduates to the UK. Therefore British products sold well in Empire countries and where there was a strong British influence, such as Canada, Australasia, South Africa, Egypt and Nigeria.

To begin with, Thackray's sent its own manufactured surgical instruments chiefly to the Mediterranean, the Middle East and West Africa; the firm were buyers for the Crown Agents, whose job was to buy for the Crown colonies. In those days, salesmen went on trips lasting, perhaps, six months, or up to two years. By 1930 the yearly total for exports was nearly £6000, about one-thirtieth of total turnover. Markets had been built up thanks chiefly to substantial leaflet advertising and to the increasing renown of the 'Moynihan School' of surgery.

Thackray's staff had increased to 100 by 1931. Since 1914 the firm had trebled its production and increased its turnover eightfold, despite generally slack trading conditions in most of the economy. Then international financial problems and a world slump led to devaluation of the pound. With fewer goods imported, it was opportune for Thackray's to expand its own manufacturing capacity.

In the early Thirties the firm therefore began to make its own hospital sterilizers, operating tables and other items of theatre furniture. Packed ready for despatch, storage became a problem. Cases were stacked on stairways and in passageways; even in the front entrance sometimes.

To make room for the extra manufacturing activity and storage at Park Street, the entire rear half of the building was demolished in 1933. It was then rebuilt to three storeys as a modern building of the time, with a fourth storey added shortly afterwards. The neo-Gothic front façade remained more or less unchanged.

Although the firm rode the Depression years well, it suffered a major blow in 1934 when Charles Thackray died suddenly at the age of 57. He failed to return from an evening walk in Roundhay Park near his home and later his body was recovered from Waterloo Lake.

His widow, Helen, had witnessed his mental anxiety for the previous two years and felt that his death would at last have given him peace. A tendency to anxiety that seemed to run in the family and the effects of his young daughter's death were both likely to have affected Charles's mental state. Nowadays, his condition would probably be diagnosed as anxiety neurosis.

Thackray died when the two (of his three) sons who had joined the business were relatively young and inexperienced. Noel was twenty-nine and his brother, Tod, twenty-seven. The man best placed to take up the reins was Mercer Gray; he had been with Thackray's since he was a newly qualified pharmacist before the First World War, and had become the most senior manager in the firm.

Ownership of Charles Thackray's share of the firm passed to Noel and Tod, and Helen Thackray was given financial security with an allocation of preference shares. (The business had grown by this time to achieve annual sales of about £200,000, equivalent to over £5million today). It was agreed that a limited company should be formed, with Scurrah Wainwright as Chairman, Mercer Gray as Managing Director and Noel and Tod Thackray as Directors of the Commercial and Manufacturing operations.

The Thirties continued to be formative years in the field of surgery and Thackray's were designing and making an increasingly wide range of instruments. It was therefore essential that the firm produce a comprehensive catalogue to replace the handful of leaflets (not to mention competitors' catalogues) they had relied on to date. In 1937, under Mercer Gray's direction, two volumes containing line drawings of every instrument Thackray's supplied were made available for the first time.

Many instruments were made to surgeons' own specifications—witness the number named after their inventor in any Thackray catalogue index. The close co-operation between surgeon and manufacturer shows up in the firm's correspondence, such as this letter from Mr Cockcroft-Barker, MB, ChB, writing to Mercer Gray in 1938 about a dilator: 'The true secret of the instrument,' which is not easy to decipher owing to Mr Cockcroft-Barker's handwriting, 'is the *curve* and also the *length* of the dilating portion.' He suggests to Mercer Gray in a post script that this 'might be a good thing to keep up your own sleeve'.[7]

Surgeons could come to Park Street to buy their instruments; they could also get to know of new products at medical exhibitions. Thackray's claims to have been first in its field to run an exhibition in conjunction with a surgeons' meeting—a practice that is widespread nowadays with clear advantages to both parties.

The pre-war instrument catalogue lists about 2500 different items (at least twenty of which were to Moynihan's design). Park Street, where all design and the majority of manufacture took place, had become totally inadequate.

A new factory would have to be reasonably nearby, so that the Managing Director could travel to the works easily; it should not be too expensive, and should be capable of expansion. A site fulfilling these criteria became available at Viaduct Road, about a mile to the west of Park Street.

As a result of the government's wartime policy of concentrating industry to make best use of resources, Leeds Dyers, to which Scurrah Wainwright was financial adviser, were looking for a buyer for their textile dyeing works. The three-storey building, alongside the River Aire and the Leeds-Liverpool Canal, was old but solidly built.

While the Viaduct Road site accommodated increased instrument manufacture, production of pharmaceuticals and dressings continued at Park Street. Drugs were produced in what was known as 'the lab', although it would hardly be recognized as such today.

'We used to prepare 20, 40 or even 80 gallons in large barrels stood on the floor. The mixtures were stirred with a big pole, filtered through asbestos and ladled by hand into buckets before being poured through funnels from the top of steps into smaller barrels,' recalled one member of staff.

The retail shop, meanwhile, dealt in smaller quantities. Apart from one or two stock items, such as cough mixtures, aspirins and 'Thackray's Pile Pills', most preparations were made up individually from doctors' prescriptions.

A visit to the doctor was expensive for many in these pre-NHS times, so the pharmacist played a much more important role in diagnosis and treatment than his modern counterpart. Often, the customer would take the recommended remedy while still in the shop, sitting on one of two chairs provided. This practice could have its drawbacks. On one occasion, a customer came in complaining of queasiness and was given—reasonably in the circumstances— a seidlitz powder, a common remedy for indigestion. The customer drank the mixture and promptly keeled over and died. In fact, the man had suffered a heart attack and the pharmacist's action was not to blame.

The shop enjoyed a reputation as a high-class chemist; Thackray's maintained their policy of dispensing only private prescriptions, even after the introduction of the National Health Service. A high standard of service was maintained by a level of staffing that would be unthinkable today. Under the Manager were an Assistant Manager, two unqualified staff who dealt with nursing home orders, four apprentices, four errand boys and two cleaners. The shop was open every day of the year, including Christmas Day. Weekday closing at 7 pm (an hour earlier than many other shops in Leeds) meant that apprentices, whose evening classes began at 6.50 pm at Leeds Central School a little further up Great George Street, had to sprint up the road after closing time.

The Second World War inevitably created high demand for drugs, dressings

Plate 9.5   The interior of the Great George Street pharmacy.

and surgical instruments, with injured servicemen returning to Britain for treatment.

Among the worst casualties were the burns suffered by airmen shot down in the Battle of Britain. Many of these young men, who included Canadians, Australians, Poles and Czechs, as well as Britons, were taken to East Grinstead hospital in Sussex—one of only four plastic surgery units in the country—which was under the direction of the gifted surgeon, Archibald McIndoe.[8] He was Consultant in Plastic Surgery to the Royal Air Force and was later knighted in recognition of his pioneering work.

At East Grinstead, McIndoe wrought miracles of reconstructive surgery; through this work he became a household name. It was Thackray's who made many of the instruments for this delicate surgery, including dissecting forceps and scissors to McIndoe's own design.

The fact that McIndoe did not take his business to London firms—which, after all, would have been a more obvious choice for a surgeon based in the South East—underlines the importance of Thackray's maintaining a presence in the capital: although it was expensive, they had to be seen as a national company, not just a provincial one.

Without the London office, it is unlikely that Thackray's would have been

256

in plastic surgery at all. As well as fostering links with surgeons at the plastic surgery centres in the South East, the London representative won profitable accounts from major London teaching hospitals. The significance of instrument sales such as these was that orders for other Thackray goods tended to follow.

One of the craftsmen who worked from surgeons' backs-of-envelopes sketches for instruments turned his skill to providing life-saving equipment to servicemen who were to be dropped by parachute across the Channel. Folding scissors, saws and wire cutters were fitted into the heels of boots, compasses were hidden in tunic buttons and Gigli saws (a flexible saw rather like a cheese-cutter) were concealed in coat collars.

Many members of staff were called up into the forces. Some of the older ones volunteered to join the Home Guard, and came to work in battledress, while at the retail shop, two firewatchers took turns to sleep on the examination couches in the orthopaedic department.

The war brought a big influx of women into the firm, to train for jobs that men had had to leave for service duties. (The foundations of training laid in the war later grew into an Apprentices School, created in 1961 out of the difficulty in recruiting suitably qualified labour, especially in connection with surgical instrument manufacture, which was more of a craft than light engineering. Latterly, sixteen-year-old school leavers served a four-year apprenticeship, of which the first year was spent at an Industrial Training Board college and the remaining three completing work experience at Thackray's.)

Hand work represented a large proportion of activity during the war and even into the 1950s. Some of the young female employees did a range of jobs: 'We used to roll up catgut [for sutures] and put it in envelopes. My least favourite job was in repairs. Broken glass syringes came in, sometimes still with blood on, and we had to knock off the broken glass with hammers.' Other duties included plaiting horsetail hair in groups of a hundred and cutting and rolling bandages from a large piece of lint.

Today, it seems surprising that even as late as the 1950s so many jobs were carried out by hand, but the business—in common with the rest of the trade—had been traditionally craft-oriented; it was not until the 1960s that this labour-intensive approach was gradually modified in favour of more highly mechanized production.

The closing years of the war saw the development of antibiotics, which was radically to change the treatment of a host of illnesses. Thackray's was awarded the important new distributorship of one of these, Sulphadiazine, developed by the pharmaceutical firm May & Baker (M & B). Vaccines, too, were undergoing major advances. Soon after the war, Thackray's were carrying stocks of Lederle's new measles vaccine with approximately four times the potency of its predecessor. Such agencies were highly profitable: turnover for the Lederle account in 1946, for instance, was almost equal to the firm's total exports.

III

The introduction of the National Health Service in 1948 was the most important single factor to affect Thackray's after the war. The Ministry of Health took over all voluntary and municipal hospitals, and the extensive re-equipping that followed led to a busy and expansive period for all sections of the business. (The Leeds Postmaster remarked that Thackray's generated one of the biggest parcel posts in the city.)

Service has been described as the lodestone of Thackray's. The firm had already established a depot to facilitate distribution in the South of England; now another was needed to supply Scottish customers promptly, and Glasgow was chosen for a second warehouse. At this time, too, a South African subsidiary was created, initially based in Cape Town. As a prosperous dominion, South Africa offered a potentially lucrative market, with the additional advantage that it had no major UK competitors.

Exports, slowed during the war, began again in earnest immediately hostilities ended. Yearly total export turnover, averaging about £50,000 during the war years, leapt to £120,000 in 1946 and continued to rise in the 1950s. Thackray's sales force was once more increased, with some representatives travelling overseas full-time.

The life of the overseas rep. was not always as glamorous as some of the exotic destinations might suggest:

'On one occasion, in Sierra Leone, the booking clerk at a rest house told me I would have to share a room. I not only shared a room, but a bed—with an American agronomist.'

It could be dangerous, too. One overseas representative contracted cerebral malaria in Africa, another tells of a narrow escape when caught in crossfire in Venezuela.

A less hazardous way of promoting Thackray's products was participation in international trade fairs. Frequently, orders for equipment would be taken at the exhibition stand but sometimes the fairs were not so much of benefit from a commercial point of view as to show the flag, encouraged by government subsidy.

In 1956 Mercer Gray died and the second generation of the three families involved in the Thackray business now assumed new responsibilities. Mercer Gray was succeeded as Managing Director, jointly, by Charles Thackray's sons, Noel and Tod. Richard Wainwright and Mercer Gray's son, Robert, were elected to the Board the following year.

A family firm, such as Thackray's, presents special problems regarding its future financial security when share ownership is divided among the families involved. To avoid the pitfall of being forced into a sale by death duties, the heads of family had established family trusts, making over some of their shares to trustees for the benefit of their children. Although commonplace nowadays, such arrangements were then quite innovative and meant that the company weathered without difficulty the financial consequences of Mercer Gray's death—and, later, Scurrah Wainwright's and Noel Thackray's.

Noel and Tod took over the managing directorship of the company in the climate of post-war prosperity. Manufacturing continued to increase and the firm once again outgrew its premises. Unable to expand at Viaduct Road because it was discovered that there were major sewers underground, the company looked elsewhere. A factory in St Anthony's Road, Beeston, in South Leeds, was up for sale. Although it had more space than required at the time, Tod Thackray was convinced that they should buy the site. He persuaded fellow directors and the Beeston factory was acquired in 1957 at a cost of £55,000 (equivalent to just over £600,000 today). It has proved to have been a shrewd investment in the light of subsequent expansion.

Manufacturing and drugs moved to Beeston and the now-empty Viaduct Road building was put up for sale. It failed to attract a buyer, however, owing to a proposed plan to straighten a dog-leg bend in the road adjoining the factory (a plan which was never carried out). In the event, therefore, the Drug Department, together with the Wholesale Pharmacy, took over the premises.

The removal of the instrument works from Viaduct Road was not without drama. A young man who had been employed at the works had been convicted of murder in 1945, a *crime passionel*, it seems. The victim's bloodstained clothing was only discovered twelve years later, when machinery was unbolted from the floor for removal.

Thackray's expansion in Leeds was followed by the acquisition of two specialist manufacturing companies, the British Cystoscope Co Ltd, in Clerkenwell, London, and Thomas Rudd Ltd of Sheffield, makers of surgical scissors. What both these companies had in common was a highly skilled workforce producing instruments to the exacting standards required of Thackray products.

Although most sections of the business had been expanding throughout the 1950s, changes in the pattern of medical practice brought about by the National Health Service had led to a decline in business at the retail shop in Great George Street. Prescriptions from nursing homes and physicians with practices in Park Square, on which the trade of the shop had depended in the past, had declined; at the same time, profit margins on products had dwindled so that the shop was not even covering its overheads.

Despite its popularity among customers, the Board could not ignore the shop's balance sheet. In January 1962, it served its last customers, sixty years after Thackray and Wainwright had started their business there and a century since it had begun as a pharmacy under Samuel Taylor's ownership.

In general, however, the post-war reconstruction period of the 1950s and 1960s was highly profitable for the medical business, with large sums of public money directed towards new hospitals and universities.

In 1961, for the first time since the National Health Service had come into being, Regional Hospital Boards were encouraged by the Minister of Health to make long-term plans for hospital building, with an allocation of more than £60 million capital expenditure for 1961–3 and further sums forthcoming by the mid-Sixties. This new attitude towards health spending virtually guaranteed Thackray's a fast-expanding home market for the Sixties and made a sound base for increasing export trade.

The 1960s were notable, too, for the important association Thackray's developed with a remarkable surgeon whose name was to become as famous as Moynihan's and McIndoe's. John Charnley, later knighted for his work in the field of total hip replacement, was an orthopaedic surgeon at the Manchester Royal Infirmary when he had first asked Thackray's to make instruments for him in 1947 as an alternative to a long-established London firm.[9]

However, his most notable collaboration with the firm concerned total hip replacement, an operation to reduce pain and restore movement to the hip by implanting a manmade replacement for the deteriorated ball-and-socket joint. Briefly, the artificial hip (or prosthesis) comprised a ball-ended stem which fitted into the patient's thigh bone and a cup which took the place of the socket (or acetabulum) in the pelvis. Charnley refined his hip replacement operation throughout his long association with Thackray's and was still working on improvements when he died in 1982 at the age of seventy.

The close collaboration between surgeon and manufacturer is revealed in Charnley's copious correspondence with the firm.[10] Sometimes he would write three or four letters in a week, concerning himself with everything from the minutiae of design to broader, commercial issues. He was without question a perfectionist and could be forthright in his criticism of Thackray's, but he was quick to apologize, too. Thackray's, though tolerant of his demands, could reply with equal vigour and an understanding developed between them.

In the pioneering days of the operation soon after the Second World War, Thackray's made the stainless steel stems, while Charnley made the sockets himself, turning them on a lathe in his workshop at home. This arrangement

Plate 9.6   Sir John Charnley, knighted for his work in the field of total hip replacement, who collaborated with Thackray's from 1947 until his death in 1982.

continued until 1963, when Thackray's took over the socket production. Interestingly, the most suitable material Charnley found for the sockets was Teflon*[11], better known for its non-stick properties in cooking pans.

Charnley had set up his own workshop in the 1950s at the Wrightington Hospital near Wigan where he was Consultant Orthopaedic Surgeon. His technicians made instruments under Charnley's close supervision and then Thackray's manufactured them. As time went on, Thackray's contributed their own design suggestions; this continual exchange of ideas was a significant factor in the advance of the hip operation.

By 1962, it became evident that Teflon was not the ideal material for replacement sockets. Charnley was impressed by a new material, a high molecular weight polythene, which he—characteristically—tested by implanting a sample in his own thigh. Only with no reaction discernible after six months did he begin to use the new material with patients.

However, he was worried that other surgeons would take up his operation before the new material had been proven. Even after five years, he allowed Thackray's to sell only to those surgeons whom he had personally approved—although the special instruments were available because they could be used for other hip operations. Such a restriction often put Thackray's in the embarrassing position of having to refuse requests for Charnley implants from eminent surgeons.

Charnley's caution did not prevent considerable demand for the product, however, and the surgeon berated Thackray's for not manufacturing in sufficient quantity. They responded by improving their manufacturing capability, so that by the end of 1968, they could write:

'As from January 1st next, we shall increase our rate of production of prostheses by 25% and our anticipated production will be 6000 per annum, which could be increased to 7000 by the end of the year. Additional production up to 10,000 per annum could be organized without too much difficulty.'

Although the mechanics of the hip replacement operation had become established in the 1950s and 1960s, recovery in some patients was hampered by infection in the wound. With Charnley's encouragement, Thackray's created a model 'clean' area for the packing of prostheses, not simply meeting British Standard requirements but setting them.

In due course, Charnley stopped making a personal selection of surgeons and any who had spent a minimum of two days learning the technique at Wrightington could buy his prosthesis. By the early 1970s, the product was made generally available and Thackray's were fully stretched to produce the quantity of Charnley hips and instruments required.

It was at this time that Noel Thackray died. The consequences of Noel's death are described in more detail later but, in essence, it led to a reorganization of the firm's management with Tod Thackray taking over his brother's role as Chairman and becoming sole Managing Director. Tod's son John became Deputy Managing Director and his nephew Paul (Noel's son) was appointed Director responsible for Interplan Hospital Projects and much of the company's purchasing activity.

The changes coincided with a period when government was encouraging industry and universities to collaborate in order to make full use of the most up-to-date techniques available. In this context, Thackray's approached Leeds Polytechnic Industrial Liaison Unit for advice on how to meet their increasing production demands. Accordingly, a general works manager was appointed in March 1971 and, shortly afterwards, Ron Frank, the management studies lecturer who had produced the works organization report, joined the company. Significantly, these two were the firm's first professionally trained managers from non-medical industry.

At the time they joined, manufacturing was craft-oriented, employing highly skilled men who could turn out excellent products. However, such craftsmanship had two inherent drawbacks: there were difficulties in achieving precision consistency and there was little flexibility of volume. The 1970s consequently saw major capital expenditure in machinery. Computer-controlled, and operated by only one technician, the new machinery could turn out large numbers of stems (50,000 a year in 1990) and a sophisticated electro-chemical process honed the metal to a high degree of accuracy.

By far the biggest expenditure, however, was in equipment for 'cold-forming' steel. This process—whereby steel is compressed between dies at much lower temperatures than conventional forging—could dramatically increase the strength of stems without enlarging them.

Although the incidence of stems fracturing in patients was extremely low, Thackray's continuously researched stronger materials. A new steel was developed, called Ortron 90*.[12] It was calculated to prolong the life of the implant so that no further operation would be necessary during the patient's lifetime. It also allowed Charnley to develop a new, narrow-necked stem.

Demand for Charnley products was high and took the company into new export fields. In the US, Thackray's was faced with building up sales against giant competitors; the volume required presented problems, too, and in 1974 an American company was granted an option to manufacture Charnley hip prostheses and sockets.

What made Charnley's contribution to orthopaedics exceptional was the combination of his undeniable skill with his gift for innovation and the will—including, as he admitted, acting as 'the scourge and flail of Thackray's'—to see it through. He was given due recognition in the citation that accompanied the honorary Doctorate of Laws awarded to Tod Thackray by the University of Leeds in May 1988:

'He and his company have contributed to some of the greatest advances in orthopaedic surgery this century. Through his long co-operation and friendship with the late Sir John Charnley, Mr Thackray and his company confronted and overcame some of the major problems in orthopaedics....Though a skilled engineer as well as a surgeon, Charnley quickly outran the resources of his own laboratory and it was through his close co-operation with Thackray and his company's engineers that low-friction total hip replacement was gradually perfected.'

By the time Charnley died in 1982, thousands of hip replacements operations were carried out annually. A huge number of implants therefore needed to be available. An exact fit for each patient would have necessitated keeping in stock literally hundreds of different designs and sizes at any one time. A revolutionary solution to the problem was devised by a Belgian orthopaedic surgeon, Professor Joseph Mulier, from the University of Leuven, who approached Thackray's with his concept of a made-to-measure stem.

Mulier's idea was for an implant that was manufactured while the patient was still on the operating table, using computer-controlled laser technology. The system had the additional advantage of not needing to be cemented in place, as the Charnley stem did, a factor which caused complications in unexpected revision cases. Together, Mulier and Thackray's developed a system which they called Identifit. It took about 40 minutes for a titanium stem to be milled and delivered to the operating theatre. The first such stem was inserted in February 1987 with generally favourable results.

IV

Changes in the management structure of the firm were touched on in relation to Charnley, but we should now look in more detail at what took place as the 1960s gave way to the 70s. It was in the prosperous years of the 1960s that the third generation of the family, John and his cousin Paul Thackray, entered the picture.

Tod's son, John, had departed from the tradition of learning the business within the company by undergoing management training, both at Edinburgh University and with a market research company in Amsterdam.

Paul, Noel's son, had intended to work for Thackray's only temporarily after Army service in a garrison medical centre abroad, but after a stint in the firm doing a range of jobs, his interest in Thackray products grew and he decided to stay on.

When John rejoined Paul in the family firm in the 1960s, all was going exceptionally well for the business. The dramatic increase in demand at home coincided with a surge of new hospitals in the oil-rich countries where Thackray's had won sizeable contracts. At this time annual exports were about equal to home sales, totalling £1,340,000 in 1971—chiefly due to Charnley products—compared with just under £250,000 in 1960. Success overseas was due in large measure to Export Director Bill Piggin, whose achievement was recognized beyond the firm when he was awarded the OBE for services to Britain's exports.

Towards the end of the decade, however, alarm bells sounded in the boardroom: the impending abolition of resale price maintenance would hit consumables and result in competitors' taking over the wholesaling of general sundries, the bulk of Thackray's business; and there was the threat of losing the US agencies which had been such a profitable source of income since the 1920s, as American companies set up their own operations here.

First, the board recognized the need to update its methods. Computerization was clearly going to be an essential part of streamlining—particularly in stock control, with about 15,000 different items stored at three different warehouses as far apart as Leeds, London and Glasgow (a problem that was resolved with the building of a new warehouse at Beeston in 1974).

Outside consultants were brought in to ease the transition to a computerized system, but most members of staff agree that, to start with, it was a fiasco. 'If

I had ordered what the computer said on day one,' claimed someone in the purchasing department, 'Thackray's would have been bankrupt.'

The extra work over two years in putting right mistakes was considerable for some. Not least for Noel Thackray, who had been closely involved with the whole programme since its introduction. Members of his family feel that that period of stress made him ill and had probably even hastened his death in 1971.

The bottom line of the company's accounts at this time showed a healthy profit, but both John and Paul Thackray felt that administration was old-fashioned and inefficient. In this respect, however, Thackray's was no different from any other of the major surgical houses. When John suggested bringing in management consultants, Tod welcomed the idea. It was at this point that Thackray's had their first contact with Leeds Polytechnic staff, whose role has already been touched on in relation to Charnley.

The appointment of a works manager and massive investment in machinery led to what unquestionably became the most efficient production line of Charnley stems in the world. Meanwhile, manufacture of replacement knees, elbows and external fixation equipment for bone fractures continued alongside, although in smaller quantity than the hip prostheses.

John and Paul Thackray sought further advice from Leeds Polytechnic Department of Management, whose brief was to look at marketing. Their report made it clear that the firm had no concerted approach and that if action were not taken quickly, the healthy position that Thackray's was in owing to a favourable market environment could soon revert to one of chaos or even decline.

A solution to the general lack of co-ordination within the firm was to restructure the business. The old 'shop' system—in which, for example, each department had its own raw materials store even though many of these were common to other departments—was replaced by a new structure, in which the company was divided by function rather than product. To put the scheme into practice, ten new managers were appointed in the early 1970s and, as John Thackray put it, 'The driving was left to them.'

Delegating management, so that the traditional linear structure was re-placed by a pyramidal one, represented a watershed in the company's organiz-ation. It ceased to be a patriarchy, and for the first time a personnel manager was appointed.

The revolution occurring within the company was mirrored elsewhere, with people working shorter hours and trade unions' influence on industry increas-ing. The 1970s saw the company's first strike. This was a remarkable event in a business with no record of industrial action throughout its long history, but less noteworthy when considered in the national context.

Throughout the country, millions of workers had been given a cost-of-living increase in the high-inflation days of the mid-1970s. About 300 of the workforce at Beeston walked out in protest at the delay in payment of their threshold award. Union members agreed to return to work after twelve days when they were offered a cost-of-living safeguard.

The otherwise good record of labour/management relations survived this hiccup and the Seventies continued to be a prosperous decade for the company. Widespread hospital building, with concomitant orders for new equipment, was good for business, and increasing profits from the sale of Charnley products were ploughed back into the company.

Towards the end of the decade, John and Paul Thackray took over as Managing Director and Deputy respectively, while Tod remained as Chairman.

A more vigorous approach to marketing led to substantial exports. Hundreds of thousands of pounds worth of equipment was sent to Middle Eastern hospitals and in 1978 the firm won a £2.5million contract for a royal hospital in Abu Dhabi. This was the first time the firm had scheduled such a project from start to finish.

The largest volume of sales was still in surgical sundries for which there was now cut-throat competition. But, as Paul Thackray put it, 'We were like a corner shop trying to compete with supermarkets.' If Thackray's were to remain competitive, they would have to specialize.

Management decided to rationalize their agencies, retaining only exclusive ones or those that complemented their own theatre products. In addition, they began to subcontract some of the more common instruments and simple hospital furniture. This strategy left Thackray's producing a minority of its own instruments for the first time and it opened the way for manufacturing to be concentrated on new winners, like Charnley, and medium-run items such as plastic surgery instruments. Foreign-made surgical instruments began to show undeniable quality as well as low prices and the company started to import a range of specialist instruments which they marked Thackray Germany.

On the whole, the rationalization strategies worked, but the decision to retain only exclusive agencies could backfire, as Thackray's found to their cost with an excellent American product, the Shiley Heart Valve. This agency achieved a turnover of £1 million; then, with little warning, it was withdrawn. Profits for the company were halved overnight.

At the end of the successful Seventies, a strong pound hit exports, and cash limits were imposed on the National Health Service. For the first time, profits dropped to break even. In common with the rest of British industry, Thackray's found themselves having to make staff redundant, dropping from a total of 750 employed to 500 over a period of three or four years—though the number of compulsory redundancies was low.

The staff redundancies and the Shiley experience made John and Paul Thackray realize that they would have to take some radical—and sometimes unpopular—decisions, among them the closure of the London office and the firm's canteen. But they acquired confidence and it was in the 1980s that they undertook what was to be the last major reorganization of the company under family ownership.

They began by splitting the increasingly unprofitable Raymed division (Thackray's drug department) into two: with Pearce Laboratories on one hand and ostomy and continence products, under the heading Thackraycare, on the other. By manufacturing fewer products and larger volumes, Pearce Laboratories, moved to a factory at Garforth on the outskirts of Leeds, could now outprice its giant competitors.

The new policy, which could conveniently—if clumsily—be called divisionalization, meant a return to division by product area, with each having its own manufacturing, warehouse, sales and marketing, but with the additional advantage of shared centralized services.

In this context, Instruments were now separated from Orthopaedics, which represented the lion's share of Thackray's business by 1985, achieving a turnover of £20 million. Expansion at Beeston took place on the proceeds of the sale of Park Street, which Leeds City Council had purchased to make way for additions to the Magistrates' Court. The Council's approach to Thackray's fortunately coincided with the need to find larger premises anyway; and the company's head office moved to a new leasehold office building in Headingley, on the edge of Leeds.

The remarkable growth of Thackraycare was a success story in its own right. It had its origins in the orthopaedic department of the retail shop in Great George Street. But it was clear to Christin Thackray (who met her husband, John, while working for Charnley product agents in her native Norway) that patients were in need of far more professional help than was available to them. Her idea was for Thackray's to employ trained nurses to work in the community, fitting the appliances and giving back-up advice.

By 1980, Thackraycare took on its first two nurses to put the concept into practice. The old brown-paint-and-cracked-lino image of the orthopaedic department was replaced by an attractive display in the basement of the Instrument Centre which had opened at 47 Great George Street two years previously.

The success of the new appliance centre lay in word-of-mouth recommendation and by 1984, two more were opened, in Surrey and in Bristol. Others, in Oxford, Southampton and Wolverhampton, followed. Most manufacturers' products were stocked and it was strict policy to recommend a Thackray product only where appropriate. Most patients were referred by healthcare professionals to the centres and the majority were seen in their own homes—an immeasurable improvement for patients.

V

At the end of the 1980s the family shareholders had to consider how the firm was to continue into the Nineties and beyond. As a predominantly orthopaedic business, accounting for about eighteen percent of the total number of hips implanted internationally, John and Paul Thackray recognized that if the company were to succeed against giant competitors, they would have to develop a global presence. They could foresee potential inheritance tax problems arising for individual shareholders, too.

Given these circumstances, most boards of directors would consider either going public or selling out. The first option was rejected because the family directors felt themselves to be unsuited to the different disciplines the stock market would have imposed. There was every likelihood, too, that Thackray's would be undervalued compared with American prices. Selling the company did not appeal to John and Paul at that time either; they had not planned to retire for another five or ten years.

Although a sale was not envisaged until the mid-1990s or possibly 2000, the company actually changed hands in 1990. What led to this unexpected turn of events?

Orthogenesis was a major investment for the company requiring millions to develop and market it. Thackray's drew up a list of some of the big names in orthopaedics and, early in 1990, approached them with a view to developing Orthogenesis as a joint venture, or possibly selling that part of the company. But no one was interested: all or nothing was the common response.

In John and Paul Thackray's view selling the whole company should be considered only if the following criteria could be met: that a high, US-level price was paid; that the buyer should have a similar ethos; that continuity of employment on the firm's present sites could be assured for the foreseeable future; that the buyer would continue to expand the company.

Among the international companies who showed interest was another family-owned business called Corange. With 90 percent of its business in diagnostic products, pharmaceuticals and biomaterials, but only ten percent of its worldwide sales in orthopaedics (through its subsidiary, DePuy), Corange found what they were looking for in Thackray's. And Corange could provide the worldwide network and financial resources that Thackray's needed to assure the company a future as successful in the twenty-first century as they had been throughout the twentieth.

Notes

[1] *Chemist and Druggist*, 14 January 1984

[2] *Kelly's Directory of Leeds*, 1902

[3] Thackray Company Prescription Ledgers, West Yorkshire Archive service, Leeds District Archives

[4] House Committee Minutes, Leeds General Infirmary Archive

[5] S. T. Anning and W. K. J. Walls, *A History of the Leeds School of Medecine; One and a Half Centuries 1831–1981*, Leeds University Press, 1982.

[6] Reality, vol. 1, no. 2, September 1961, Thackray Company Archive, Thackray Medical Museum.

[7] Unpublished correspondence, Thackray Company Archive, Thackray Medical Museum.

[8] H. McLeave, *McIndoe: Plastic Surgeon*, 1961.

[9] W. Waugh, *The Man and the Hip*, 1990.

[10] J. Charnley, Manchester Collection (Medical), John Rylands University Library of Manchester.

[11] *Registered Trade Mark.

[12] *Registered Trade Mark.

CHAPTER 10

The Economy of Leeds in the 1990s[1]

Malcolm Sawyer

T HE preceding chapters show clearly that over the last hundred years Leeds has changed enormously, both as a city and in economic terms. The creation of the Metropolitan District in 1974 was largely due to the recognition that surrounding areas were linked inextricably to the city in economic terms. Beyond that, the West Yorkshire conurbation is ever more tightly bound together and Leeds, though it is located on the north-eastern edge geographically, is its functional centre: the short-lived county of West Yorkshire was an embodiment of this concept. Today it is therefore impossible to look at the economic prospects of the city in isolation, and certain aspects of the economy of Leeds may look unbalanced unless we are aware of their links to the wider region. Structural changes locally often reflect those that have occurred nationally, and do not indicate decline in themselves, especially given the diversity and flexibility which have always characterized the local economy. The job of this chapter is to look at the state of that local economy today, to look at the problems which certainly exist, and to point out the possible sources of growth.

Asa Briggs devoted a chapter of his book, *Victorian Cities*, to Leeds, and called it 'a study in civic pride'.[2] The city has traditionally based its prosperity on firms with strong local roots which exported to the rest of the country and further afield. The picture is no longer so simple. Shifts in consumer demand and competition from abroad has led to the decline and sometimes the death of many such firms, especially in the clothing industry, as the story of Burton's has shown. Other firms have expanded away from a regional base into national and international operations, as with the Leeds Permanent Building Society. In yet other cases, firms like Tetley's have become part of a multinational operation through acquisition. Moreover, as Leeds has consolidated its position as the capital of Yorkshire and Humberside, major public utilities and financial institutions have established their regional headquarters in Leeds. Even so, it is reckoned that there are over 20,000 companies in the Leeds Metropolitan District, and they vary greatly in size, as Table 10.1 shows. Only 1 per cent

Table 10.1   Distribution of Size of Firm in Leeds (by Employment), 1993

Size of firm by number of employees	Number of firms	Total number of employees
over 1000	17	26866
500–999	29	19493
200–499	92	26447
100–199	176	23499
Total of above	314	96305

Source: Leeds Development Agency.

employ over 200 people, 10 per cent employ between 25 and 100, and the remaining 89 per cent employ 24 or less.[3] The universities, the health service, the city council, and the civil service are not included in this table, but they are among the largest employers of labour. The figures given here for branch operations that are part of large national or international organisations apply only to employment in Leeds.

This shows that in terms of large employers, the local economy does not conform at all to stereotypes of northern industrial cities. Five of the seventeen listed organizations which employ over a thousand people are public utilities, and a sixth is the British Library's branch at Boston Spa. Three others are financial institutions, and while the Leeds Permanent Building Society and the Yorkshire Bank are long-established firms with strong roots in the area, the latter has recently been acquired by a multinational, the National Australia Bank. The third, which serves a national market and could in theory be located anywhere, is First Direct. It has been established only recently by Midland Bank, which is itself owned by Hong Kong and Shanghai Bank. A further four of the largest companies are manufacturers, Waddingtons, Tetley's, A.E. Turbines, and Elida Gibbs, and they all produce for sale into a national and international market. The remaining four, apart from Yorkshire Post Newspapers, are all retail distributors. The Leeds Industrial Co-operative Society is the local arm of a national organisation, Kay and Company are a national mail order firm, and Asda operates nationally but has its headquarters in Leeds.

Amongst the firms included in Table 10.1, forty-three have been identified by the Leeds Development Agency as being under foreign ownership, and they employ nearly 14,000 people, which is less than 5 per cent of the workforce. In the largest size group, we have seen that two, both financial institutions, are foreign owned. They employ 2550, and the establishment of First Direct has been the largest inward investment in employment terms. Figures for the other size categories are seven (4410 employees), fourteen (3944 employees) and twenty (2813 employees) respectively and the vast majority of them are in the manufacturing sector. Foreign ownership of firms in Leeds has been historically very low even by comparison with the local region, with no major foreign multinational presence before the 1980s. A range of long established local firms have been taken over by foreign companies in the past few years, however, and of the companies featured in this book, Chas F. Thackray was bought by Boehringer Mannheim of the USA in 1990 to form Depuy Thackray, and Tetley's is now part of Carlsberg-Tetley, owned on an equal basis by Allied-Lyons and Carlsberg A/S of Denmark. Other notable examples of the growing, though still relatively small, presence of multinational companies come from the acquisition of Howson Algraphy by Du Pont (USA) and of Wabco Automotive by Kelso (USA). In the engineering sector, Airmaster Engineering were acquired by BMD-Garant (a branch of the Danish firm A.P. Moller), West Yorkshire Foundries by Eisenwerk Bruhl of Germany, and a division of Carclo Engineering by Hoescht, also of Germany.

The pattern of employment by sector in the Leeds economy in 1981 and 1991 is given in Table 10.2 and the figures show a dramatic shift in the composition of employment in Leeds during the 1980s. Thus, tourism is now as important as clothing in terms of the numbers employed. The growth of the financial sector has brought it to the fore as a substantial employer and the provision of public services continues to be highly significant. The first four entries cover mineral extraction and manufacturing, which had been the backbone of the Leeds economy in the first half of the century, and their share declined by nearly one-third from 31.6 per cent in 1981 to 22.1 per cent in 1991. Estimates of employment in manufacturing industry as a whole in the early 1950s vary from nearly 150,000[4] to just over 114,000 jobs.[5] By the early 1980s the figure was only just above 80,000, and a decade later it had fallen to 61,000. The formerly dominant trades of clothing and textiles accounted for around 7000 jobs in 1983–4, and while engineering remained rather more important with around 25,000 jobs,[6] this was still a shadow of its former position.

The decline in manufacturing employment of around 28 per cent echoes national trends and it now accounts for less than a fifth of employment in the Leeds area. The contraction was strongest during the recessions of the early 1980s and the early 1990s, and it stemmed in part from marked increases in productivity, but the closing down of firms and sectors has also contributed in Leeds as elsewhere. The Leeds Development Agency have listed major expansions and contractions of employment in manufacturing firms employing over 100 people between 1981 and 1991, and the only recent major start-up in manufacturing which is recorded is that of Exsa (UK), which manufactures yarns from polyester and nylon. Twenty seven firms are recorded as significantly increasing employment as well, thereby creating 3230 new jobs. The three

Table 10.2   Employment by Sectors in the Leeds Economy, 1981, and 1991

	Sept. 1981	*Sept. 1991*	*Change*	*% change*
Energy & water supply				
	12287	7417	−4870	39.6
	4.1	2.4		
Extraction, manufacturing: minerals and metals				
	10885	9477	−1408	−12.9
	3.6	3.0		
Metal goods, vehicle industries etc.				
	34363	25372	−8991	−26.2
	11.0	7.6		
Other manufacturing industries				
	40239	29395	−10844	−26.9
	12.9	9.1		
Construction				
	15370	13335	−2035	−13.2
	5.0	4.3		
Distribution, hotels & catering, repairs				
	61834	69607	7773	12.6
	20.6	22.3		
Transport & communication				
	18411	18078	−333	−1.8
	6.2	5.8		
Banking, finance, insurance, leasing etc.				
	27465	45729	18264	66.5
	9.1	14.8		
Other services				
	79711	94234	14523	18.2
	27.4	30.7		
Total				
	300572	312644	11774	3.9

Note: For each sector the first set of figures refers to the absolute number of employees, the second set of figures to the share of that sector in total number of employees. The employment figures do not include agriculture where there were a substantial number of self-employed as well as around 1000 employees.
Source: Information supplied by Leeds Development Agency (based on National Online Manpower Information System, NOMIS)

largest increases came from Silver Cross, producers of prams, pushchairs and nursery equipment, Moores Furniture, kitchen and bedroom furniture, and Symphony Group, kitchen furniture. The first two are located well outside the city of Leeds at Guiseley and Thorp Arch, Wetherby, respectively. This reflects a trend for larger manufacturers to look outside the city centre for premises because there are very few sites of any size available there. Seven firms relocated their activities to other areas, in fact, with Centaur Clothing moving to Goole (490 jobs lost), E.J. Arnold to Nottingham (520 jobs) and RHM to Halifax (290 jobs). These contributed to the significant reductions in employment recorded by sixty seven manufacturing firms amounting in all to the loss of 18,000 jobs, nearly a thousand of which were lost at Vickers Defence alone. There were nineteen closures, and a notable loss was Systime Computers and its 1200 jobs. In 1980 there were five pits in the south-east part of the Leeds area, and as recently as 1989 they employed 1,900 people,[7] but by 1992 they had all closed. The knock-on effects of the recent wave of pit closures is put at 400 lost jobs in the Leeds area, but this is slight in comparison with over 30,000 for the Yorkshire region as a whole, reflecting the fact that the industry had already contracted sharply since the turn of the century.

Employment in the financial sector grew by over two-thirds during the 1980s, and this was again consistent with the national experience. The dominance of London as a financial centre within the UK is well-known, but there are a number of regional financial centres and Leeds can be clearly identified as one of them.[8] Such a centre will usually be the headquarters of a small number of locally active financial institutions with employment in the range of 20,000 to 35,000.[9] Leeds is the headquarters of the Yorkshire Bank, the four major clearing banks all have their regional offices there, there is one of the few branch offices of the Bank of England, and there are thirteen foreign banks. The Leeds Permanent and the Leeds and Holbeck are amongst the top twenty building societies and they have their headquarters in Leeds. This reflects the extent to which the building society movement has been centred in West Yorkshire, where five of the largest twenty building societies are based. Leeds is not a centre of employment in the insurance industry and there are no major life insurance companies with headquarters in Leeds, but the local or regional presence of national companies in other parts of the finance sector are substantial employers. In addition, since financial institutions require the services of legal and accountancy firms, six of the UK's top legal firms are based here, and sixteen of the twenty largest accountancy practices had offices in Leeds in 1985. Employment in accountancy, including auditors and tax experts, nearly doubled in the decade up to 1991, rising from 2000 to 3800. Some of these relocations and start-ups provide services to customers nationwide, not just to local or regional customers, the clearest example of which is First Direct, which provides telephone banking services around the clock to the whole country and is Leeds' fasting growing employer in 1993. It is perhaps symbolic of the changes in Leeds that their new premises are being built on a site previously occupied by Waddingtons. A partial listing of important relocations of financial sector operations to Leeds is provided in Table 10.3.

Many would argue that due to a combination of indigenous growth and inward investment, the financial sector over-expanded during the second half of the 1980s, with its credit boom and with the explosion of property prices. It is therefore unlikely that there will be a similar expansion during the 1990s.

Table 10.3   Some Recent Major Relocations of Financial Companies

AA Customer Services	160 employees
Barclays Direct Mortgage Services	250 employees
First Direct	260 employed in 1989 rising to 1400
GRE Personal Financial Management	72 employees
Natwest Switchcard	200 employees
Royal Insurance (UK)	330 employees

Source: Information from Leeds Development Agency.

Moreover, the Leeds financial sector is not much involved with the trading of financial assets such as stocks, shares, and foreign investments, but rather with the provision of financial services. As such its growth will be closely bound up with the sectors for which these services are provided.

Bigger in employment terms than any of the finance sector firms are the local public sector organizations and the privatized public utilities. Leeds City Council itself employed 35,000 in 1993, over 10 per cent of the work force. The Area Health Authority employed over 14,000 in 1989, together with a share of the 15–20,000 employed in the related field of social care, though many of those work for Leeds City Council.[10] The next four largest employers are utilities: Post Office (3900), British Gas (2200), British Telecom (2000) and Yorkshire Electricity (1810). Such organizations generally provide goods and services for the residents of the city and the region, rather than producing for export to outsiders. Thus Leeds gains from being a regional centre, but its prosperity is linked with that of the region. In contrast, the relocations by central government of the Benefits Agency Central Services, NHS Management Executive and DSS Central Adjudication Services have brought around 2000 jobs to Leeds which are not tied to regional needs. There are also several major further and higher education institutions, notably the University of Leeds which employs around 4500 people and the Leeds Metropolitan University which employs another 2400. Additional employment is generated in the city and region through the spending power of their students. Figures are not available for Leeds alone, but the substantial numbers of students attending such institutions are likely to be much larger than those leaving the city to get their education elsewhere. In the Yorkshire and Humberside region, 19,500 students stayed within the region, 31,000 went to other regions, whilst nearly 53,000 came into the region for their higher education.[11]

Around 300,000 people currently work in Leeds, which is about 35 per cent of the total for West Yorkshire.[12] 54 per cent are male, almost all working full time, and 46 per cent are female, of whom just over half work full time.[13] For much of its history female participation in the paid work force of Leeds tended to be above the national average, but it has now slipped below it,[14] largely due to the decline of the clothing industry. Generally the north of England has a relatively small proportion of self-employed people and compared to the UK average of 11.5 per cent of the economically active population, Leeds has only 9.6 per cent and West Yorkshire 9.8 per cent. Employment expanded over the decade ending in 1991 by 3.9 per cent, which compares with 1.4 per cent for the Yorkshire and Humberside region and a national figure of 1.6 per cent.[15] At the same time population fell by 1.6 per cent and this relative and absolute expansion in employment is one of several indicators which suggest that the Leeds economy has been performing comparatively well over the past decade or more.

The growth of employment which has occurred recently, together with the decline in population, has helped to keep the level of unemployment in Leeds slightly below the national average. In the Leeds travel to work area at the end of 1992, those registered unemployed accounted for 9.1 per cent of the workforce, as compared with 10.6 per cent for the whole of the UK. This amounts to 35,036 people registered as unemployed, of whom 78 per cent were male, which reflects the fact that as many women work part time and are not eligible for unemployment benefit, they do not register. Generally it is the young who are most affected, with one-third of the unemployed being under 25 years of age. Unemployment is spread unevenly over the Metropolitan District, and is mainly concentrated in the inner city areas. Table 10.4 gives the distribution of unemployment across the Metropolitan District by parliamentary constituency and shows the high levels of unemployment in Leeds Central and Leeds East. These are approximately halved in the outer constituencies of Elmet and Pudsey, and if comparisons between smaller areas could

Table 10.4   Unemployment in Areas of Leeds (December 1992)

Parliamentary Constituency	Male	Female	Total
Leeds Central	5732	1423	7155
Leeds East	4856	1135	5991
Leeds North East	3035	993	4028
Leeds North West	2427	799	3226
Leeds West	3886	1069	4955
Morley and Leeds South	3071	915	3986
Elmet	2328	723	3051
Pudsey	2162	690	2852
Leeds Metropolitan District	28073	7902	35975
Leeds Travel-to-Work-Area	27329	7707	35036

Note: The Leeds Metropolitan District is not exactly coterminous with the sum of the constituencies listed.
Source: Department of Employment, Employment Gazette, June 1993.

be made, the differences in the rates of unemployment would almost certainly be even greater. The council wards of City and Holbeck, University, Harehills, Chapel Allerton, Burmantofts, Richmond Hill and Headingley have particularly high concentrations.[16]

The growth of the service and financial sectors means that in broad terms the composition of the local and national economies are rather similar and the Leeds economy has therefore faced locally many of the problems of the British economy as a whole, particularly the decline of the manufacturing base and substantial unemployment. It must be said that the prospects for the British economy to the end of the century are not particularly rosy given that the balance of trade position and the failure to tackle the economy's inflationary bias both point towards relatively high levels of unemployment and like most areas and regions, Leeds is now more dependent on decisions taken outside of the area: some made by distant consumers, but large firms which operate nationally and internationally increasingly control investment and employment decisions. In a world where regional and national frontiers have become of much less significance for economic activity than hitherto, it is therefore easy to say that the future of Leeds is closely bound up with regional, national, and international developments but Leeds retains some unique characteristics and some possibilities for the people of Leeds to influence their future destiny still exist, especially as the economy of Leeds and the surrounding region has begun to diversify again, and its industrial structure now has many sectors which are generally identified as growth sectors rather than decaying sectors. Much clearly depends on the prosperity of the regional economy, but the Yorkshire and Humberside region as a whole performed slightly worse than the UK average during the 1980s in that the regional GDP grew at an annual average rate of 2.1 per cent during the 1980s, compared to a UK figure of 2.3 per cent.[17] We must, however, remember that this is a large and very diverse region, including areas like South Yorkshire which was particularly badly hit by the closures of many parts of its major industries of steel and coal.

It is perhaps some small comfort to find that Yorkshire and Humberside as a whole did not suffer quite as badly as the rest of the country from the recession of the early 1990s, declining by 2.3 per cent and 0 per cent in 1991 and 1992 respectively compared with national figures of 2.6 per cent and 0.6 per cent. Another reflection of this trend is that though the regional unemployment rate was 0.8 per cent above the national average in 1981, and though the gap widened to 1.5 per cent at the height of the boom in 1988, it had been eliminated by the beginning of 1993. There is no consensus on the outlook for the Yorkshire and Humberside region. Two recent forecasts predict slower growth than the rest of the UK, while another suggests it will be faster.[18] During the 1980s despite needing to overcome its structural inheritance of sunset industries, one survey concluded that if each of the industries in existence at the start of the 1980s had performed in line with the national performance, employment would have declined in this region by 5.3 per cent, but it actually achieved a 3.6 per cent rise.[19] The gap between GDP per head in West Yorkshire and the UK average narrowed very marginally in the period 1981 to 1989, and the ratio stood at 93.1 per cent in 1989. If those favourable forces continue to operate then there would indeed be good prospects for the region.

Industries which have been in long term decline, notably mining and clothing are now so small that further decline will not have a large impact, and Leeds is no longer so heavily reliant on its traditional industries. It is, however, true that the industrial base of Leeds, and of the Yorkshire and Humberside region as a whole, is characterized by relatively low technology industries. Firms involved with high technology in Leeds have been estimated to provide around 6700 jobs, which is around 2 per cent of the total.[20] Another source reports that employment in firms making or delivering new technology products or services was 11,300 in 1987, with a third of those in telecommunications, which was under 4 per cent of employment in Leeds as compared with a national figure of over 5 per cent.[21] This has left a relatively weak industrial research and development base and a low level of technologically-based activities, and there have been few signs of any inward movement of high technology firms or of the indigenous growth of such firms. There is also a weak infrastructure for collaborative research and development.[22]

This may be linked to the general levels of education and training of the workforce, for high technology industries clearly require highly educated scientists and engineers, even though many of the jobs in such industries may call for relatively low levels of skill, and many firms provide on-the-job training. But more generally, the type of industries which can grow and the nature of the jobs which can be created depend heavily on the education and training of the workforce and though the picture is mixed, there are signs that it is not as well educated and trained as nationally. Over half the Leeds workforce has no qualifications and one third of managers have no educational qualifications.[23] The level of educational attainment, particularly as measured by the proportion of children remaining in education after the age of sixteen and continuing into further and higher education, is relatively low. The largest proportion of highly qualified people is among those working in banking, finance, and public services and many of them probably come from outside the area, but the level of graduates in the regional workforce as a whole is below the national average, so there seems to be a brain-drain from the region.[24]

The significance of the rather small role played by transnational corporations in Leeds can be seen in a variety of ways, on the other hand. The presence of transnationals can bring employment in industries that use relatively advanced technology, often training their workers in new skills and using modern management techniques. As such their presence can be seen as advantageous and it may spark off local initiatives in time, but it does leave local employment subject to decisions made elsewhere, and local factories may be viewed as dispensable within the strategic plans of the parent company. The presence of multinational companies is unlikely to diminish in the coming years, but the question is more what type of multinationals will be attracted to Leeds, what efforts should be made to attract particular types, and what sort of jobs will they provide. The creation of good quality jobs will require a well-trained workforce, but if firms in high-tech industries can be induced to come to the area, the training they provide will itself be a useful contribution to escaping the low-skill trap.

It is easy to say that there have been some dramatic changes in the Leeds economy during the decade which has been the focus of this chapter, and even more so in the century covered by this book. Whether the nature of those changes has been on balance beneficial and whether the pace of change has been faster than in previous decades we leave to others to debate. However, change has always been a factor in the success of the Leeds economy, and recently it has overcome some considerable structural weaknesses with the decline of many sunset industries. The local economy is in a stronger and more diversified position to face the future challenges, and there are plenty of opportunities to be seized. Thus, Yorkshire has often been seen as lacking involvement in or concern for Europe, but the arrival of the Single European Market and the probable expansion of the European Community to include Eastern European countries and the rest of Scandinavia offers north-eastern England the chance to revive traditional trading links with these areas via the Humber ports, and this would clearly benefit Leeds. Economists at the Henley Centre identified Leeds in July 1990 as a UK location having above average potential for dynamic growth in the run up to the next century, and in October 1992 a forecast from Business Strategies supported this optimism by showing Leeds as the fastest growing employment centre in the UK over the 1990s. The City Council is committed to supporting the local economy and to making Leeds 'one of Europe's leading business centres', so there is every reason to look forward with confidence to another hundred years of growth and change.

Notes

[1] In writing this chapter, I have received considerable help from Stan Kenyon, (Director of Planning, Leeds City Council), Chris Tebbutt (Leeds Development Agency) and Adam Tickell (School of Geography, University of Leeds). They cannot be held responsible for the use

279

which I have made of the material which they have kindly supplied to me, nor for the opinions expressed in this chapter, for which I alone am responsible.

[2] Asa Briggs, *Victorian Cities*, 1963. Briggs was Professor of Modern History at the University of Leeds when the book was written.

[3] The Leeds TEC Ltd: *TEC Performance Related Funding for Education*, March 1993. Note that *Leeds* is generally intended in this chapter to refer to the area covered by the Leeds City Council. However, in some cases, where stated, figures relate to the Leeds travel-to-work area. Some slight differences in figures in the text arise from this cause.

[4] Leeds Development Agency, *Economic Development Strategy*, 1992.

[5] Calculated from W. G. Rimmer, 'Miscellany', *Thoresby Society*, volume L, part 2, no. 113, 1967, table 7.

[6] Leeds, *Economic Development Annual Statement 1993/84*, pp. 10 and 12.

[7] Employment Committee: Employment consequences of British Coal's proposed pit closures, volume 2: Minutes of evidence and appendices HC 263-II, p. 436.

[8] The others being Birmingham, Bristol, Edinburgh, Glasgow, Liverpool, and Manchester.

[9] A. Tickell, *Leeds And The Regional Financial System*, School of Geography, University of Leeds, 1993.

[10] LDA, *Strategy*, p. 17.

[11] Central Statistical Office, *Regional Trends*, 28, 1993, table 5.12.

[12] The sources of data (unless otherwise stated) are *Regional Trends*, 28, and Department of Employment, *Employment Gazette*, various issues.
Regional Trends gives a figure of 298.1 thousand in employment including the self-employed for the Leeds district in April 1991. The Census of Employment figures on which table 10.2 is based give rather higher figures of 312,600 employees to which the self-employed of circa 30,000 needs to be added.

[13] Figures from Leeds City Council, *Economic Development Annual Statement 1993/94*: that source gives rather higher employment figures for Leeds of 360,000.

[14] 'A third of the borough's work force, a proportion that was above the national average as in other West Riding towns, was female', referring to the situation throughout the second half of the 19th century, Rimmer, 'Miscellany' op. cit.

[15] Both 1981 and 1991 were years of recession and hence figures for those years tend to understate typical employment levels, though the trend in employment levels should not be too distorted by the end dates used.

[16] The Leeds TEC Ltd: *TEC Performance Related Funding for Education*, March 1993.

[17] National Westminster Bank, *Economic and Financial Outlook*, March 1993.

[18] Cambridge Economics forecast covering the period 1993 to 2005 suggests that growth in the region will be 97 per cent of the UK average, whilst PA Consulting put the figure at 91 per cent for the period 1994 to 2001. In contrast, Nat West Bank estimate the figure as 105 per cent for the period 1993 to 1997. Information derived from Coopers and Lybrand, *UK Economic Outlook*, April 1993.

[19] Cambridge Economics, Regional Economic Prospects, as quoted in Cooper and Lybrand, *ibid.*

[20] LDA, *Strategy*.

[21] *Ibid.*, p. 20.

[22] *Ibid*, p. 6.

[23] Leeds TEC: *Performance Related Funding*.

[24] In West Yorkshire, the proportion of pupils aged sixteen staying on in education rose from 55 per cent in 1981 to 73 per cent in 1991, figures which are close to the English average of 57 per cent and 73 per cent respectively. However a higher proportion of school leavers had no graded results at GCSE in 1991, 9.3 per cent in West Yorkshire compared with a 7.5 per cent average for England. In West Yorkshire, 20.5 per cent of school leavers had one or more A-levels (21.1 per cent in England) and a further 10.8 per cent had five or more GCSE grade A to C (14.8 per cent in England).

INDEX

284

Guiseley, 273
Guiseley Gyle, 140

Habitat, 200
hair care, 233
hair care products, 233
hair dyes and tints, 233
hair preparations, 233–4
hair product market, 233–4
hair products, 234
hair sprays, 234
Halifax Building Society, 57, 66, 73, 75, 79
Halpern, Ralph, 196, 212
Halton, 1
Hammonds, Bradford, 136
Harehills, 10
Harrison and Townshend, 149
Harrogate, 2
Hartman brothers, 164
Harvey, John Martin, 147
Headingley, 14, 277
Healey Baker, 209
Heaton's, 18
Heinz, 162, 176
Hemingway, 137
Henley Centre, 279
Henry Holding Limited, 194
Hepworth, 16, 18, 187, 189
Hetherington, Alistair, 24
Hicks, Rupert, 164
higher education, 278
Hirst, C H, 156
HMSO, 16
Hoescht, 272
Holbeck, 10
Holbeck Rugby Union Football Club, 14
Hong Kong and Shanghai Bank, 271
Hope Inn, Lands Lane, 125
Hope Mills (Water Lane), 153
Hopple Plastics Inc, 178
horselads, 129
Horsell, Frank and Co Ltd, 150
Horsforth, 1
House of Questa, 178
housing, 9–10, 20
Housing Act, 1909, 9
Howard and Wyndhams, 152

Howson Algraphy, 272
Huddersfield, 119, 122
Hudson Road, 186, 192, 201
Hudson Road Mills, 14, 192, 193, 197, 198, 202, 204
Hull, 118, 119, 122
Hulme, 135
Humble (brewer), 113
Hunslet, 113
Hunslet Lane, 112
Hurwitz, Emmanuel, 210
Hydro-Chemie, 165

ICI Metals, 168
Ilkley, 123, 126
Imperial Tobacco, 160, 173
Ind Coope, 122, 129, 136
Ind Coope Tetley Ansell Ltd, 136
Independent, 42, 50
infant mortality, 8
International Card Co, 170
International Paper Co, 166
Irish community, 8
ITV, 25, 235

Jackson of Sunderland, 137
Jackson shops, 198
Jackson the Tailor, 16, 197, 210
Jacobson brothers, 197, 211
Jacques, Thomas, 112
Jaycare Ltd, 178
Jenkinson, Henry Ltd, 168
Jewish community, 9, 10, 191
jigsaw puzzles, 160

Karno, Fred, 146, 147
Kay and Company, 271
keg beers, 137
Keighley, 145, 157, 159
Kelso, 272
Key Estates Limited, 194
Kinder Scout, 136
Kirkstall, 168
Kirkstall Brewery Co, 122
Kleinwort Benson, 176, 178, 210
Kurl-Out, 238

Lackey, Clifford, 136
lager, 138

285

shampoo, 218, 223
Sharp v Wakefield, 124, 125
shaving creams, 218, 230
shaving soap, 230
Sheepscar, 17, 113
Sheffield, 10, 27, 42, 54, 70, 90, 115, 117, 118, 119, 121, 122, 135, 187, 188, 191
Sheffield Corporation, 135
Sheffield Gas Light Company, 90
Sheffield Telegraph, 42, 54
Shipley, 123, 126
shower gels, 234
Signal, 237
silicate of soda, 219
silk-screen printing, 165
Silver Cross, 273
Simon, Ets J-M, 170
skin care market, 234
Skol lager, 138, 139, 142
Smith, Adam, 187
Smith, John, Tadcaster brewery, 115, 122
Smith, Samuel, Tadcaster brewery, 122
snooker, 209
soap, 217–41 passim
soap hard, 225, 230
soap flakes, 223, 230
soap industry, 219–23
soap makers, 219–23
soap manufacture, 219–23
soap powders, 230
soap producers, 219–23
soap production, 223, 225
Soap Trust, 221–2
Solidox, 223, 235
Sowerby Bridge, 3
Sparkla, 229–30
Spencer, Cyril, 212, 213
Spink, George, 154, 167
SR, 223, 235
St Ann's, Headingley, 140
Staffordshire, 121
Station, Guiseley, 140
Stead and Simpson, 17
steam engines, 4, 14
steam lorry, 129
Stephens, R B, 147, 153
stock market, 136
Stoke Newington, 145, 152, 162, 172
Storehouse Group, 200

street lamps, 81
street lighting, 83
Subbuteo, 145, 171
Suit-making, 186–90, 200–5
suits, made-to-measure, 188, 190, 206
suits, ready-made, 187, 190
Sumrie, 18
Sun, 42, 43
Sunday Chronicle, 33
Sunday Express, 25, 33
Sunlight, 234
Sunsilk, 234, 236
Sure, 234
Swillington, 203
Sykes, William, 112, 113
Symphony Group, 273
Systime Computers, 274

Tadcaster, 2, 115, 122, 127
Tadcaster Tower Brewery Co, 122
tailoring, 186–9, 196–8
tailoring, trade, 18, 186–213 passim
tailoring, wholesale bespoke, 188, 190, 206
tallow, 219, 226
tanning, 16–7
Taylor, Mr Fred, 155
Taylor, Samuel, 244, 247
telecommunications, 278
telephone banking services, 274
television, 141
Temperance Building Society, 67
Tempest, J S, 122
Temple Newsam, 1, 12
Tetley, Joshua and Son, 12, 112–44, 271
Tetley's Brewery Wharf, 123, 142
Tetley Bitter, 142
Tetley family, 125
Tetley Pub Company Ltd, 112
Tetley territory, 123, 126, 129
Tetley Walker Ltd, 136, 137
Tetley, profits, 128, 133
Tetley, Brigadier Noel, 136
Tetley, Charles Francis, 122, 127
Tetley, Joshua, 112–44
Tetley, William, 112
textiles, 14, 272
Thackray, 18

Thackray, Charles Frederick, 244–5, 247, 253, 390
Thackray, Charles Noel, 245, 254, 259, 262
Thackray, Charles Paul, 262, 264, 266
Thackray, John Pearce, 262, 264, 266
Thackray, William Pearce (Tod), 245, 254, 259, 262, 263
Thackraycare, 267–8
The Economist, 65
Theatre Museum, 147
Theatre Royal, 147
Thornton, Charles, 4
Thorp Arch, 273
Thyne of Edinburgh, 163
tied houses, 120–6
Times, 28, 30, 34
Tit Bits, 30
tobacco, 124
Toby, 150
toilet soap, 230
toilet water, 230
toiletries, 224, 228
toothpaste, 218, 233–5, 237
Top Man, 199
Top Shop, 198, 199
Totopoly, 171
Tower Press, 171
Town & Country Building Society, 75
trading stamps, 172
trams, 11, 12, 13
transnational corporations, 278–9
transport costs, 133
Trixie, 223
Turner, W E, 149
turnpike roads, 3
Twink, 233
Typographical Association, 158

UDS, 211
Underwood Typewriter Co, 154
Unilever, 217
Unilever Associated Companies Ltd, 217, 218, 223, 227, 228, 235
Unilever Export, 224
Unilever Home Soap Executive, 217, 223
Unilever Toiletries, 224
Unilever, Toiletries Division, 224

Union Mills, 151, 152
United Newspapers, 51
United Provincial Newspapers, 25

vacuum-formed plastic containers, 166
Vaizey, John, 129, 133
Vale of York, 3
Valentines of Dundee, 171, 174, 175
Van Den Berghs, 173, 176
Vaseline, 234
Vauvelle, Achille, 155, 160
Venus soap, 234
Vickers Defence, 274
Vickers Business Forms, 177
victuallers, 116, 117, 118, 120
Videomaster, 171, 174
Viscount printing presses, 44, 47
Vivian, G S, 156

Wabco Automotive, 272
Waddington Auxiliary Board, 167
Waddington International Company Ltd, 166
Waddington, John, 146, 149, 155
Waddington, John Ltd, 153
Waddington, John PLC, 16, 19, 145-85, 271, 274
Waddingtons, 145–85
Waddingtons Ltd, 146
Waddingtons, Research Department, 165
Wade Lane, 15, 147
Wade Street, 147
Wainwright, Henry Scurrah, 245–6, 247
Wainwright, Richard Scurrah, 246, 259
Wakefield, 1, 2, 123, 126
Wakefield Road, 153, 154, 158, 164, 165, 168
Wales, 129
Walkden, 201
Walker Cain, 136
Walker, James, 209
Walker's Thirty Shilling Tailors, 188, 191, 201
Wansbrough, A W, 210
Wapping, 220
Warrington, 135, 136, 220
Watmough, 177
Watney, Combe, Reid, 126

Watney Mann, 134, 136
Watson's, 152
Watson's marketing, 234–7
Watson's raw material prices, 220, 221, 222
Watson's, prize wrapper scheme, 235
Watson's, profits, 229
Watson's, women's employment, 238–9
Watson, Charles, 219
Watson, Eric, 168
Watson, George, 219
Watson, Horace, 152
Watson, Joseph I, 219
Watson, Joseph and Sons Ltd, 217, 222, 226
Watson, Joseph II, 220
Watson, Norman, 156, 157, 161, 171, 173
Watson, Victor H I, 147, 149, 150, 151, 152, 153, 156, 157, 164, 165–7
Watson, Victor H II, 145, 167, 176, 177, 178
waxed-paper, 166
Wellington Road, 9
Wellington Street, 15, 45, 114
West Riding, 133, 136
West Riding Quarter Sessions, 125
Westbourne Park Building Society, 64, 65
Wetherby, 2, 271
Wharfedale, 2
Whitaker, 129, 134, 135
Whitbread, 129, 133
Whitehall Road, 217, 218, 230, 231, 232, 237
Whitelaw, David, 171
Widnes, 220
wines and spirits, 131
Woodhouse, 10
Woodhouse Carr, 15
woollen industry, 17

woollen trade, 3
Woolwich Building Society, 66, 67, 73, 75
Woolworths, 161
World Cup, 1966, 171
World War I, 100, 123, 125, 127, 150–1, 191, 192, 197, 200, 202, 249–50
World War II, 163, 192, 195, 197, 217, 224, 226, 227, 237, 239, 255–7
Worsley, 201
worsted industry, 14, 17
Worthington, 129
Wrightlington Hospital, 261, 262

York, 123, 126
York Minster, 155
York Street gasworks, 86
Yorkshire, 115, 117, 136
Yorkshire and Humberside, 275, 276, 277, 278
Yorkshire Bank, 271
Yorkshire breweries, 118
Yorkshire Conservative Newspaper Company Limited, 25
Yorkshire County Cricket Club, 14
Yorkshire Electricity, 275
Yorkshire Evening News, 30, 41, 46, 51
Yorkshire Evening Post, 7, 25, 30–3, 38, 42, 52
Yorkshire Factory Times, 1, 8
Yorkshire House-to-House Electricity Company, 87, 88
Yorkshire Newspaper Society, 44
Yorkshire Post, 6, 7, 24–54
Yorkshire square, 127, 137, 138
Yorkshire TV, 25, 28, 43
Yorkshire Weekly Post, 30

Zimmerman Brothers, 191

291